Faculty of Color
in Academe

Related Titles

Faculty Work and Public Trust: Restoring the Value
of Teaching and Public Service in American Academic Life
    James S. Fairweather
    ISBN: 0-205-17948-7

Emblems of Quality in Higher Education:
Developing and Sustaining High-Quality Programs
    Jennifer Grant Haworth and Clifton F. Conrad
    ISBN: 0-205-19546-6

Writing for Professional Publication:
Keys to Academic and Business Success
    Kenneth T. Henson
    ISBN: 0-205-28313-6

Revitalizing General Education in a Time of Scarcity:
A Navigational Chart for Administrators and Faculty
    Sandra L. Kanter, Zelda F. Gamson, and Howard B. London
    ISBN: 0-205-26257-0

The Adjunct Professor's Guide to Success:
Surviving and Thriving in the College Classroom
    Richard E. Lyons, Marcella L. Kysilka, and George E. Pawlas
    ISBN 0-205-28774-3

Multicultural Course Transformation in Higher Education: A Broader Truth
    Ann Intili Morey and Margie K. Kitano (Editors)
    ISBN: 0-205-16068-9

Sexual Harassment on Campus: A Guide for Administrators,
Faculty, and Students
    Bernice R. Sandler and Robert J. Shoop
    ISBN: 0-205-16712-8

Designing and Teaching an On-Line Course: Spinning Your Web Classroom
    Heidi Schweizer
    ISBN: 0-205-30321-8

Leadership in Continuing and Distance Education in Higher Education
    Cynthia C. Jones Shoemaker
    ISBN: 0-205-26823-4

Shaping the College Curriculum: Academic Plans in Action
    Joan S. Stark and Lisa R. Lattuca
    ISBN: 0-205-16706-3

FACULTY OF COLOR IN ACADEME

Bittersweet Success

Caroline Sotello Viernes Turner
University of Minnesota

Samuel L. Myers, Jr.
University of Minnesota

Allyn and Bacon
Boston • London • Toronto • Sydney • Tokyo • Singapore

Executive Editor: Stephen D. Dragin
Series Editorial Assistant: Bridget McSweeney
Editorial-Production Service: Omegatype Typography, Inc.
Manufacturing Buyer: Dave Repetto
Electronic Composition: Omegatype Typography, Inc.

Library of Congress Cataloging-in-Publication Data

Turner, Caroline Sotello Viernes.
    Faculty of color in academe : bittersweet success / Caroline
Sotello Viernes Turner, Samuel L. Myers, Jr.
      p.   cm.
    Includes bibliographical references (p.   ).
    ISBN 0-205-27849-3
    1. Minority college teachers—Selection and appointment—United
States.   2. Afro-American college teachers—Selection and
appointment.   3. Hispanic American college teachers—Selection and
appointment.   I. Myers, Samuel L.   II. Title.
LB2332.72.T87   2000
378.1'2—dc21   99-12507
                                                              CIP

Printed in the United States of America
10 9 8 7 6 5 4 3 2 1   03 02 01 00 99

CONTENTS

PREFACE

On the brink of the twenty-first century, our nation continues to struggle with the challenge of becoming a multicultural society. Although our society takes pride in the opportunities for mobility offered to its citizens, inequities based on racial and ethnic difference continue to exist. This book focuses on those inequities, which continue to be documented within the professorial workplace in higher education. Today, with race-based scholarships under scrutiny, affirmative action losing support, and efforts to achieve diversity and equity in higher education contested, there is an urgent need to reexamine the issues of successful recruitment, retention, and development of faculty of color in the academic workplace. Statistics detail dismal participation and completion rates for African Americans, Latinos, and American Indians in the American educational system. Low representation rates for people of color among tenure-track and tenured faculty ranks follow this pattern. Even though the record appears far better for the Asian Pacific American population, exclusion continues to be a theme addressed by Asian Pacific American faculty in this study and other published work.

In choosing to study issues of faculty of color in academe, we do not mean to discount the severity of the problems that confront students of color at the elementary and secondary school levels or in undergraduate and graduate programs. The issues at these fundamental levels of education have a direct impact on the supply of faculty of color. The focus of this book, however, is to examine the status and learn from the experiences of faculty of color who, despite those barriers, are currently employed in predominantly white colleges and research universities. Among the various institutions of higher learning, the major research universities are of particular interest. It is within these institutions that the results of dismantling affirmative action in California and Texas first appear in the media. This is not surprising because major research universities play a significant role in our society. They educate the faculties and set the cultural climate for the rest of the academic enterprise (Alpert, 1985). Even more importantly, the major research universities are gateways to positions of significant influence in the United States (Arenson, 1997; Carnegie, 1989; Duster, 1991; Johnson, 1992). These prestigious institutions have guarded privilege in this country for over two centuries, and they are very often a significant part of the path taken by most people who come to occupy powerful positions.

This book draws on a comprehensive study of African American, Asian Pacific American, American Indian, and Latino faculty in eight midwestern states. The study was conducted in states that were members of the Midwestern Higher Education Commission from 1993 to 1995: Illinois, Kansas, Michigan, Ohio, Wisconsin, Nebraska, Missouri, and Minnesota. We intend to present critical perspectives emerging from our data with the hope of contributing to a comprehensive understanding of issues surrounding successful recruitment, retention, and development of faculty of color in higher education. These perspectives come from the voices of faculty of color themselves; from statistical data collected for our study; and from a comprehensive analysis of data presented in the literature. A thorough examination of these data not only reveals the continued underrepresentation of faculty of color in the nation's colleges and universities, but, equally significantly if more subtly, the persistence and the personal and professional effects of a decidedly chilly work environment.

Challenges to the successful recruitment, retention, and development of faculty of color include significant barriers within academia itself that discourage people of color from becoming productive and satisfied members of the professoriate. Our findings and analysis show that the predominant barrier is racial and ethnic bias resulting in unwelcoming and unsupportive work environments for faculty of color. There are also, however, positive workplace experiences that strengthen the commitment of faculty of color to remain in academe. Furthermore, it is important to note that ours is a study of successes, not failures. In spite of the high probability of failure in preparing for the professoriate, all faculty interviewed for this study, as well as faculty quoted in the literature, have earned tenure-track and tenured positions in higher education. Yet their well-articulated experiences point to the continued exclusion and isolation of these successful scholars, even among those who are not only tenured but hold high-level, high-profile academic appointments.

Ultimately, it is you, the reader, who must decide whether the issues raised in this book document a crisis that you, as an individual, must address. We, on the other hand, stand to make the case for action. To be honest, our reporting and thinking here is partly an attempt to come to some answers as to how we can constructively engage in the struggle for equality and justice within our own spheres of influence. This is not done without some apprehension on our part. We are part of a system that we praise and that we criticize. We benefit and have benefited from the support provided to us by those who are and have been our academic colleagues. This is a multifaceted, multiracial, and multicultural group. We hope that what we say here is challenging while at the same time it does not devalue our appreciation for our nation and for those who have helped us obtain our present status within the academy. Certainly the opposite is true. What would devalue that appreciation would rather be the failure to confront the barriers to the full realization of the ideals we share with those who have supported us. It is in the name of those ideals—of social justice and intellectual integrity—that we have undertaken this work.

Acknowledgments

We want to express our appreciation to the professors, policy makers, and administrators who participated in this study. Without their cooperation and willingness to share information through personal interviews and institutional surveys, this book would not have been possible. Faculty shared details about their professional lives while institutional representatives sent us information about their faculty development programs. Others provided us with access to programmatic documents as well as access to their faculty development program sites and participants. Because we promised anonymity to study participants, we are not able to name them or their institutions here. However, we wanted to acknowledge our indebtedness to them.

We wish to thank Steve Dragin, editor, and the following reviewers for Allyn and Bacon who provided us with excellent ideas for developing our manuscript: Estela Mara Bensimon, University of Southern California; Bob Boice, SUNY Stonybook; Janet Dawson-Threat, University of Missouri–Columbia; Mary Howard-Hamilton, University of Florida; and Carolyn J. Thompson, SUNY Buffalo. We also thank our faculty colleagues who supported us in this endeavor with their advice and ideas, among them professors John Creswell, University of Nebraska; Daryl Smith and Jack Schuster, Claremont Graduate University; and Karen Seashore Louis and Tim Mazzoni, University of Minnesota. We are particularly grateful to professors Estela Bensimon, University of Southern California; Naomi Scheman, University of Minnesota; and policy maker Tina Tsuei for their willingness to read manuscript drafts and provide us with many ideas for improvement. The Office of the Associate Vice President for Multicultural Affairs and the Roy Wilkins Center, Humphrey Institute, University of Minnesota, provided financial support for Caroline Turner to pursue this book project. Special thanks to Rusty Barcelo, Robert Jones, and Josie Johnson for their unwavering support of this effort. We also want to thank David Murphy and Diane Berube of the Midwestern Higher Education Commission (MHEC), the St. Paul Companies, and the McKnight Foundation for their support of the Minority Faculty Development Project. That MHEC report was reviewed and critiqued at various stages in the project and we are especially grateful to the Oversight Committee: Roger Clark, Josie Johnson, Sharon Tolbert-Glover, Mary Pickard, Ronald McKinley, Michael O'Keefe, David Powers, and Phillip Sirotkin, and the Steering Committee: Carol Anderson, Sherri Coe-Perkins, John Creswell, Dolores Cross, Lucille Davis, Douglass Day, James E. Facen, Greg Frost, John L. Henderson, David Hinton, Rachel Lindsey, Charles E. Morris, K. C. Morrison, Emma Palmer, Chernoh M. Sesay, Glenn Stevens, John A. Taylor, and Judith Trent, for their suggestions and comments. Valuable research and consulting support was provided by Allan Malkis, research associate, The Urban Coalition, St. Paul, Minnesota; Daniel M. Pasquini, research associate, National Research Council; and Jeff Dykehouse, University of Michigan.

The project was ably assisted by a dedicated and committed research staff from the Roy Wilkins Center, Humphrey Institute and from the Department of Educational Policy and Administration, University of Minnesota. We want to recognize Melanie Peterson-Hickey, Linda Heyne, Willie Johnson, and Tina Tsuei for their participation in project data collection and analysis. Andriana Abariotes, Chanjin Chung, Mohamed Darif, Todd Graham, Amanda Jameson, Fred Marsh, Lan Pham, Nathan Tiller, and David Waithaka assisted in the statistical analysis. Claire Cohen provided editorial assistance, Judy Leahy provided administrative oversight for the project, and Mary Lou Middleton managed the final preparation of the manuscript.

We also wish to acknowlege our family and friends who provided day-to-day inspiration in endeavors such as these. Caroline Turner would like to particularly thank Ruby G. Turner, Nathan J. Turner, Dion T. Harris I, Dion T. Harris II, Jose and Gabriella Garcia, Rosie Lopez, Liz Garcia, Monica Santa, Margaret Garcia, Diana Ruud, Gloria Williams, Jose S. Garcia Jr., Rosemary McGuire, Mary Von Bank, and Don Koukal. Myers is indebted to Sheila D. Ards, Angela Myers, Andrea Myers, Marion Myers, and Samuel L. Myers, Sr. for their constant inspiration and support throughout the project.

1

FACULTY OF COLOR IN ACADEME

On the Brink of the Twenty-First Century

On the brink of the twenty-first century, our nation continues to struggle with the challenge of becoming a multicultural society. Although our society takes pride in the opportunities for mobility offered to its citizens, inequities based on racial and ethnic differences continue to exist. This book focuses on those inequities, which continue to be documented within the professorial workplace in higher education. Today, with race-based scholarships under scrutiny, affirmative action losing support, and efforts to achieve diversity and equity in higher education being contested, there is an urgent need to reexamine the issues of successful recruitment, retention, and development of faculty of color in the academic workplace. Statistics detail dismal participation and completion rates for African Americans, Latinos, and American Indians in the U.S. educational system. Low representation rates for people of color among tenure-track and tenured faculty ranks follow this pattern. Even though the record appears far better for the Asian Pacific American population, exclusion continues to be a theme addressed by Asian Pacific American faculty in this study and other published work.

In choosing to study issues of faculty of color in academe, we do not mean to discount the severity of the problems that confront students of color at the elementary and secondary school levels or in undergraduate and graduate programs. The issues at these fundamental levels of education have a direct impact on the supply of faculty of color. The focus of this book, however, is to examine the status and learn from the experiences of faculty of color who, despite those barriers, are currently employed in predominantly white colleges and research universities.

Why study faculty? We wholeheartedly agree with Green (1989) when she asserts that "faculty are the core of the institution...A diverse faculty is essential to a pluralistic campus...faculty create the curriculum [as well as create and legitimize knowledge] and determine the quality of experience in every classroom [and in every department]" (p. 81). In academe's attempts to enhance diversity, it is imperative then that the representation and well-being of faculty of color be strengthened.

Among the various institutions of higher learning, the major research universities are of particular interest. It is within these institutions that the results of dismantling affirmative action in California and Texas, the dazzling plummet of the number of African American students in the entering law school classes, first appear in the media. This is not surprising because major research universities play a significant role in our society. They educate the faculties and set the cultural climate for the rest of the academic enterprise. Even more importantly, the major research universities are gateways to positions of significant influence in the United States. Such prestigious institutions have guarded privilege in this country for more than two centuries, and they are very often a significant part of the path taken by most people who come to occupy powerful positions.

This book draws on a comprehensive study of African American, Asian Pacific American, American Indian, and Latino faculty in eight midwestern states. The study was conducted in states that were members of the Midwestern Higher Education Commission (MHEC) from 1993 to 1995: Illinois, Kansas, Michigan, Ohio, Wisconsin, Nebraska, Missouri, and Minnesota.

This study approached three fundamental questions: (1) To what extent is there underrepresentation of faculty of color? (2) What factors contribute to this underrepresentation? (3) What do we know about possible solutions to the underrepresentation of faculty of color in higher education?

We sought to address these questions through an econometrics analysis, individual and group interviews, a study of exemplary programs, and an institutional faculty development survey. We also undertook a thorough examination of the literature documenting the continued underrepresentation of faculty of color in the nation's colleges and universities.

Challenges to the successful recruitment, retention, and development of faculty of color include significant barriers within academia itself that discourage people of color from becoming productive and satisfied members of the professorate. Our findings and analyses show that the predominant barrier is racial and ethnic bias resulting in unwelcoming and unsupportive work environments for faculty of color. There are also, however, positive workplace experiences that strengthen the commitment of faculty of color to remain in academe.

In this book, we attempt to present critical perspectives emerging from our data with the hope of contributing to a comprehensive understanding of issues surrounding successful recruitment, retention, and development of faculty of color in higher education. These perspectives come from the voices of faculty of color themselves, from statistical data collected for our study, and from a comprehensive analysis of data presented in the literature. Furthermore, it is important to note that ours is a study of successes, not failures. In spite of the high probability of failure in preparing for the professorate, all faculty interviewed for this study, as well as faculty quoted in the literature, have earned tenure-track and tenured positions in higher education. Yet their well-articulated experiences point to the continued exclusion and isolation of successful minority scholars, even among those who are not only tenured but hold high-level, high-profile academic appointments.

We believe that this book will add to an understanding of the subject because we have examined the issues of underrepresentation of faculty of color, blending our academic interests and methodological approaches. We analyze higher education administration and policy, human relations, and social justice, within the context of public affairs, and have used qualitative and quantitative research approaches. Not only does this book present personal narratives of the real-life experiences of faculty of color, it also includes quantitative analyses of the underrepresentation of faculty of color through the use of national data sets and large sample surveys.

Our goal is to allow—and challenge—the reader to appreciate the nature and consequences of the persistent underrepresentation of faculty of color in higher education, and to envision a broad new agenda for addressing the problem. We believe that today's passive approaches will not correct the persistent inequities in academia. More direct and active approaches must be embraced.

STRUCTURE OF THE BOOK

Chapter 2, "Snapshots from the Literature: Elements Influencing the Workplace Environment," presents our comprehensive review of the literature. This includes a discussion of (1) the historical legacy contributing to the maintenance of racial and ethnic barriers in education, (2) continued resistance to faculty diversity and affirmative action, (3) the common themes and recommendations emerging from selected survey and narrative studies, (4) an examination of the literature on faculty of color by racial and ethnic group, and (5) some reflections on the literature reviewed.

The literature provides a rich and varied look at the numbers and circumstances of faculty of color from a variety of research and ethnic perspectives. The chapter presents our synthesis and summary of much of the recent literature, as well as providing information, authors, and articles of interest.

We have found that the individual studies reported in existing literature on the recruitment, retention, and development of faculty of color lack cross-disciplinary and mixed-method approaches. We realize also that it is impossible to capture the nuances of academic life for every individual. We try, however, to present a portrait of faculty life through the lenses of large national data sets, paper and pencil surveys, narrative data, and from our own experiences as faculty of color in academe.

Chapter 3, "The Nature and Extent of Minority Faculty Underrepresentation," examines some of the measurement and empirical issues associated with the underrepresentation of faculty of color in higher education. Several definitions of minority faculty underrepresentation are reviewed to identify the most appropriate measurement methodology for assessing the extent of faculty underrepresentation in higher education. The main definition utilized in this analysis is the ratio of the percentage of faculty from specific demographic groups to the percentage of the general population ages twenty-four to seventy who are members of that same group. The population subsets were ethnic/racial group, gender, age cohort, immigration status, citizenship, and by individual member state.

We detail the results of computations using Equal Employment Opportunity Commission (EEOC) data, U.S. Census Public Use Microsample (PUMS) data, as well as other sources of information on the employment of individuals with advanced degrees in higher education.

The central conclusion is that the underrepresentation of African Americans, American Indians, and Latinos/Latinas cuts across different measures of representation, age cohorts, fields of study, and reference groups. Indeed, we also find nontrivial underrepresentation of native-born Asian Pacific Americans in the critical age groups in which tenure and career advancement are expected.

Chapter 4, "A Chill in the Air: In the Words of Faculty of Color," describes, from the perspective of study respondents, what it is like to be a faculty member of color. Respondents articulate how they experience the "campus climate" in which they work. Unfortunately, they describe many manifestations of racial and ethnic bias in the workplace.

Chapter 5, "Minority Faculty Hiring—Equality of Opportunity?," describes, in a sense, how the environment of exclusion continues to exist for faculty of color. This chapter presents evidence that underrepresentation is not attributable to a "revolving door" phenomenon, as some contend, but that institutions simply are not hiring faculty of color.

This chapter examines the relationship between commitment—tangible versus rhetorical—to affirmative action policies and actual success in hiring faculty of color. Predictably, those institutions with the largest budget allocations for minority faculty development hire the most faculty of color. This chapter concludes, however, that for faculty of color institutional attitudes remain very important to overall representation. Experiences reported by faculty of color regarding chilly climates indicate that if students of color are to pursue academic careers and faculty of color are to be highly productive, their institutions must not only recruit them more aggressively but must nurture and affirm them after they are hired.

Chapter 6, "Why Stay? Current Rewards and Promising Efforts," gives us the opportunity to learn some lessons from people who remain in academe despite the "chill." Most of the faculty of color interviewed report "chilly climates" but nevertheless indicate that they plan to stay in academia. This chapter provides many comments that reflect the study participants' commitment to their academic careers and the positive experiences that keep them in the academic environment. In addition, they cite ways in which colleges and universities can enrich the lives of faculty of color and increase the impetus to stay, and this section of the book focuses on the positive workplace experiences our respondents identified and defined—although there may be a myriad of other factors that help retain faculty of color study respondents.

In addition to the recommendations of our study respondents, we examine several exemplary programs designed to address the problem of underrepresentation of faculty of color. Most of the programs are "pipeline" programs designed to increase the number of doctorates of color, and we identify three categories of emphasis: fellowships, special hiring programs, and mentoring and networking programs. We briefly describe one program to represent each category. These programs are presented as examples of each type— not necessarily better or worse than other such programs. In fact, we commend all programs that attempt to "go the extra mile" to recruit, retain, and develop faculty of color.

Finally, this chapter explores Duke University's much publicized effort to increase the number of black faculty. Although seen as a failed attempt, this dramatic and commendable effort begun in 1988 provides lessons that we discuss in this chapter.

Chapter 7, "Market Forces: Ph.D. Pipelines versus Competitive Wages," comprehensively examines two common explanations for the underrepresentation of minority faculty in higher education: the absence of qualified candidates with Ph.D.'s and the attractiveness of academic employment relative to employment outside of academia. There is some merit to both explanations.

Our findings challenge the widely held view that the cause of the underrepresentation of minority faculty is an undersupply of minority Ph.D.'s, and this chapter presents our analysis and conclusions in detail.

Chapter 8, "Moving beyond Myths and toward Community Diversity: Conclusions and Reflections," presents some thoughts on addressing the elusive issues and challenges highlighted by our research. We speak a little more about "academic angst" as it is experienced and compounded for minority faculty. We discuss the nature of privilege in academia and the importance of acknowledging the authenticity of other experiences, and we briefly revisit the question of the present and future role of affirmative action.

The literature, our statistical analyses, and our field study lead to the inevitable conclusion that higher education remains resistant to change, even in the face of insurmountable evidence that something is wrong and continues to be wrong, and despite our present efforts to make things right. Why are existing interventions not working and how can we forge new paths?

In Chapter 8 we discuss how achieving diversity will require many new approaches—new perspectives as well as new strategies—rather than "more of the same." We consider alternatives to present strategies for improving the representation and circumstances of minority faculty, and what we might do to build on the most promising among them. We raise critical questions about the organizational change processes required for true diversity, and the need for support both within and external to institutions of higher education. We also examine some of the underlying assumptions and myths—within ourselves and within our institutions—that prompt us to maintain the status quo.

We share our ultimate conclusion that to achieve meaningful diversity higher education must abandon a "business as usual" approach and embrace the highly unusual; that only by bringing to bear our great variety of perspectives and disciplines—along with a true commitment to change—can diversity and pluralism become reality.

SOME PRELIMINARY MATTERS
FOR THE READER

Williams (1991) talks about her rationale for using the categories of black and African American when describing her experience in academe. We agree with her view that terms such as *black* and *white* do not begin to "capture the rich ethnic and political diversity of my subject. But...that the simple matter of the color of one's skin so profoundly affects the way one is treated...that the decision to generalize from such a division is valid" (p. 256). She states that the term *minority,* although she uses it, implies "a certain delegitimacy in a majoritarian system," and prefers to use the term *African American* because "it effectively evokes the specific cultural dimensions of my identity" (p. 257). In this book several categories are used depending on the author, the speaker, and preferences. In all cases, speaking about any racial or ethnic population, the category used does not capture the full cultural dimensions of the people being described.

Many authors share similar concerns about definition or lack of definition for other groups. For example, Nakanishi (1995) defines Asian Pacific Americans as "immigrants, refugees, and the U.S. born descendants of immigrants from Asia, including Pakistan and the countries lying east of it in South Asia, Southeast Asia, East Asia, and the Pacific Islands" (p. 684). Aguirre and Martinez (1993) use the term "Chicano to identify a population that consists of persons of Mexican origin, whether born in the United States or Mexico" (p. xvii). In deciding not to further define the term *Chicano,* the authors state that such an attempt would be monumental and would divert from the specific topic of their writings. Valdes and Seoane (1995) state that "there is currently no consensus within the Hispanic community as to how its members should be collectively referred to...Often the terms Latino and Hispanic are used interchangeably...Hispanics may be of any race...most trace their ancestry to a Spanish-speaking country" (p. 8). Oppelt (1990) describes definitions typically used to refer to the American Indian population. "The term 'Indian' is unacceptable to, and is even seen as derogatory by some descendants of the original Americans. Some prefer to be called Native Americans...[but some may misinterpret this term as meaning anyone born in North America]. In spite of its geographic inaccuracy, some descendants of the first Americans still prefer...Indian...there is no one term preferred by all first Americans" (p. ix).

Obviously, attempts to even designate race and ethnicity are complicated. In examining one part of an intricate web, we acknowledge that the aggregation of data by racial and ethnic group is problematic in that there exists a great deal of diversity within each group. We are well aware, as Padilla (1994) correctly points out, that more research is needed in order to clearly understand intragroup variability. However, for the purposes of this study, we typically use the terms *African American, Asian Pacific American, Latino,* and *American Indian.* We have included thorough descriptions, as defined and described by the Census Bureau of Racial Statistics, of each population in Chapter 2 entitled "Snapshots from the Literature." We have used these categories because the existing data collected, both qualitative and quantitative, primarily used these terms.

We also felt strongly that we should use terminology typically used by our study respondents. We do not want to offend anyone by our use of language, and apologize if we do so. In Green's (1989) words, "we only hope that readers will keep their sights on the challenge and the solutions rather than the vehicle of expression. Language has its limitations, human potential has few" (p. xvii).

Furthermore, we use the term *people of color* or *faculty of color* to refer to persons of African American, American Indian, Asian Pacific American, and Latino origin. In doing so, we understand that people of color do not constitute a monolithic group. (We recognize that whites are also members of a distinct racial category.) And certainly by using the individual racial and ethnic categories we do not intend to imply that all persons so "designated" experience anything in a uniform way. Rather these categories are used in order to use existing data to distinguish between groups, identify some common themes, and make overall statements about the varying experiences of the identified groups.

We do not, in this book, explore the interlocking relationships that connect race, gender, and class; and given the boundaries of our research we do not claim to capture the full complexity of the issues at hand. We do hope, however, to share critical insights gleaned from our research to promote further understanding of the complicated web that produces negative workplace environments for many faculty of color in predominantly white colleges and universities.

We also use general terms to designate departmental affiliation and administrative position of our survey participants and interviewees. This is done, in large part, to provide anonymity for study participants quoted in this book.

The term *diversity* in this book is interchangeable with *pluralism.* Although we recognize the importance of the coexistence of multiple ethnic and racial groups within academe, we also urge, as noted in Green (1989), that members of all groups explore, understand,

and try to appreciate one another's cultural experiences and heritage. Simply but strongly put "Diversity connotes passive coexistence; pluralism is a dynamic atmosphere of collaboration...a key goal is to move beyond diversity to pluralism" (p. xvi).

As for some general notes about our presentation of material throughout the book: Often a theme introduced in one section of this book will reappear in another section because it applies to different sets of data. We hope that the reader will appreciate that such repetition, rather than being redundant, illustrates the pervasiveness of issues across data sets.

Finally, this text includes many direct quotes from our own study's individual faculty interviews and from the published literature. We feel it is extremely important to allow study participants—through us and other authors of color—to speak directly to our readers. It is their voices that both underlie and eloquently illustrate the major premises of this book.

2

SNAPSHOTS FROM
THE LITERATURE

Elements Influencing
the Workplace Environment

Most of the literature reviewed for this book points to a change in the manifestations of racism. Today they are the less visible, more subtle slights and exclusions, which are no less real for being difficult to prove. No longer are hate-filled faces a part of public displays at predominantly white institutions, nor are pictures of elected officials barring the entrance of African American students. Blatant rules excluding minorities from faculties of predominantly white universities—as Harvard excluded the eminent W. E. B. DuBois—are no longer on the books. Overt racism has gone underground, out of the glare of the journalists and the television cameras that captured the raw emotions of the civil rights movement in the 1960s.

The conflict now seethes at a deeper level. No longer legally sanctioned as institutional policy, bias and enmity take the form of campus racial incidents, hate speech, and hostility to multicultural curricula. Today the continuing conflict may be revealed in lawsuits filed by faculty of color contesting tenure and promotion decisions. Although some have successfully challenged a biased system

SEE

Tenure, Discrimination, and the Courts T. L. Leap (1995)

Academics in Court: The Consequences of Faculty Discrimination Litigation G. R. LaNoue and B. A. Lee (1987)

and secured tenure through the courts, the mere fact of these legal challenges, and the fact that they are successful at all, signals continued racism, and toxic environments in academia. These lawsuits are, in our view, only the tip of the iceberg. Many faculty of color continue to do their jobs and succeed at them within an unwelcoming and exclusive academic environment. Countless studies and reports bear witness to this troubling nationwide trend.

This chapter presents the results of our comprehensive literature review. Included are discussions of (1) the historical legacy that has helped maintain racial and ethnic barriers in education, (2) faculty diversity and affirmative action, (3) continued resistance to faculty diversity, (4) themes and recommendations emerging from selected survey and narrative studies, (5) an examination of the literature on faculty of color by racial and ethnic group, and (6) some reflections on the literature reviewed. Because there has been much recent discussion about affirmative action in the literature, a section devoted to summarizing some of that discussion is included here.

We have also included pertinent quotes from our own interviews as a reminder that what may sometimes appear to be intellectual abstractions are based on very real human experiences.

HISTORICAL LEGACY

Since its earliest beginnings, the American public school system has been deeply committed to the maintenance of racial and ethnic barriers. Higher education, both public and private, shared this outlook. Philosophers of the common schools remained silent about the education of minority children...White educators profited from the enforced absence of black and other minority competitors for jobs. Planned deprivation became a norm of educational practice.

Weinberg (1977, p. 1)

Not only were minority scholars excluded from full participation in the academy, historical accounts of their exclusion are almost entirely absent from the standard histories of the United States and American education. Thus, the legacy of segregation and exclusion continues today, handed down through the generations. Contemporary scholars continue to lack exposure and access to information concerning the contributions of people of color to various streams of knowledge. Such resources are not readily available in many doctoral programs and any scholarly inquiry in this area must be somewhat extraordinary.

Weinberg (1997) documents incidents of racism against African Americans, and also includes some discussion on the plight of Mexican Americans, American Indians, and Puerto Ricans in academic settings. Regarding the early experiences of minority faculty in white academia, he states: "White academia ensured its ignorance by excluding eminent minority scholars from university faculties" (p. 4). Not only were minorities excluded from faculties but they were excluded from academic discourse altogether, as white scholars failed to include important contributions from minority scholars in their works. Weinberg points to the submergence of works by W. E. B. DuBois, Carter G. Woodson, and Horace Mann Bond in research on the educational history of African Americans.

According to Weinberg, early scholars from other minority groups fared even worse than early African American scholars, as their contributions to education were unpublished or even unrecorded. Olivas (1988) writes that the history of exclusionary employment has created learning environments that are citadels of segregation. Brown (1994) notes

> *We must have diversity in scholarship. Indians get censored even before we get in print. More outlets are needed to publish articles on minority concerns.*
>
> American Indian male tenured humanities college administrator

that strict exclusionary hiring practices, sanctioned by custom and law in both private and public higher education, continued well into the mid-twentieth century for all minority groups including black Americans, American Indians, Hispanics, and Asian Americans. Thus, the lack of representation of minorities throughout the range of disciplines continues to exist. It is not surprising that many faculty of color describe a lack of respect, lack of publication opportunities, and lack of recognition for their scholarship.

SEE

"The Impasse on Faculty Diversity in Higher Education: A National Agenda" S. V. Brown in *Minorities in Higher Education* M. J. Justiz, R. Wilson, and L. G. Bjork (Eds.) (1994)

"Latino Faculty at the Border: Increasing Numbers Key to More Hispanic Access" M. A. Olivas *Change* (1988)

Given the situation, those of us who have achieved some success in academia must consciously cast a wider net than our traditional training demanded. We must make that extraordinary effort to identify and acknowledge the work of scholars of color in our own work. Long before we began this book, one of our colleagues, a senior scholar of color, criticized our limited citations in an earlier work. We recognized a lack of knowledge; the educational experience failed to introduce such inclusive scholarship. Because of this early criticism, including scholarship from culturally diverse scholars became very important to our work.

> **SEE**
>
> *Racial Oppression in America*
> R. Blauner (1972)
>
> "The Emperor Has No Clothes: Rewriting 'Race in Organization'"
> S. M. Nkomo *Academy of Management Review* (1992)

The discussion of racism in the academy has gone on for many years. Blauner (1972) addressed the sociological context of institutional racism contending that a broader (as opposed to individually based) and more sociological definition of racism "focuses on the society as a whole and on structured relations between people rather than on individual personalities and actions" (p. 277). From this standpoint, "the University is racist because people of color are and have been so systematically excluded from full and equal participation and power—as students, professors, administrators, and particularly, in the historical definition of the character of the institution and its curriculum" (pp. 277–278).

Twenty years later, writing for the *Academy of Management Review,* Nkomo (1992) focused on the need to rewrite race into the study of organizations because organizational dynamics are not race neutral. Nkomo contends that race is not merely a demographic variable but that the very concept of race and its historical and political meaning must be understood in order to use race as an analytical concept for understanding the nature of organizations.

The works of Blauner and Nkomo suggest indicators that might be observed on a daily basis in order to assess the inclusiveness of departmental climates for people of color. For example, regarding curriculum, Blauner cites an informant who noted the absence of any work by a black or Chicano on any other faculty member's required or suggested reading list, despite the department's emphasis on urban and minority problems. In our own study, one respondent recently observed interviews for positions in urban education and reported being very mindful of the candidate's knowledge or ignorance of diverse scholars, writers, and practitioners in the field. In "job talks," candidates should display knowledge of work done by diverse scholars in the field. Otherwise their thorough knowledge of their fields as well as their ability to contribute to an inclusive departmental environment should be questioned. Unfortunately, hiring authorities rarely apply such a standard.

An anthology of writings on faculty and faculty issues in colleges and universities by Finnegan, Webster, and Gamson (1996) acknowledges the social barriers that precluded or limited access to professional opportunities for African American scholars prior to the Civil Rights Act of 1964. The work illustrates the abundance of research (beginning in 1942) focusing on white male faculty and the paucity of studies involving faculty of color in academia prior to the 1980s. Other recent anthologies have collected and presented articles documenting the historically unwelcoming environment for faculty of color.

> **SEE**
>
> *Faculty and Faculty Issues in Colleges and Universities* D. E. Finnegan, D. Webster, and Z. F. Gamson (Eds.) (1996)
>
> *The Racial Crisis in American Higher Education* P. G. Altbach and K. Lomotey (Eds.) (1991)
>
> *Racial and Ethnic Diversity in Higher Education* C. S. Turner, M. Garcia, A. Nora, and L. I. Rendon (Eds.) (1996)

FACULTY DIVERSITY AND AFFIRMATIVE ACTION: CONTINUED RESISTANCE

> *By adopting affirmative action policies, an organization tacitly acknowledges the inadequacy of equal opportunity. Those who have "made it" in the system must acknowledge that one contributing factor may have been privilege—subtle and covert, but nonetheless real and important. Exposing meritocracy as an illusion threatens all who would like to see their own achievements as determined by merit alone.*
>
> Crosby and Clayton (1990, p. 72)

Wilson adds to the works of Weinberg, Brown, and Olivas in documenting the historical legacy that continues to exclude certain racial and ethnic groups from full participation in education. He notes that attempts, such as affirmative action, have been made to work toward parity and inclusion of people of color within higher education. However, such efforts continue to be met with resistance. Wilson (1995) quotes former Secretary of Labor Robert Reich who identified the job market pressures as the source of much of this resistance. Reich observed that "angry white males" were "venting their frustrations at minorities and women when the real problem they face (along with everyone else) is an increasingly competitive global economy that has produced massive changes in the domestic economy and drastically altered the nature and demands of the job market" (p. 16).

SEE
"Affirmative Action: Yesterday, Today, and Beyond" R. Wilson American Council on Education (1995)
"I'm White and They're Wrong" P. Begala *George* (1997)
"For Richer, for Poorer: Faculty Morale in Periods of Austerity and Retrenchment" S. P. Kerlin and D. M. Dunlap *Journal of Higher Education* (1993)

Begala (1997) supports the position that reaction to affirmative action occurs in a context of shifting privilege. He writes, "Don't believe the old canard about how unqualified people benefit from affirmative action. That may have been true in the past, when only the inbred progeny of the eastern moneyed elite received preferential treatment" (p. 88). Olivas points out that today's most senior faculty directly benefitted—that is, they attained and have maintained positions of privilege—in markets and institutions in which competition from women and minorities did not exist.

These perspectives point to an existing but unacknowledged preferential system for whites now and in the past. Such comments are reiterated over and over again in the debates surrounding affirmative action.

Kerlin and Dunlap believe that the interests of the corporate sector increasingly influence many aspects of American higher education; that the missions of colleges and universities have shifted toward serving "technocratic, economic, and private research interests" as opposed to "public interest" educational objectives such as quality undergraduate teaching. Global competition, private interests, and a history of exclusion in higher education combine to fuel the fires of contention within higher education today.

We agree with those who believe that—ultimately—affirmative action issues in higher education are not fundamentally legal questions but are political, societal, and educational issues. Wilson (1995) sums it up well in his article for the American Council on Education: "The questions confronting the academy are whether diversity is a legitimate goal; whether achieving a diverse student [or faculty body] is an educational value; and what is the educational role and purpose of higher education" (p. 19).

Executive Order 11246 and Higher Education

On September 24, 1965, Lyndon B. Johnson issued Executive Order 11246, which ordered all government contractors to take affirmative action, seeking to ensure the termination of occupational segregation by race mandated by Title VII of the Civil Rights Act of 1964. Executive Order 11246 required federal contractors, including universities contracting with the federal government, to ensure that all employment applicants be treated without regard for their race, creed, color, or national origin.

According to Ethridge, it was not until Labor Department Orders were issued in 1970 and 1971—Order Number 4 and Revised Order No. 4—that there was real impact on higher education. In combination they required that government contractors with fifty employees or more and government contracts of $50,000 or more, including nonconstruction contractors, prepare affirmative action plans with goals and timetables for hiring women and minorities.

In 1973 the American Association of University Professors endorsed affirmative action in faculty hiring and charged the professoriate with promoting diversity to remedy past discrimination. Wey (1980) writes about the resistance of major research universities to comply with this directive. For example, she states that in 1975 faculty members from the University of California system testified before the president of the United States and the Commission on Civil Rights. These faculty members argued against the implementation of affirmative action in higher education.

SEE

"There is Much More to Do" R. W. Ethridge in *Affirmative Action's Testament of Hope: Strategies for a New Era in Higher Education* M. Garcia (Ed.) (1997)

"Asian-Americans in Academia" N. Wey in *Political Participation of Asian Americans* Y. H. Jo (Ed.) (1980)

SEE

"Recruitment and Retention of Minority Faculty and Staff" R. Wilson *AAHE Bulletin* (1987)

"Faculty Issues: The Impact on Minorities" J. E. Blackwell *The Review of Higher Education* (1988)

Wilson and others have long observed an ongoing pattern of resistance to the meaningful inclusion of minorities in the higher education mainstream. Blackwell (1988) sees the opposition to affirmative action in higher education as a complex and subtle phenomenon, in that verbal support is often inconsistent with institutional behavior. He cites a number of means by which affirmative action in faculty recruitment is subverted. These include transmitting negative signals during the interview process, failing to include minorities on search committees to review the curricula vitae of applicants, having no tenured minority faculty on search committees free to voice opinions without fear of reprisal, and continuing to use white male networks as a primary recruitment tool for faculty positions.

Affirmative Action "On the Line"

Today, amid challenges to affirmative action practices and policies, a review of all related federal and state laws is taking place. A special report in *The Chronicle for Higher Education* on April 28, 1995 related that affirmative action is said to be "on the line." Alarm about the legal attacks on affirmative action is based on the prematurity of abandoning it; the knowledge

"Anticlimax" may be the best word to describe the status of the now 17-year-old effort to desegregate the faculties of predominantly white colleges and universities...the impact of affirmative action in terms of increased African-American and Hispanic faculty...is still minimal...the prospects for diversity look extremely dismal unless the institutions find ways to make affirmative action a reality and not just a rhetorical exercise.

Washington and Harvey
(1989, pp. 39–40)

that even *with* legally mandated affirmative action, progress in incorporating minorities in academia has been excruciatingly slow. Literature examining the status of faculty of color in higher education consistently documents continued underrepresentation and racial and ethnic bias.

In their 1989 book, Washington and Harvey address the failure of affirmative action policies to remedy the underrepresentation of both African American and Hispanic faculty at predominantly white institutions. In their view, increased hate speech, racially motivated incidents on campuses, and growing polarization along color lines signal the need for greater efforts—not reduced attention—to promote parity in the nation's college faculties. They contend that the motivation for parity comes from a "higher sense of national necessity that supersedes narrow self-interest" (p. 40). Given the minuscule progress made in diversifying faculty, Washington and Harvey state that "the chances of significantly decreasing the level of [African American and Hispanic faculty] participation is very great if affirmative action policy is abandoned" (p. 41). Unfortunately, it appears as if we will have a chance to see if that prediction comes true.

Myers (1997) describes recent federal court decisions such as *Croson v. City of Richmond* and *Poderesky v. Kirwan* as shaping "the dismantling of affirmative action in America" (p. 26). He goes on to say that college officials, embracing the language of diversity, have drastically

> **SEE**
>
> "Why Diversity Is a Smoke Screen for Affirmative Action" S. L. Myers, Jr. *Change* (1997)

downplayed the language of affirmative action in their promotional materials. By the same token, minority business set-aside programs have been replaced with disadvantaged business programs and "diversity goals." Myers (1997) concludes that the reframing of "affirmative action" into "diversity goals" has in fact served as a "smoke screen for the elimination of all real efforts to assist African Americans and other underrepresented minorities" (p. 27).

In Texas, according to the State Attorney General's Office, the *Hopwood* reverse-discrimination case had the effect of barring any use of race in admissions and scholarships at state colleges and universities. In a similar vein, the University of California Board of Regents adopted a measure that banned the use of preferences in admissions. The 1996 passage of the California Civil Rights Initiative, Proposition 209, is another example of the dismantling of affirmative action. Proposition 209 amends the California State Constitution to eliminate all statewide affirmative action programs based on race or sex in public employment, public education, and public contracting. In our view, such developments are modern-day manifestations of the historical legacy excluding racial and ethnic groups from full participation in education and in the economy.

While we question the reframing of affirmative action into diversity goals, we are impressed by the significant support garnered by such goals. One striking example is the resolution taken by the Association of American Universities, representing sixty-two leading North American universities. This public commitment refers to the importance of diversity in university admissions, but the principle may be reasonably applied to diversity of faculty as well. The association's resolution follows.

We speak first and foremost as educators. We believe that our students benefit significantly from education that takes place in a diverse setting. In the course of their university education, our students encounter and learn from others who have backgrounds and characteristics very different from their own. As we seek to prepare students for life in the twenty-first century, the educational value of such encounters will become more important, not less, than in the past…

As presidents and chancellors of universities that have historically produced many of America's leaders in business, government, the professions, and the arts, we are conscious of our obligation to educate exceptional people who will serve all of the nation's different communities.

[Excerpt] Resolution by the Association
of American Universities, from Arenson (1997, p. A17)

This expressed commitment to diversity is encouraging indeed. We hope that the members of the association see racial, ethnic, and other types of diversity as important in faculties as in student populations.

Tierney (1997) argues eloquently for such a mission in American public higher education, and describes the challenge to higher education presented by the current affirmative action debate as one of "…developing more proactive policies that help academia serve the public good by advancing diversity and fostering the public culture so that everyone is able to participate…Democracy is the practice of self-determination. Public education is the central means we have used to enable all citizens to participate in the democratic public sphere" (p. 193).

Karabel (1997) states that in order for affirmative action to survive, we must emphasize that the expansion of the "pool of talent beyond earlier boundaries and fostering inclusion in a society wracked by division, has made America a better country than it was in 1965" (p. 30). If we chose to "let the chips fall where they may," Karabel says, "the imposition of 'color blind' policies [given prevailing definitions of merit] will lead to levels of segregation in leading institutions of higher education not seen in over a quarter of a century" (p. 29).

> **SEE**
>
> "The Parameters of Affirmative Action: Equity and Excellence in the Academy" W. G. Tierney *Review of Educational Research* (1997)
>
> "Can Affirmative Action Survive?" J. Karabel *Tikkun* (1997)

Small Changes: Ongoing Patterns of Resistance?

Villalpando, in a work to be published, documents statistical underrepresentation of scholars of color and observes that "the extensive talent of scholars of color has yet to be fully recognized by higher education...By limiting their representation, we also exclude their contributions to widening our overall knowledge base" (p. 20).

Given evidence from our study, as well as in much of the literature, it is not surprising that a 1997 work entitled *Race and Ethnicity in the American Professoriate 1995–1996* published by the Higher Education Research Institute, Graduate School of Education and Information Studies in Los Angeles shows that faculty of color accounted for about 10 percent of the professoriate, inching up from 9 percent in 1989, with nonwhites concentrated in the two-year colleges or in non-tenure-track positions. The study

> **SEE**
>
> "Scholars of Color: Are They Really a Part of the Emerging Composition of the Professoriate?" O. Villalpando *UCLA Journal of Education and Information Studies* (in press)
>
> *Race and Ethnicity in the American Professoriate, 1995–96* H. S. Astin, A. L. Antonio, C. M. Cress, and A. W. Astin (1997)

was based on a nationwide survey of 33,986 faculty respondents, of whom 8.7 percent (or 2,943) represented several racial/ethnic group categories: African American/Black; American Indian; Asian American/Asian; Mexican American/Chicano; Puerto Rican American; Other Latino.

SEE

"Proportion of Minority Professors Inches Up to About 10%" A. Schneider *The Chronicle of Higher Education* (1997)

Minorities in Higher Education: Fourteenth Annual Status Report [American Council on Education] D. J. Carter and R. Wilson (1996)

The Voice of Hispanic Higher Education The Hispanic Association of Colleges and Universities (1996)

According to this report and others, faculty of color continue to report experiences of subtle discrimination in the workplace, such as seeing their work devalued if it focuses on minority issues. Furthermore, subtle but pervasive discrimination in the review and promotion process produces the largest differences in stress levels between white faculty and faculty of color. Astin (1977) notes her surprise at the findings: "I was expecting the picture to look brighter...The proportion of minority professors is so small that they're invisible in so many ways" (p. A13).

As our own study results suggest, once hired, faculty of color continue to experience exclusion, isolation, alienation, and racism resulting in uncomfortable work environments in predominantly white university settings. Indeed, Astin's study finds that, compared with white faculty, faculty of color, including Asian American faculty, are less satisfied with nearly every aspect of their jobs. Factors related to job satisfaction receiving "less satisfied" responses from faculty of color included autonomy/independence, professional relations with faculty, overall job satisfaction, opportunity to develop new ideas (compared with all other respondents, Asian Americans were least satisfied on this factor), job security, and quality of students.

Carter and O'Brien documented these conditions in their 1993 research brief entitled Employment and Hiring Patterns for Faculty of Color. The study was conducted over a ten-year period, from 1981 to 1991. They concluded that "the growth in the employment of faculty of color has been uneven, and their overall representation remains relatively small" (p. 1). Their study points to unsupportive academic environments as an important factor in the nonretention of faculty of color, and to a "revolving door" explanation for underrepresentation. Although our own statistical analysis does not show that minorities, once hired, leave at higher rates than their white counterparts, our interviews bear out—and we are in complete accord with Carter and O'Brien and others who demonstrate—that minorities face daunting obstacles and hostile environments in mainstream academia. Our data lead us to conclude that there is, indeed, a chilly climate, and that although it may serve to discourage potential academics, it does not cause many faculty of color to abandon their academic careers once undertaken (see Chapter 4, "A Chill in the Air," and Chapter 6, "Why Stay?").

SOME COMMON THEMES AND RECOMMENDATIONS

In developing this book we made a comprehensive search of literature germane to the issue of the recruitment and retention of faculty of color, and we identified and reviewed hundreds of books, articles, and other relevant publications. The literature—whether involving statistical studies, field investigations, or other forms of scholarly inquiry—documents continued underrepresentation of faculty of color in American colleges and universities.

These materials also reveal a number of common themes. The image of a pipeline is frequently used to describe the links between the availability of faculty of color, the training of minority graduate students, the accessibility of undergraduate education for minorities, and the success of minority students at the elementary and secondary school levels. The presence of "leaks" in this pipeline provides one explanation for underrepresentation. A number of studies indicate that the problem of underrepresentation is one of supply, and that the solution is to increase the number of doctoral recipients of color.

Although certainly an important part of the solution, we believe this approach does not address the barriers within academia

SEE

Increasing Minority Faculty: An Elusive Goal S. V. Brown (1988)

"Faculty Issues in the 1990's: New Realities, New Opportunities" J. H. Schuster *New Directions for Higher Education* (1990)

"Participation and Degree Attainment of African-American and Latino Students in Graduate Education Relative to Other Racial and Ethnic Groups: An Update from OCR Data" G. E. Thomas *Harvard Educational Review* (1992)

"Tomorrow's Professoriate: Insuring Minority Participation Through Talent Development Today" H. G. Adams [Paper presented at the Engineering Dean's Council Student Pipeline Workshop, American Society for Engineering Education] (1988)

"Faculty Issues: The Impact on Minorities" J. E. Blackwell *The Review of Higher Education* (1988)

that hinder the recruitment and retention of faculty of color. As part of our literature review, selected quantitative survey studies were examined as well as several narrative studies and essays. Results of these different types of studies complemented one another so the findings will be presented together. Speaking to the issue of campus environment for faculty of color, several researchers, including ourselves, have identified many institutional barriers to the recruitment, retention, and the development of faculty of color. Researchers also provide a wide spectrum of recommendations. Those most commonly made had to do with proposed reevaluations of hiring, tenure, and promotion policies and practices. Not to dismiss or belittle other very important concerns presented here, but due to the preponderance of writings related to hiring, tenure, and promotion policies, more lengthy discussion of these topics will be reported. Certainly all of the following concerns brought forward by the literature combine with other study data to form an interlocking web that weaves and shapes the experiences for faculty of color in academia. These elements combine to contribute to the creation of the academic environment within which these faculty work.

Isolation and Lack of Mentoring Opportunities

Faculty of color find themselves outside the informal networks of the department. A sense of isolation is among the most commonly reported problems in the literature as well as in our own study.

> *I don't feel like a part of the department. I have been alienated from my department for a number of years…It is not an environment that's nurturing for me.*
>
> Male African American tenured social sciences college-level administrator

Although merit and autonomy are touted as institutional values in the academy, a major contributor to success in the professoriate is association with senior colleagues. Without such affiliation, faculty of color are isolated and struggle through the socialization process alone.

Most studies recommend an improvement in professional development opportunities for minority faculty, to improve retention, tenure, and advancement prospects, and alleviate many of the "quality of work-life" problems. The literature discusses many worthwhile options, but the single most common recommendation for improving minority faculty retention is mentoring.

It is hard to overstate the value placed on this intervention throughout the literature. Bjork and Thompson (1989) recommend "structuring mentor relationships with senior faculty recognized for excellence in teaching, research, publishing, and service, areas critical for new faculty in meeting tenure expectations" (p. 350). Granger (1993) writes that "mentoring is a means by which a senior faculty member can provide moral support, assistance in developing expertise, and guidance in gaining access to resources and securing faculty positions" (p. 133). Blackwell (1989) sees mentoring to be of particular importance to minority faculty because "...Mentoring means using one's own experiences and expertise to help guide the development of others. It is a close, interpersonal relationship...[the mentor] offers encouragement and constructive criticism" (p. 429).

Occupational Stress

The existing underrepresentation of men and women of color and the desire of universities to have minority representation on committees combine to place formidable responsibilities on the shoulders of faculty of color. Faculty of color are involved in a Catch-22; they feel they cannot refuse to serve on committees, but heavy service loads mean less time for the research that is the focus of tenure review (see the source box: Garza; Menges & Exum; Smith & Witt).

Several studies point out that faculty of color often have different demands placed on their time and energy than what is expected from white faculty members. For example, faculty of color

SEE

The New Faculty Member: Supporting and Fostering Professional Development R. Boice (1992)

Retaining and Promoting Minority Faculty Members: Problems and Possibilities J. Spann (1990)

"Hiring, Promoting and Retaining African American Faculty: A Case Study of an Aspiring Multi-Cultural Research University" M. W. Clague. Paper presented at the annual meeting of the Association for the Study of Higher Education (1992)

"Mentoring: An Action Strategy for Increasing Minority Faculty" J. E. Blackwell *Academe* (1989)

"The Next Generation of Faculty Minority Issues" L. G. Bjork and T. E. Thompson *Education and Urban Society* (1989)

"A Review of the Literature on the Status of Women and Minorities in Higher Education" M. W. Granger *Journal of School Leadership* (1993)

Tenure-Track Faculty Study E. M. Bensimon, K. A. Ward, and W. G. Tierney. Prepared for the Penn State Commission for Women (1994)

SEE

"Second Class Academics: Chicano/Latino Faculty in U.S. Universities" H. Garza *New Directions for Teaching and Learning* (1993)

"Barriers to the Progress of Women and Minority Faculty" R. J. Menges and W. H. Exum *Journal of Higher Education* (1983)

"A Comparative Study of Occupational Stress among African American and White University Faculty: A Research Note" E. Smith and S. L. Witt *Research in Higher Education* (1993)

are often asked, and feel compelled, to serve on more committees than white faculty members. This was borne out in our own study. Although aware that they may decline some committee work, faculty of color feel they are expected to accept committee invitations, particularly when an opportunity to address minority issues is involved. They do not want to be seen as disinterested. (Faculty responses regarding committee and community service concerns are elaborated further in Chapter 4, "A Chill in the Air.") Astin, Antonio, Cress, and Astin (1997) report that the personal goal of promoting racial understanding accounts for the biggest difference between faculty of color and white faculty in their study. We feel this finding adds further insight into the reluctance of faculty of color to decline committee assignments. Smith and Witt (1993), documenting that black faculty have higher stress levels relating to research and service than do white faculty, recommend the development of techniques to reduce job-related stress as one means to increase retention.

Institutional Racism

SEE

"Asian Pacific Americans in Higher Education: Faculty and Administrative Representation and Tenure" D. T. Nakanishi *New Directions for Teaching and Learning* (1993)

"Racism in America: The Old Wolf Revisited" M. Reyes and J. J. Halcon *Harvard Educational Review* (1988)

Faculty of color find that research on minority issues is not considered legitimate work, particularly if articles are published in journals that are not mainstream. Just as our study respondents described, other studies find that the research interests of faculty of color are denigrated, either because the research area is not traditional or because the faculty themselves are seen as inferior due to race or ethnicity. Due to continued exclusionary practices within institutions of higher education, Verdugo (1995) describes such institutions as "segregated citadel(s)" (p. 101).

Garza (1993) conducted a national survey of 238 Latino faculty and found that 40 percent of the Chicano and Puerto Rican faculty in his study felt that colleagues devalued their research, particularly if it related to their own racial/ethnic group; 44 percent felt that research by Chicanos and Puerto Ricans was generally seen as inferior within their department. According to these respondents, the top three reasons for the denial of tenure for many Latino faculty were department politics, racism, and an insensitivity to their research interests.

Delgado (1989) reports the results of a job satisfaction survey of 106 minority law professors initially interviewed and over 50 interviewed the following year: "The picture that emerges from the data is sobering. Many minority professors report a decline in civility and toleration of difference at the nation's law schools. A high percentage described their work environments as racist or subtly racist" (p. 352).

SEE

"Reflections of a Black Social Scientist: Some Struggles, Some Doubts, Some Hopes" J. Mitchell *Harvard Educational Review* (1982)

The Leaning Ivory Tower: Latino Professors in American Universities R. V. Padilla and R. C. Chavez (1995)

"The Changing Composition of the Faculty: What Does It Really Mean for Diversity?" J. F. Milem and H. S. Astin *Change* (1993)

"Success in Doctoral Programs: Experiences of Minority and White Students" M. T. Nettles *American Journal of Education* (1990)

"Faculty-Faculty Mentoring and Discrimination: Perceptions among Asian, Asian American, and Pacific Island Faculty" R. G. Sands, A. L. Parson, and J. Duane *Equity & Excellence* (1992)

"Minority Law Professors' Lives: The Bell-Delgado Survey" R. Delgado *Harvard Civil Liberties Law Review* (1989)

The "Token Hire" Misconception

Faculty of color report that colleagues expect them to be less qualified or less likely to make significant contributions in research. Some have noted a pervasive attitude of complacency: the belief that hiring one person of color in a department is sufficient. This contributes further to the isolation being "the one" in a department (see the source boxes: Reyes & Halcon; Mitchell; Bronstein; Granger; Padilla & Chavez; Sands, Parson, & Duane). Kulis and Miller (1988) say that tokenism "in its various manifestations should be identified and abolished," and the "concomitants of tokenism, such as committee overload, professional isolation, and marginality, should be monitored and redressed" (p. 32).

Racial and Ethnic Bias in the Recruitment and Hiring Process

SEE

"Challenges, Rewards, and Costs for Feminist and Ethnic Minority Scholars" P. Bronstein *New Directions for Teaching* (1993)

"Are Minority Women Sociologists in Double Jeopardy?" S. Kulis and K. A. Miller *The American Sociologist* (1988)

"Racial/Ethnic Minority and Women Administrators and Faculty in Higher Education: A Status Report" J. G. Ponterotto *New Directions for Student Services* (1990)

"Minority Faculty Recruitment Programs at Two-Year Colleges" R. D. Opp and A. B. Smith. Paper presented at the Annual Meeting of the Council of Universities and Colleges (1992)

"Faculty Issues: The Impact on Minorities" J. E. Blackwell *The Review of Higher Education* (1988)

Our study suggests that the absence of aggressive hiring strategies may contribute more to the underrepresentation of faculty of color than the leaving of faculty of color. Ponterotto (1990) suggests the following:

"Necessary qualifications" should be defined carefully. Does excellence in the field include being able to relate to, mentor, and be a role model for minority students, or would this just be a nice extra in a candidate?... For example, which of the following two candidates is more qualified for the job of full professor: a generally good teacher with seventy-three articles published in academic journals, or a generally good teacher with thirty-nine articles published and an exemplary reputation for mentoring minority students and attracting them to the campus? In this example, an important question is what constitutes a "qualified" candidate. (p. 71)

Opp and Smith (1992) make the interesting proposal that institutions should cancel positions when people of color are not in the candidate pool. They also recommend that (1) state incentive programs should be developed to target funds for enhancing minority faculty recruitment, (2) minorities should be hired as chief academic administrators of institutions, and (3) minorities should be appointed to boards of trustees of institutions.

Blackwell (1988) points to elements necessary to the successful recruitment of faculty of color based on the experiences of the University of Massachusetts, which ranked first among all New England colleges and universities in percentage of minority faculty (approximately 13.4 percent). Blackwell attributes this success to the unqualified priority assigned to affirmative action by the university's chancellor, the authority delegated to the affirmative action officer, and the monitoring roles performed over the past seventeen years by the association of black faculty and staff of the university.

Several essays (see the source boxes: AAUP; Bronstein; Cooper & Smith; Granger; Graves; Nakanishi; Wilson) speak to the importance of recruitment plans and policies for increasing the number of faculty of color. The American Association of University Professors (AAUP, 1982) recommends that "a plan for the recruitment of minority persons and women should be developed by each department and approved by the affirmative action officer" (pp. 18A–19A). The AAUP report also suggests many possible elements of such a plan, including the following:

- Search committees should consider going beyond those institutions from which faculty for the institutions have been traditionally recruited. Consistent use of the same few institutions may perpetuate a pattern of discrimination in faculty hiring.
- In recruiting faculty, the standards should be the same for all candidates. White males should not be considered on "promise" and all other of comparable education and accomplishments on "achievement." Search committees should be sensitive in reading letters of reference for indications of bias.
- The fact that the pool of minority persons and women candidates for a particular vacancy is small should not be used as an excuse for not attempting to recruit for such candidates.

Another recommendation for recruitment is provided by Graves (1990) in her essay on black women in higher education:

Many national professional organizations have a Black and/or minority caucus (e.g., the Black Caucus of the Society for Research in Child Development, the section on the Psychology of Black Women of the American Psychological Association). Furthermore,

in many professions there are parallel Black and/or minority pro-
fessional organization (e.g., National Medical Association, the
Black Psychologists Association). These groups maintain direc-
tories of minority professionals and, in some cases, of minority
graduate students. Contact with such groups, instead of reli-
ance on the… "old boy"…networks, would greatly increase the
probability of identifying promising Black female candidates.
(p. 7)

SEE

"Affirmative Action Plans,"
Academe 15a–20a American
Association of University
Professors (1982)

"Challenges, Rewards, and
Costs for Feminist and Eth-
nic Minority Scholars" P.
Bronstein *New Directions for
Teaching* (1993)

"Lessons Form the Experi-
ence of the Evergreen State
College: Achieving a Di-
verse Faculty" R. Cooper
and B. L. Smith *AAHE Bulletin* (1990)

"A Case of Double Jeopar-
dy? Black Women in High-
er Education" S. B. Graves
Initiatives (1990)

"Making the Short List:
Black Candidates and the
Faculty Recruitment Pro-
cess" R. A. Mickelson and
M. I. Oliver in *The Racial
Crisis in American Higher Ed-
ucation* P. G. Altbach and K.
Lomotey (Eds.) (1991)

Mickelson and Oliver (1991), in "Making the Short List: Black Candidates and the Faculty Recruitment Process," recommend that institutions not limit their recruitment efforts to the elite universities. They contend that blacks are excluded from faculty employment because they are less likely to graduate from the elite institutions, and that hiring committees tend to view degrees from universities such as Harvard, Princeton, and Stanford as proxies for individual merit. Their findings indicate that the inference may be valid for white students of privileged backgrounds, but that equally meritorious black students may not necessarily gravitate to the top institutions, and may be more widely dispersed throughout schools of all rankings. They conclude:

The assumption that quality rises to the top may reflect some truth in the case of male majority students, but such assumption is flawed in the case of blacks and other members of minor-ities who continue to meet barriers to obtaining the prerequisites for higher education, and to higher education itself. Because of family obligations, community ties, hostile social and racial cli-mates on elite campuses, inadequate social and psychological support systems at leading schools or limited financial support, well-qualified minority group members may enroll in a wide variety of schools rather than following the path that leads to elite universities. (pp. 161–162)

An example of this phenomenon from our own study involves an American Indian male tenured in the social sciences who holds a top-level position in university administration. Observing that "faculty who got here are the survivors," he recalls his first encounter with postsecondary education:

I just planned to graduate from high school and become a car mechanic…then I won some awards and received some scholarship money…[An admissions officer at a prestigious private elite university said], "Most of the parents of our students here make more than $100,000 a year. That will probably be some social distress for you. I see that you are good academically… Well, yes, you're good enough for us but you could be better."

I was seventeen or eighteen years old and I was furious. I left and went to another [less prestigious] university. So I, by good fortune, had a bad taste for what that admissions officer did and ended up in a place where the station may have been a little bit lower, but my relative position in it seemed all the more higher and successful and that's good feedback to get when you are developing and growing.

Mickelson and Oliver suggest first that recruitment committees cast their nets more widely, and also that there should be more postdoctoral training programs at elite universities to address biases in the hiring process. Because access to top research institutions remains limited for scholars of color, Mickelson

> **SEE**
>
> "Diversity in the Faculty 'Not Like Us': Moving Barriers to Minority Recruitment" P. Light *Journal of Policy Analysis and Management* (1994)

and Oliver strongly conclude that the fault lies with racially and ethnically biased faculty recruitment and search practices. An essay by Light (1994) further illuminates issues related to the recruitment and hiring of minority faculty. He states that the "tendency to search for minority candidates who mirror ourselves is easily the greatest— though hardly the only—obstacle in the path of recruiting a more diverse faculty...Where we often fail is in valuing differences" (p. 179). His conclusion, which reflects some of the optimistic reasoning underlying our own work, is as follows:

> *Ultimately our success in minority faculty recruitment depends on inviting and valuing candidates who are less like us. There is a great strength in doing so, if only because our students are increasingly not like us. This is not to argue that embracing different kinds of training and careers will not be difficult. But if we treat it as a function of valuing and interpreting the same kinds of differences that motivate our research, we will be able to build institutions that push us all forward on our teaching, research, and service, precisely because no one is just like us. (p. 179)*

SEE
Blacks in College J. Fleming (1988)
"Improving Black Student Access and Achievement in Higher Education" W. Allen *The Review of Higher Education* (1988)
How College Affects Students E. T. Pascerella and P. T. Terenzini (1991)

National studies, such as Fleming's *Blacks in College* and Allen's "Improving Black Student Access and Achievement in Higher Education" as well as Pascarella and Terenzini's *How College Affects Students*, provide further elaboration on the academic development for young students of color within an all too often hostile and, at best, indifferent predominantly white college campus environment.

Racial and Ethnic Bias in Tenure and Promotion Practices and Policies

The literature documents the pervasive theme—and our study respondents report—that the talents and contributions of faculty of color are devalued or undervalued, and that this racial and ethnic bias carries over to the tenure and promotion process.

Astin (1982) asserts that hiring and promotion criteria should be revised to credit a wider variety of accomplishments and types of service than are traditionally recognized. Similarly, Garza (1993) maintains that institutions "need to reassess what constitutes rigorous and legitimate scholarship, and its relationship to institutional barriers that may help maintain ethnic and racial social division" (p. 40). Johnsrud and Des Jarlais (1994) similarly recommend that departments be required to update and clarify tenure and promotion criteria, and also suggest that department chairs be trained to provide performance reviews to probationary faculty that explicitly address progress toward tenure.

Several authors of narrative studies discuss the need for a change in the promotion and tenure policies for faculty. Such change includes (1) acknowledgment and reward for additional demands on faculty of color, (2) acknowledgment and reward for faculty of color who may invest more of their time in teaching and service activities, and (3) acknowledgment and reward for the research of faculty of color.

One example of special demands already discussed involves excessive committee assignments. Another is the expectation that faculty of color be the "ethnic" resource for the entire institution. In an essay by the Committee on Policy for Racial Justice, the importance of such service is acknowledged. However, the authors maintain that faculty of color will continue to be pressed into additional services as long as they are so scarce, contending also that they should be rewarded for their special contributions.

Graves (1990), like Astin (discussed earlier), provides an example of how the personal goals of faculty of color differ from those of their white faculty colleagues. She asserts that black faculty tend to value teaching more and have different research interests than the other faculty. And Garza (1993) cites the devaluation of those research interests as one of the institutional barriers that maintains ethnic and racial social divisions.

For these reasons, several authors recommend a reevaluation of promotion and tenure policies. "It is time for universities

SEE

Minorities in American Higher Education, Recent Trends, Current Prospects, and Recommendations A. W. Astin (1982)

"Barriers to Tenure for Women and Minorities" L. K. Johnsrud and C. D. Des Jarlais *The Review of Higher Education* (1994)

The Inclusive University: A New Environment for Higher Education The Committee on Policy for Racial Justice (1993)

"The Situation of Black Education Researchers: Continuation of a Crisis" H. T. Frierson *Educational Researcher* (1990)

"Women and Minority Faculty Experiences: Defining and Responding to Diverse Realities" L. K. Johnsrud *New Directions for Teaching and Learning* (1993)

"The Status of Women and Minorities in the Professoriate: The Role of Affirmative Action and Equity" K. M. Moore and M. P. Johnson *New Directions for Institutional Research* (1989)

"The Survival of American Indian Faculty: Thought and Action" W. Stein *The National Education Association Higher Educational Journal* (1994)

and colleges to reevaluate existing tenure policies," writes Blackwell in 1988. He continues:

> *(T)enure policies should assign at least the same weight to teaching as to research competence. In addition, if institutions are committed to participatory democracy and to the value of faculty involvement in governance, they must find ways of rewarding service. Finally, as long as minority faculty members are expected to respond to the needs of minority students over and above regular duties, that work should be factored into the scale of values used to determine merit for tenure. (p. 41)*

Frierson (1990), Graves (1990), Johnsrud (1993), and Moore and Johnson (1989) make similar recommendations. The American Association of University Professors recommends that the criteria to be used in the promotion and tenure processes be made clear to faculty and reviewed with faculty on a regular basis. Stein (1994) and Garza (1993) recommend that institutions rethink their notion of what constitutes rigorous and legitimate scholarship, and carefully examine their views on minority research and scholarship.

Bensimon, Ward, and Tierney (1994), through interviews and surveys, have found that junior faculty in general often do not have a clear understanding of promotion and tenure requirements. Among their recommendations are that (1) communication about the promotion and tenure process be improved, (2) the contribution of teaching, research, and service to evaluation for promotion and tenure be made explicit, and (3) faculty be assisted in developing realistic and balanced workloads. Clague (1992) used a combination of interviews, surveys, and document analysis to do a case study of one institution. She supports the development of a long-term strategic personnel policy for scouting, recruiting, hiring, and creating conditions to support promotability. Frierson (1990) also recommends that institutions provide opportunities for professional growth and development for black faculty.

Leap (1995) reviewed court cases relating to tenure and discrimination and observes:

> *The pressures associated with achieving tenure are even more intense for faculty who must deal with discrimination linked to racial, sexist, or other prejudices...The process of reappointment,*

*promotion, and tenure at many colleges and universities is sur-
rounded in uncertainty, a condition that is conducive to surrep-
titious discrimination. (p. 3)*

Boice (1992a) and Astin (1982) elaborate further on these
themes. According to Boice, "feelings of isolation dominate the
experience of [all] new faculty. But most new faculty do not report
having suffered the condescension of racist, sexist, and careerist
remarks" (p. 256). Boice goes on to say that faculty of color "feel
pressure to give up their racial ethnic identities, discouraged from
studying their own cultures and problems as colleagues express
doubts about whether such research is 'real.'" They are "reminded
again and again of the dominant culture in academia to which [they]
are expected to become socialized" (p. 257). Boice concludes that the
entrenched elitism of campuses is "the chief obstacle to treating
women and members of minorities as equals who merit the collegial
supports traditionally accorded to white males" (p. 265). Astin
(1982) states that "affirmative action may never work until universities reward successes of individuals who recruit and support minority
faculty" (p. 263). However, he observes the present professorial values work against diversity: "Professors value the demonstration of intellect [narrowly defined] over the development of intellect…we
favor students and colleagues who arrive with the proper intrinsic
motivation, manifest brilliance, and social tone" (p. 262).

These barriers as well as general conditions of professorial life
(e.g., lengthy tenure processes, below-market salaries) may combine to encourage minority doctoral recipients to pursue careers in
government or industry rather than academia.

A BIRD'S-EYE VIEW—LITERATURE ON FACULTY OF COLOR BY RACIAL AND ETHNIC GROUP: FINDINGS AND RECOMMENDATIONS

Here a brief demographic overview provides a snapshot description
of the diversity found within each population we are studying. The
information presented was derived from 1993 reports published by
the Bureau of the Census, Racial Statistics Branch, Population Division, Washington, DC. Categories used by the Census Bureau are

also used here to report data by racial and ethnic group. These statistics do not take into account the nation's mixed-race populations, further complicating the study of racial and ethnic issues. One of the faculty we interviewed has this to say about Census Bureau classifications and biracial issues:

> We refused to classify our son as either Asian or White. You know, he's both...We've got to stop using some of these categories. They're obsolete. Within my own community and in other [minority] communities, there's a tendency to want to hold on to these classifications because it provides all of us with a social identity...I am saying, wait a minute. We want to take biological characteristics and attach social meaning to them. How far can you take this?
>
> Female Asian American tenured social sciences

Although unable to capture the full texture of experiences from all perspectives, we attempt to provide an opportunity for the reader to examine the experiences of faculty of color represented in these studies. We hope to provide clearer portraits of individual faculty of color within the broadly sketched Census Bureau categories. Faculty participating in these studies provide uniquely authentic perspectives, and their descriptions of their own academic lives give meaning to the demographic data. It is important to note that although we cannot capture all of the complexities inherent in diversity, the bulk of the literature reviewed here, whether in statistical or narrative form, documents a commonality of experience for faculty of color. The literature represents a wide variety of research approaches, thematic approaches, racial/ethnic focuses, and historical or contemporary perspectives. Nevertheless, it appears that, on the whole, there is ample evidence that faculty of color perceive discrimination and exclusion, which constitute barriers to their recruitment and retention.

Asian and Pacific Islander Americans

Asian Americans
In the 1990 census, Asian Americans numbered 6.9 million, a 99 percent increase over the 1980 census. This growing population includes Chinese, Filipinos, Koreans, Asian Indians, Japanese, Viet-

namese, Cambodians, Laotians, Hmong, and Thai. Smaller populations of Burmese, Sri Lankans, Bangladeshi, Malayans, Indonesians, and Pakistanis are also part of the Asian American grouping. In 1990, the largest proportions of Asian Americans were Chinese (24 percent), Filipino (20 percent), and Japanese (12 percent) followed by Asian Indians (12 percent), Korean (12 percent), Vietnamese (9 percent). Newer immigrant groups—Laotian, Cambodian, Thai, and Hmong—each accounted for 2 percent or less of the Asians in America.

Most Asian Americans live in the West (54 percent), and approximately 66 percent of Asian Americans live in just five states—California, New York, Hawaii, Texas, and Illinois. At the college level, by 1990, 38 percent of Asians had graduated with a bachelor's degree or higher, compared with 20 percent of the total population. Asian Indians had the highest attainment rates, and Cambodians, Laotians, and Hmong had the lowest. Japanese had the highest per capita income at $19,373 and Hmong had the lowest at $2,692.

Overall, despite higher educational attainment and higher median family income, Asian Americans experience poverty rates slightly higher than the U.S. population as a whole. About 14 percent of Asian Americans lived in poverty in 1989, a rate slightly higher than the 13 percent rate for the entire nation. Hmong and Cambodian families had the highest poverty rates, 62 percent and 42 percent, respectively. The lowest poverty rates were for Filipino (5 percent) and Japanese (3 percent) families.

Pacific Islanders

The Pacific Islander population in the United States grew 41 percent between 1980 and 1990, from 259,566 to 365,024. Hawaiians, the largest Pacific Islander group, were 58 percent of the total Pacific Islander population. Samoans and Guamanians were the next largest groups, representing 17 percent and 14 percent, respectively, followed by Tongans (5 percent) and Fijians (2 percent). Other Pacific Islanders, including Palauans, Northern Marina Islanders, and Tahitians, each constituted less than 0.05 percent of Pacific Islander Americans. Eighty-six percent of the Pacific Islanders live in the West, with approximately 75 percent living in just two states, California and Hawaii. Eleven percent of Pacific Islanders were college graduates compared with 37 percent of all Asians and Pacific Islanders and 20 percent of the total U.S. population. The per capita income for Pacific Islanders ($10,342) is below the national average ($14,143). Their poverty rate is higher (17 percent) than that for all Asians and Pacific Islanders (14 percent).

Together the percentage of Asians and Pacific Islanders in the total U.S. population nearly doubled during the 1980s, from 1.5 percent to 2.9 percent.

Asian Pacific American Faculty

SEE

Asian Americans in Higher Education: Trends and Issues E. Escueta and E. O'Brien (American Council on Education Research Briefs V2 N4) (1991)

Our discussion of the Asian Pacific American experience in academia is not meant to be an exhaustive survey of the literature. It is presented, rather, as a brief overview of the literature by and/ or about Asian American faculty reviewed for this book. Most studies and reports examining workplace issues for Asian American faculty focus on Asian Americans other than Pacific Islanders. Work is needed to give voice to the Pacific Islander experience. Indeed, nearly all of the studies pointed out that grouping Pacific Islanders with other Asian Americans tends not only to mask their diverse cultures but also make invisible their diverse needs. Asians are lumped together in naive ways. Escueta and O'Brien (1991) note that Asians comprise some twenty nations and sixty ethnic groups, with concomitant differences in cultures and needs.

Escueta and O'Brien found that even though their numbers have increased, Asian American faculty have low tenure rates, are concentrated in non-tenure-track positions, and are grossly underrepresented among administrators of higher education.

SEE

"Special Focus: Asian Pacific American Demographic and Educational Trends" S. Hune and K. S. Chan in *Minorities in Higher Education: Fifteenth Annual Status Report* D. J. Carter and R. Wilson (Eds.) American Council on Education (1997)

Hune and Chan (1997) indicate that the number of Asian Pacific American (APA) faculty declined between 1991 and 1993. This decrease was attributed to the removal of Asian nonresident aliens from the APA racial category. Like Escueta and O'Brien, they find low tenure rates, non-tenure-track positioning, and low numbers of APAs in administrative positions. Hune and Chan report that APA faculty salaries "generally are lower than those of their white counterparts, even when rank and college affiliation are taken into consideration" (p. 59). They note, additionally, wide gender gaps among this population: women primarily in the junior faculty ranks and men primarily at the full-professor level. According to Hune and Chan, APA faculty also experience the less quantifiable forms of discrimination: revolving doors, glass ceilings, and chilly climate. Limited English proficiency and cultural biases in leadership styles are also discussed as potential career impediments.

In "Confronting the Myths: Asian Pacific American Faculty in Higher Education," Cho (1996), describes "beyond parity" types of discrimination faced by APA faculty. In this she includes denial of tenure and promotion, professional and disciplinary tracking, the absence of APAs at the executive and managerial levels in higher education (which she terms "academic caste"), sexual and racial harassment, accent discrimination, and inclusion of foreign nationals in affirmative action "counts."

According to Cho, parity is the balance between baseline representation (the percentage representation of an eligible disadvantaged minority group in the relevant labor, business, or applicant pool) and the actual percentage (their percentage representation in employment, contracting, or university admissions). Her discussion of the concept of parity and using it to infer that all APAs are well represented as compared with other groups of color in higher education is very informative. Parity suggests that APAs are successful and, therefore, do not suffer from bias or discrimination in the academic workplace; that they do not need supports such as affirmative action. Cho's views on parity are provocative and very useful in unpacking some of the complexities of studying workplace issues for all faculty of color. Cho (1996) says:

> *Just as the presumption that "under-parity necessarily evinces discrimination is wrong, so is the presumption that parity necessarily means no discrimination."...the related assumption that over-parity representation must be indicative of success, and by extension, an absence of discrimination...over-parity representation and discrimination against APAs are by no means mutually exclusive. (p. 34)*

Cho goes on to point out that (1) numbers showing overparity in some fields or disciplines mask related underparity in other fields; (2) overparity status at the entry level does not mean overparity status higher up on the promotion ladder; and (3) inferences drawn from an aggregated overparity status serve to make invisible the varied needs of a heterogeneous population. This discussion is excellent and leads one to understand how representation can be coupled with discrimination. The concept of parity speaks to a statistical picture of numerical "inclusion" but does not say anything about the quality of that inclusion. The texture of academic life for APA faculty is best explored by speaking directly with or reading the works of APA faculty. This emphatically includes the writings of Sumi K. Cho.

In a dissertation entitled *Asian Women Leaders of Higher Education,* Ideta (1996) interviewed ten women of Chinese, Filipina, and Japanese backgrounds. She states that there are only

> *two known Asian women presidents of higher education institutions in the nation, constituting the smallest ethnic minority group in comparison to female presidents of African American, Hispanic, and American Indian descent...[One theme emerging from her study was] the women's ability to become stronger and more determined in pursuit of their goals when confronted by discriminating situations of racism, classism, and sexism.* (p. viii)

This work elaborates on the intersection of race, class, and gender among Asian women faculty pursuing executive and other high-level administrative positions in higher education. Ideta's work contributes to the continuing discussion of the status of Asian Americans in higher education, particularly shedding more light on gender gap issues.

Finally, Nakanishi and his associates (1995) have written several articles and a source book entitled *The Asian American Educational Experience,* coedited in 1995 with Nishida. The book includes a section addressing higher education issues and experiences, and discusses promotion and tenure processes as they relate to Asian American faculty, particularly the promotion and tenure battle waged and won by Professor Nakanishi himself. His successful challenge is documented in the November 1990 issue of the *Amerasia Journal* published by the University of California, Los Angeles (UCLA) Asian American Studies Center. Although there is some suggestion that inappropriate political pressure was brought to bear on UCLA to grant tenure in this case, these accounts nonetheless describe the flaws in the process from an Asian American perspective. It is unclear, however, if Professor Nakanishi's challenge or any of the other successful tenure suits brought by faculty of color have caused the tenure process to be modified.

> **SEE**
>
> "Asian Pacific Americans and Colleges and Universities" D. T. Nakanishi in *Handbook of Research on Mulitcultural Education* J. A. Banks and C. A. Banks (Eds.) (1995)
>
> *The Asian American Educational Experience* D. T. Nakanishi and T. Y. Nishida (Eds.) (1995)

In "Asian Pacific Americans and Colleges and Universities," Nakanishi points out ways in which institutions of higher education may prospectively limit the numbers of Asian American faculty through discriminatory practices that limit their admission as undergraduate students. In his view, Asian Pacific Americans legitimately suspect bias in admissions policies; that if they are *seen* as having achieved success, institutions move to make certain that they are not "overrepresented." Nakanishi (1989) refers to this as "a quota on excellence" (p. 38).

He then uses the pyramid as a metaphor to explain the systematic pattern of underrepresentation of the Asian American population in higher education—a pattern that is similar to other underrepresented populations. According to Nakanishi (1995):

> *As in other groups of color and women, there is a substantial decline in the representation of Asian Pacific Americans as one moves up the academic pyramid from high school graduation to freshman admissions, to graduate admissions, and then to the ranks of faculty and administrators...On the other hand, at most major universities in the United States, Whites reflect the opposite, upward pattern of increasing representation in the academic pyramid. (p. 686)*

Although Asian Americans are the fastest-growing minority in academia and no longer qualify for affirmative action on most campuses, they should not be perceived as free from discrimination. The reports, essays, and studies indicate that they are often made to feel unwelcome and that they must still struggle to obtain equitable treatment in the academic workplace.

American Indians and Alaskan Natives

There were nearly 2 million American Indians, Eskimos, and Aleuts living in the United States in 1990, representing an increase of 38 percent over the 1980 total. Projections show growth of the American Indian (including Eskimos and Aleuts) population reaching 4.6 million by 2050. Nearly one-half of the American Indian population lived in the West in 1990, 29 percent in the South, 17 percent in the Midwest, and 6 percent in the Northeast. With over 500 tribes, the American Indian population varies greatly in tribal size and tribal customs and beliefs. In 1990 the only tribes with more than 100,000 persons were the Cherokee, Navajo, Chippewa, and Sioux. The Choctaw, Pueblo, and Apache had populations of at least 50,000 persons. The Iroquois Confederacy, Lumbee, and Creek all had 43,000 or more persons. Most tribes have populations of less than 10,000.

American Indians were less likely than the U.S. population as a whole to have completed a bachelor's degree or higher (20 percent). About 9 percent of the American Indian population attained this level of education in 1990 as compared with 8 percent in 1980. The proportion of American Indian persons and families living below the poverty level in 1989 was considerably higher (31 percent) than that of the total population (13 percent). In 1990 the median family income for American Indians was $21,750 compared with $35,225 for the total U.S. population.

American Indian Faculty

Studies, reports, and essays documenting the status and experiences of American Indian faculty are scarce. Due to their small numbers, many projects examining the experiences of faculty of color do not include American Indians. In most national education data American Indians have either been ignored or placed in the "other" category. Much more needs to be done to document their experiences in academia. The literature that does focus on American Indians generally does not include the experience of Alaskan Natives.

In the demographic and educational trend analysis cited earlier in this chapter, Pavel, Swisher, and Ward (1994) find that the proportion of American Indian and Alaskan Native full-time faculty increased slightly from 0.3 percent to 0.4 percent from 1981 to 1991. Cross and Shortman's (1995) demographic analysis of tribal college faculty underscores the need to increase the number of American Indian and Alaskan Native instructors. They stress the importance of nurturing young, talented tribal members to achieve this goal. Part of that nurturing must take place within postsecondary institutions, in which students will receive bachelor's and master's degrees, with mentor relationships between American Indian and Alaskan Native students and faculty members at both the tribal college level and the four-year institutions they will attend.

In his examination of American Indian faculty issues, Stein (1994) applies the findings of Pepion (1994) about the disconnect between nonminority and minority faculty perceptions of the tenure process. In fifty interviews with majority and minority faculty and administrators, Pepion had found "a pattern of contrasting opinions on the part of majority and minority faculty regarding the atmosphere of the department, the institution, and the unique contributions of minorities to those environments" (p. 96). According to Pepion, although majority faculty believe the department or institutional climate to be accepting of minority faculty, they downplay or deny the unique scholarly contributions of minority faculty. Contributions by minority faculty are referred to in terms of collegial and social contexts rather than in scholarly or intellectual contexts. Minority faculty, on the other hand, feel ambivalent about the academic

SEE

"Special Focus: American Indian and Alaska Native Demographic and Educational Trends" M. Pavel, K. Swisher, and M. Ward *Minorities in Higher Education* (1994)

"Tribal College Faculty: The Demographics" K. P. Cross and P. V. Shortman *Tribal College* (1995)

SEE

Ideologies of Excellence: Issue in the Evaluation, Promotion, and Tenure of Minority Faculty K. Pepion Dissertation, University of Arizona in "The Survival of American Indian Faculty: Thought and Action" W. Stein *The National Education Association Higher Educational Journal* (1994)

environment and point to the influence their cultural backgrounds bring to their approaches to research, teaching, and service. However, minority faculty describe their unique contributions as having little advantage to their professional advancement.

Stein reports finding the same contradictory perceptions between nonminority faculty and American Indian faculty; that most nonminority faculty think that minority faculty face no barriers to promotion and tenure, and that, in fact, being a minority is of benefit in the promotion and tenure process. In contrast, American Indian faculty responding to Stein's American Indian Faculty Survey overwhelmingly report that they must work twice as hard as their non–American Indian counterparts to prove themselves. According to Stein's findings, many American Indian faculty become faculty through circuitous routes, coming from careers in other sectors of education, tribal government, and federal government, and often have well-developed skills of benefit to their hiring institution. For instance, they report that universities often expect them to participate in grant writing and, if successful, to administer the resulting program. Respondents also indicated that they are expected by students, colleagues, and administrators to serve as mentor, advisor, and role model to all American Indian students, and other minority students on campus. None of these activities, however, is highly weighted for tenure and promotion. Stein refers to this as a situation of perceptions and misperceptions.

Based on his findings, Stein makes the following recommendations for the recruitment and retention of American Indian faculty: (1) Institutions must make serious and creative efforts to hire more American Indian faculty; (2) they must create promising career paths leading to faculty positions for American Indian students; (3) once an American Indian faculty member is hired, there must be efforts to retain him or her, such as mentoring or other support programs; (4) institutions must rethink their attitudes about research done by American Indian faculty; and (5) American Indian faculty must be rewarded for community involvement and other services in the tenure and promotion process.

Cross (1991) states that "one of the least known segments of American higher education is the American Indian/Alaska Native... professoriate...Faculty in the 1990s will play an increasingly important role in the education and economic advancement of our tribal communities" (p. 13). His study indicates that American Indian fac-

ulty are virtually ignored in the literature and lost in the educational pipeline.
He notes also that American Indian
women fare better in higher education
than American Indian men.

SEE

"Pathways to the Professo-
riate: The American Indian
Faculty Pipeline" W. T.
Cross *Journal of American
Indian Education* (1991)

In addition to the economic and social hardships faced by American Indi-
ans who aspire to the professoriate, there are also value conflicts
between American Indians and the mainstream culture. Cross
(1991) states, for example, that "the social value and preeminent
goal in life for many American Indians is the survival of the Indian
people" (p. 22). Mainstream education values individual success,
whereas the American Indian commitment is to community. Cross
concludes that "further research is required in order to more fully
understand the means necessary to cultivate additional Indian faculty and to better understand the contributions and potential contributions of Indians who are not serving in that capacity" (p. 23).

Hispanics

In 1990 there were 22.4 million Hispanics in the United States, almost 9 percent of the nation's nearly 250 million people. The Census Bureau's projections suggest rapid growth of this population,
with 81 million projected by the year 2050. Between 1980 and
1990 the Hispanic population grew by 53 percent, over seven times
the growth of the population as a whole. A higher birth rate and
substantial immigration from Mexico, Central America, the Caribbean, and South America have contributed to this growth. The
Mexican population nearly doubled, and both Cuban and Puerto
Rican populations grew at a rate at least four times greater than the
rest of the nation. In 1990 nearly 90 percent of the Hispanic population lived in ten states. The four states with the largest proportion of Hispanics were California, Texas, New York, and Florida.

Hispanics come from many different origins. The Mexican
American population is the largest (61 percent), followed by Puerto
Ricans (12 percent) and Cubans (5 percent). Central Americans represented about 6 percent of the total Hispanic population. This
population includes Costa Ricans, Panamanians, Hondurans, Nicara-
guans, Guatemalans, and Salvadorans. South Americans represented
nearly 5 percent of the Hispanic population. This population

includes Chileans, Argentineans, Peruvians, Ecuadorians, and Colombians. Dominicans, Spaniards, and other Hispanics each were over 2 percent of the Hispanic population.

In 1990, 9 percent of the Hispanic population earned bachelor's degrees or higher, compared with 21 percent of the non-Hispanic population. Also, Hispanic adults were less likely than non-Hispanic adults to complete high school or college. Percentages attaining bachelor's degrees or higher vary widely by subgroups: Spaniards (21 percent), South Americans (20 percent), Cubans (17 percent), Mexicans (6 percent), Puerto Ricans (10 percent), and Central Americans (9 percent).

In 1990 the median family income for Hispanics was $25,064, lower than the median family income of $35,225 for all Americans. Just over two of every ten Hispanic families were living in poverty in 1990 compared with less than one out of ten non-Hispanic families.

Latino Faculty

SEE

The Voice of Hispanic Higher Education 5 The Hispanic Association of Colleges and Universities (1996)

"Ethnic Minority Scholars, Research, and Mentoring: Current and Future Issues" A. M. Padilla *Educational Researcher* (1994)

An October 1996 publication of *HACU: The Voice of Hispanic Higher Education* reports: "While Hispanic full-time faculty employment increased by a reported 62 percent over the past decade, the nation's fastest growing minority group still accounts for less than 3 percent of all full-time faculty" (p. 1). Consequently, the HACU is urging minority student-faculty mentoring programs to encourage Hispanic students to pursue faculty careers. The HACU also reports that the tenure rate among Hispanic faculty showed a 4 percent decline from 1983 to 1993. The HACU supports nationwide partnerships between business and academia to stimulate the development of future minority faculty in specific fields such as business. Establishment of campus-to-campus support networks for prospective faculty is being pursued.

Padilla (1994) also highlights the importance of mentoring to enhance the comfort level of ethnic students pursuing doctoral work, as well as to support junior faculty. He characterizes institutional and faculty demands that graduate students compare research on ethnic populations with research on white populations as a "cross cultural comparison trap" (p. 25). Regarding research methodologies, Padilla supports research that calls for the "development of an empirically and theoretically based approach that focuses on intra-group variability than [the] examination of intergroup differences" (p. 25). For a true ethnic scholarship to develop, Padilla argues the importance of ethnic journals, ethnic associations, and the development of ethnic paradigms. He concludes that:

> *There are still pervasive attitudes in academia about what constitutes cutting edge research and who is empowered to do it. As we move into the 21st century, ethnic research and scholarship must play a more prominent role in defining what constitutes a worthwhile intellectual pursuit… (p. 26)*

Olivas (1988) characterizes the presence of Latino faculty in higher education as "the single most important key to any hope for increasing Latino access" (p. 6). He contends that Latino faculty remain at the border, in large part, due to the historical legacy of racism toward Latino populations. Olivas points out that departments attribute the absence of Latino faculty, in large measure, to the lack of qualified minority candidates for faculty openings. However, he challenges us to examine the track records of these departments granting doctorates to Latinos to see if they are part of the problem or part of the solution. Olivas notes that the "consumers…are also the producers; why don't they see their responsibility to graduate more Latino [doctorates]?" (p. 7).

According to Reyes and Halcon (1991), institutional racism involving minority faculty is generally covert and "often masked by adherence to a mystical academic meritocracy regarding professional qualifications that subtly favors whites" (p. 168). In an earlier publication, Reyes and Halcon (1988) categorize examples of covert racism in higher education in an effort to shed light on what they deem "the most pervasive form of racism in higher education" (p. 302). These categories are discussed elsewhere in this book. Though Reyes and Halcon suggest that their findings may apply to all minority faculty, their writings focus on the experience of Chicano faculty.

SEE
"Racism in America: The Old Wolf Revisited" M. Reyes and J. J. Halcon *Harvard Educational Review* (1988)

Further testimony to the continued overt and covert racism affecting Latinos in academia is offered in *The Leaning Ivory Tower* by

Padilla and Chavez. This text portrays the professional lives of fifteen Latino faculty. Exclusion, isolation, and alienation are themes emerging from the descriptions of their experiences. Many instances of exclusion, isolation, and alienation described by the faculty who contributed their stories fall into the categories identified by Reyes and Halcon, and echo the issues raised by respondents in our own study. One statement among these real-life narratives is particularly compelling. It captures the ambivalent feelings expressed by many faculty of color. Ana M. Martinez Aleman states the following:

> *I am struck by my lived contradiction: To be a professor is to be an* anglo; *to be a* latina *is not to be an* anglo. *So how can I be both a Latina and a professor? To be a Latina professor, I conclude, means to be unlike* and *like me. Que locura! What madness! (p. 74)*

<table>
<tr><td>

SEE

"Actuando" A. M. Martinez Aleman in *The Leaning Ivory Tower: Latino Professors in American Universities* R. V. Padilla and R. C. Chavez (Eds.) (1995)

</td><td>

She goes on to say that "as Latina/o professors, we are newcomers to a world defined and controlled by discourses that do not address our realities, that do not affirm our intellectual contributions, that do not seriously examine our worlds. Can I be both Latina and professor without compromise?" (pp. 74–75).

</td></tr>
</table>

These questions and contradictions are explored in great depth by the Latino faculty members contributing their stories to this volume, often voicing viewpoints previously unexplored in the literature on higher education. These faculty strive to maintain their identities and resist assimilation. The importance of networking and mentoring is mentioned several times in these essays as key components of their individual progress.

Richard Verdugo (1995)—not an academic but a national public policy maker—describes the Catch-22 aspiring Hispanic faculty may face: "For Anglos I was a 'minority scholar,' and to Chicano scholars I was not really in their camp...several Chicano scholars were concerned that my research was not 'Hispanic' enough" (p. 105).

Because our interviews and literature review focused primarily on sitting faculty members, we have not explicitly examined how this kind of dilemma may discourage promising scholars from ever entering the professoriate. It is, however, important to know how many people of color are deterred from academia due to this and other irreconcilable pressures.

Aguirre (1987) points to disturbing organizational practices that may limit the participation of Latino faculty at departmental or program-chair levels while fostering their participation in more visible but peripheral minority service activities. This "organizational

> **SEE**
>
> "An Interpretive Analysis of Chicano Faculty in Academe" A. Aguirre, Jr. *The Social Science Journal* (1987)

logic" channels Chicano faculty into a limited-opportunity structure in academia. Although this practice is not necessarily objectionable in all cases, Aguirre points out that it may have negative consequences for the career mobility of senior and junior Chicano faculty:

> *Since the participation of Chicano faculty in minority-oriented service activities does not necessarily decrease as they ascend the academic ladder, the role of Chicano faculty as sponsors in maneuvering [other] Chicano faculty into nonminority-oriented activities is limited. (p. 77)*

Aguirre and Martinez (1993) describe the situation of Chicano faculty as follows:

> *The institutional relationship between Chicano faculty and administrators in academia places them in a situation of relative isolation, referred to as "barrioization." [Apart from the scholarly life of the academy]...Chicano faculty feel constrained by institutional de-*

> **SEE**
>
> *Chicanos in Higher Education: Issues and Dilemmas for the 21st Century* A. Aguirre and R. O. Martinez (*ASHE-ERIC Higher Education Reports, No. 3.*) (1993)

> *mands that prevent them from participating in institutional sectors that are closer to mainstream decision making....As peripheral participants in academia, Chicano faculty are unable to develop networks that could alter the perceptions whites hold of them. (p. 61)*

SEE

"Community and Group Identity: Fostering Mattering" D. G. Smith *Higher Education Exchange* (1994)

"Multiculturalism: The Crucial Philosophical and Organizational Issues" P. J. Hill *Change* (1991)

The Diversity Project: Final Report T. Duster (1991)

This is reminiscent of recommendations by Smith (1994), Hill (1991), and Duster (1991) for collaborative efforts that maximize positive interactions among faculty across racial and ethnic groups as well as across disciplines. More such activities are needed to reduce the racial and ethnic stereotyping that tends to occur when people are isolated from one another.

American Blacks/African Americans

According to the 1990 census, the American black population grew by 13 percent between 1980 and 1990, to nearly 30 million, representing nearly 12 percent of the U.S. population. In addition to natural increase, immigration from Caribbean and African countries contributes to the growth of the black population. American blacks are located in all states. However, this population is largely urban and most live in the twenty largest metropolitan areas of the nation. The ten cities with the largest black population are New York City, Chicago, Detroit, Philadelphia, Los Angeles, Houston, Baltimore, Washington DC, Memphis, and New Orleans.

Eleven percent of blacks had earned a bachelor's degree or higher in 1990, compared with 22 percent of whites and 20 percent of the U.S. population as a whole. In 1989 the median income for all black families was $22,430 compared with the median family income for the total population of $35,225. In 1989, 8.4 million black Americans were below the poverty rate, or 29.5 percent compared with 13 percent of the total population.

African American Faculty

SEE

Black Women in the Academy: The Secrets to Success and Achievement S. Gregory (1995)

In her survey of 182 members of the Association of Black Women in Higher Education, Gregory (1995) provides information on the status of black women faculty in the academy. She points out that "black women faculty continue to be concentrated among the lower ranks, primarily nontenured, promoted at a slower rate, paid less than their male and White female counterparts…" (p. 11).

Like so many other studies of faculty of color, Gregory (1995) concludes that "it is evident that we still have much work to do to encourage the permanence of black women scholars. Regardless of talent, a faculty member cannot reasonably function in an inhospitable academic environment" (p. 96). Gregory recommends the transformation of tenure and promotion criteria by exploring ways to expand the definition of scholarly activity and to place more importance on teaching, service, and curriculum development activities. Other ways in which departments can promote the careers of black female faculty include (1) encouraging service activities with systemwide visibility and providing faculty incentives and rewards for service overload; (2) accepting differences in teaching styles and research emphasis; and (3) encouraging collaborative projects by providing resources and funding.

An article by Cross (1994) questions the validity of the pipeline argument for the inability of research universities to recruit black faculty members. To do this, he uses Harvard University as a model to illustrate "a severe challenge affecting almost all the highest ranked universities in the United States" (p. 42). Although

SEE

"Black Faculty at Harvard: Does the Pipeline Defense Hold Water?" T. Cross *The Journal of Blacks in Higher Education* (1994)

Harvard has some very distinguished faculty among its ranks, Cross points out that the departments of chemistry, mathematics, physics, biology, and computer science have no black faculty members, despite the existence of several hundred black Ph.D.'s teaching in these fields in other highly rated institutions. Although Cross agrees that there are few newly conferred black Ph.D.'s in these areas, he contends that this should not be the only place for universities to look for potential faculty members. As Light (1994) and Mickelson and Oliver (1991) contend, there is a need to cast the net widely, and in different arenas, when recruiting faculty of color. Cross argues that in addition to recruiting from the pool of new black Ph.D.'s, tenure-track faculty can come through lateral appointments from other institutions, as well as from large numbers of distinguished African or Caribbean-born scholars teaching abroad. Indeed, Cross points out that in the past, over 71 percent of Harvard's new arts and science faculty have come from other universities in this country or from abroad. To those who would say that there is a "no raid policy" in effect, Cross replies that Harvard regularly recruits scholars from other universities especially in the areas of African American literature and black studies. He strongly supports the need for institutions of higher education to expand their net and recruit black professors in other areas as well. Cross (1994) argues that such lateral hirings will, in the long run, increase the demand for African American scholars throughout the higher education system.

> *When institutions of the caliber of Berkeley, Harvard, MIT, and Yale hire laterally from other institutions, a kind of suction effect is created. New opportunities for black academics open up further down the line...Demand creates its own supply. And, as this occurs, increasing numbers of young blacks will arm themselves with Ph.D.s in response to the exciting new opportunities that open up. (p. 46)*

SEE

"Black Faculty in Academia" K. W. Jackson in *The Racial Crisis in American Higher Education* P. G. Altbach and K. Lomotey (Eds.) (1991)

Jackson (1991) contributes further to the thoughts presented by Cross. He agrees with Cross that the pool of potential black candidates for faculty positions is small and getting smaller. However, he places some of the blame for this situation on racist perceptions, which not only restrict access for those with credentials to become faculty members, but also stifle the professional growth of black faculty already in academia "such that they become less visible signs of success" (p. 145). Jackson contends that these two observations are related.

> *The experience surrounding the fairly small number of black faculty presently in academia significantly impacts the decision of potential candidates to choose academia as a career option. In turn, there are fewer individuals to help alleviate the isolated conditions and subsequent experiences of those black faculty presently in the system such that more individuals would see this profession as a positive career option...This interrelatedness implies that solutions directed solely toward increasing the number of black students enrolled in graduate programs, thereby increas-*

ing the number of potential faculty members, may be overly sim-
plistic. There must be a simultaneous effort to reduce the isolated
circumstances of black faculty… (p. 146)

Frierson (1990) writes that the presence of black faculty is a significant predictor of enrollment and graduation of black graduate students. Thus, an increase in the numbers of black faculty is critical but, due to barriers encountered in preparation for faculty positions, the production of black Ph.D.'s continues to worsen. He encourages current black faculty members to support one another and to create professional networks. He also suggests that black senior faculty provide assistance to black junior faculty as well as graduate students and undergraduates. Although these suggestions are directed to black faculty members themselves, Frierson (1990) sees the need for institutional action.

> **SEE**
>
> "The Situation of Black Education Researchers: Continuation of a Crisis" H. T. Frierson *Educational Researcher* (1990)
>
> "A Program on Institutional Research on Graduate Education" K. S. Louis and C. S. Turner *New Directions for Institutional Research* (1991)
>
> *Promotion and Tenure: Community and Socialization in Academe* W. G. Tierney and E. M. Bensimon (1996)

The presence of racism in the institution should be acknowledged
as a reality and should be addressed forthrightly when it is raised
as an issue…institutions should make every effort to ensure that
Black faculty will have opportunities for professional growth and
development…nonscholarship demands should be kept minimal
[and be the type that] bring about greater professional
visibility…[During the tenure process] acknowledge the extra
burden and demands placed on Black faculty. (p. 16)

Many authors reiterate themes brought out by other sources and by other racial/ethnic groups discussed in other sections of this book. They acknowledge that white faculty can also experience many stressors in the academy, but that race and ethnic bias adds further stress to an already challenging tenure system. In their work, these scholars refer to this extra burden as "cultural taxation" or "the price of talent" (see the source boxes: Padilla; Tierney & Bensimon; Louis & Turner).

Pervasiveness of the Problem

In our view, it is quite meaningful that even "seasoned veterans" who achieve high scholarly recognition comment on the additional difficulties in their work environment that relate to race or ethnic background.

Such situations have also been documented for television audiences. Two videotapes, "Racism 101" (1988) and "Shattering the Silences" (1996), portray racial and ethnic barriers encountered by faculty of color. "Racism 101" is part of the *Frontline* series produced by the Public Broadcasting System. Among other vignettes, it presents the story of an African American faculty member harassed by students at Dartmouth College. According to the film, students published a description of this professor as "a used Brillo pad" and proclaimed him, along with many female and other minority faculty, as among the worst professors at the university. They also had face-to-face confrontations with this faculty member, including an incident that occurred during class as his students looked on. One student who observed the classroom confrontation made the following comment about the experience: "In that moment it just let me know that there are people in this world that will hate you just because of your color. I mean hate you—not dislike you or choose not to be friends with you, but hate you." The university president and colleagues came to this professor's defense. The president stated: "When the *Dartmouth Review* year after year attacks women and members of minority groups, it is virtually impossible not to conclude that its true target is diversity."

The students were found guilty of harassment and invasion of privacy. Nonetheless, this situation provides a well-documented example of overt harassment of minority faculty.

Almost ten years later, "Shattering the Silences," a Public Broadcasting System documentary, explored the experiences of eight scholars of color in the humanities and social sciences. Faculty members describe the challenges and opportunities afforded them by the academic workplace, recounting personal experiences. As with the scholars interviewed for this study, both positive and negative situations are explored, with an overarching theme being the additional stresses encountered by those who find themselves in an environment in which they are one of very few, if not the only, faculty of color in their departments. Female faculty also talk about choices they must make related to marriage and children. These situations, along with racial/ethnic exclusion, compound the challenges women of color must overcome in order to succeed as faculty members in predominantly white, male environments. The film also highlights the unique research questions and approaches these faculty bring to the academic workplace.

Examples of the pervasiveness of such situations continue to be documented in study after study. According to Reyes and Halcon (1991) in *Practices of the Academy: Barriers to Access for Chicano Academics,* racism involving faculty of color in institutions is not usually as overt as the Dartmouth example. Instead, they find, it is generally covert and "often masked by adherence to a mystical academic meritocracy regarding professional qualifications that subtly favors whites" (p. 168). In an earlier publication, Reyes and Halcon (1988) categorize examples of covert racism in higher education in an effort to shed light on what they deem "the most pervasive form of racism in higher education" (p. 302). They are:

> Tokenism: The assumption is that minority faculty are "mere tokens…hired without the appropriate credentials, experience, or qualifications…[Thus] there is unspoken pressure put on minority academics to continually prove that they are as good as white academics" (p. 304).
>
> The Typecasting Syndrome: "An underlying attitude that [minorities] can only or should only occupy minority-related positions" (p. 304).
>
> The "Brown-on-Brown" Research Taboo: If you are Chicano and study Chicano literature, for example, then such "research interests are dismissed as minor or self-serving. The general perception is that minority related topics do not constitute academic scholarship and that they are inappropriate and narrow in scope…[whereas] white-on-white research is accorded legitimacy…" (p. 307).
>
> The Hairsplitting Concept: "A potpourri of trivial technicalities, or subjective judgment calls, which prevent minorities from being hired or promoted" (p. 308).

These "syndromes" aptly describe the manifestations of bias most commonly noted by the faculty of color who participated in our study (presented in detail in Chapter 4).

That academic rank does little to diminish the burdens of racial and ethnic bias is borne out in our study, and even more acutely by the revelations of scholars of color who have achieved public prominence—scholars with high name recognition, stellar credentials, degrees from prestigious institutions, and publications in the most prestigious journals.

Franklin (1989), a prominent historian, winner of the Presidential Medal of Freedom, and the chair of President Clinton's Advisory Panel on Race Relations, presents his view of the role of the scholar in addressing racism:

> *For the young scholar, appropriately impatient with the slow pace of change in a society that seemed reluctant to make equality a universal attribute, activism was most attractive. Signing protests, joining the Selma marchers, demonstrating against the evils of racism were ways in which the black historian could make common cause with fellow sufferers. There were, however, other ways to bear witness that utilized the professional skills I had acquired. I could provide background and context for the problems of the day...using one's skills to influence public policy. (p. x)*

As part of Professor Franklin's efforts to confront the professional challenges he faced, including his inability to have lunch with a white colleague while working at the Library of Congress, which Franklin deemed "one of the minor inconveniences" (pp. 304–305), he wrote a 1968 essay entitled "The Dilemma of the American Negro Scholar." He concluded then and again in 1989:

> *I recognized then, as I do now, that while a black scholar has a clear responsibility to join in improving the society in which he lives, he must understand the difference between hard-hitting advocacy on the one hand and the highest standards of scholarship on the other. (p. ix)*

Even scholars who make such distinction in their own work tend to be judged within the academy as though advocacy were the driving force behind their work and the view of their scholarship is inevitably compromised. No wonder Franklin himself, in a 1995 interview, states "I'm not very optimistic [about racism in the

United States]." In fact, a 1997 article in the *AARP Bulletin*, recounts this incident:

In 1995, the same night he [Franklin] was to receive the nation's highest civilian honor—The Presidential Medal of Freedom—he was approached at Washington's prestigious Cosmos Club, where he has been a member since 1962, by a woman who wanted him to get her coat from the cloak room...he pauses and shakes his head...He turns to history to explain such behavior. Slavery, as awful as it was, was not the main evil. "The real problem was the development of an ideology of white supremacy"... (p. 20)

Professor Franklin nevertheless continues to work toward an ideal saying that he is "cautiously optimistic." Whether one agrees with the way he addresses these issues or not, we believe that he eloquently conveys the added burdens facing scholars of color within a professional environment that reflects a racist society. Unfortunately, as a result of our research, we believe that many of the tensions he describes, although they may appear in the various forms discussed by Reyes and Halcon and others, remain a reality for many of today's faculty of color.

bell hooks is a public intellectual, a prolific writer (her first book was written at age nineteen) and a professor. Interviewed by reporter Sian Griffiths for an article appearing in *The Times Higher Education Supplement,* she describes her own dilemma:

For an intellectual working in the field of African American Studies the dilemma is even more acute; for how can you speak and interpret the culture of this other black America if your own life has diverged from their daily reality? (p. 20)

bell hooks has made a choice not to write solely for the narrow academic audience but to write for the widest audience. Thus, her work faces criticism from other scholars. However, this is her way of resolving the dilemmas of her professional life. She believes that assimilation, although touted as an answer to racial divisions, is dehumanizing, that it requires eradication of one's blackness so that a white self can come into being.

SEE

"Unity in Diversity: Thirty-Three Years of Stress" C. M. Pierce in *Black Students: Psychosocial Issues and Academic Achievement* G. L. Berry and J. K. Asamen (Eds.) (1989)

"Reflections of a Black Social Scientist: Some Struggles, Some Doubts, Some Hopes" J. Mitchell *Harvard Educational Review* (1982)

Chester M. Pierce, Professor of Education and Psychiatry at Harvard, states that black professionals must find satisfactions in the workplace despite racism. He concludes that "to do this means the acceptance of constant extra stress in all undertakings" (p. 311). Pierce (1989) says that "each colored minority member experiences daily stresses as he or she negotiates existence" (p. 296). Potential outcomes of such stress are articulated by Jacqueline Mitchell, a black social scientist, who describes her academic career as full of "contradictions and ambivalent feelings" that were not a result of personal problems but of "being a minority in a white-dominated society." In describing her experience as a graduate student, Mitchell (1982) explains, "My minority student colleagues and I tried to support each other as we dealt with the terrible bind: if I fail, the minority students fail; if I succeed, I only highlight a general minority student failure by being an exception and thus jeopardize my membership in minority culture" (p. 35). Mitchell goes on to describe the price she pays for her success in academe: "I have begun to experience feelings of anxiety and futility, emotions that paralyze and inhibit my creativity and productivity…What ensues is a state of double marginality…belonging to and feeling a part of two worlds, yet never at home in either" (p. 38).

Review of the Literature on Faculty Diversity: Some Reflections

Overall, the literature highlights the isolation and obstacles to socialization that faculty of color face. As we have seen, the published research provides a wide spectrum of recommendations. The most common have to do with a reevaluation of hiring, promotion, and tenure policies. Yet existing programs and proposed strategies to enhance development of faculty of color concentrate primarily on fellowship programs for graduate students of color. In addition, institutional attempts to provide retention programs for faculty of color focus on "fixing" the minority faculty member through special orientation programs and special seminars on how to publish and how to gain tenure. We believe that these attempts to support faculty of color are very necessary, but that institutions of higher education must also pursue organizational change in order to recruit, retain, and incorporate faculty of color. In our view, there is a disconnect—as identified in the literature and our own study—between the problems confronted by faculty of color and the solutions that have been proposed and implemented. A colleague makes this observation:

> *A lot of time is spent on racial and ethnic bias. That's an institutional problem. The solutions look like they answer pipeline and access issues. We've got to figure out a way that the solutions answer what's found in the data.* (personal communication)

That said, we want to underscore the need to design remedies to address issues of workplace environment and deficient promotion and tenure practices, and at the same time support the importance of finding ways to stimulate the supply of faculty of color. The problem of underrepresentation demands that we address it from many angles. The present focus tends to be on fellowship programs and "self-help" to be accomplished by faculty of color themselves. However, the broader academic community must develop approaches to alleviate some of the problems identified throughout the literature that are clearly environmental and institutional in nature.

Many existing efforts to address the underrepresentation of faculty of color are commendable and have made a difference (attested to in part by faculty respondents in Chapter 6, "Why Stay?"). We, therefore, argue against discontinuing these efforts, including affirmative action, out of hand. Nonetheless, it is also apparent that we cannot restrict ourselves to those paths that have yielded little or no systemic change, and we must find other paths as well.

Existing interventions appear to have little overall effect, and we must suspect that—despite glimmers of hope—we have failed to reach the heart of the problem. In the following chapters we attempt to identify the true nature of the problem—and the most promising solutions—from historical, statistical, and personal perspectives.

3

THE NATURE AND EXTENT OF MINORITY FACULTY UNDERREPRESENTATION

It is widely recognized that minority faculty are severely underrepresented in American higher education. Educational apartheid during the years before *Brown v. Board of Education* virtually assured that there were few if any racial minorities on

I have no doubt whatsoever that discrimination is "alive and well" in the academy and that, at whatever level of conscious or subconscious behavior, it serves to thwart minority hires and (all the more insidiously, I believe) their retention…

Male White tenured social sciences

the faculties of predominantly white colleges and universities. Although in the years following World War I there was a handful of African American faculty appointments at white universities, for most of the century that followed the Civil War, blacks were virtually excluded from teaching positions at white colleges and universities.[1]

The watershed event affecting appointment of minority faculty at white colleges and universities was *Adams v. Richardson* in 1973. This case, brought by the NAACP Legal Defense Fund, challenged the segregated, dual system of higher education and the underrepresentation of minority faculty, staff, and students at white institutions in

---

[1]See Brown (1994); Bond (1972); Fleming, Gill, and Swinton (1978).

southern states. Later the representation of minorities in institutions of northern and border states was found to be equally inequitable. The mandate of *Adams* was to dismantle the segregated, dual system of education and to increase the percentages of minority faculty, administration, and students.

In direct response to the *Adams* challenge, states developed and implemented plans and timetables to increase minority presence at public institutions of higher education. The result was a measurable increase in the numbers of minority faculty employed by American colleges and universities.

Although minority hiring increased between 1973 and 1977, from 1977 to 1983 African American faculty numbers actually *declined* in most of the states covered by the *Adams* decision.[2] This failure to sustain minority hiring might be viewed as a failure of the court's mandate, but, in fact, it does not rob *Adams* of its significance. For the first time states—both those specifically covered and those not covered by the order—felt the threat of federal action and, in response, made concerted efforts to hire minority faculty. Minority faculty underrepresentation at colleges and universities was, for the first time, not simply a moral or social issue. In the 1970s it became a legal issue, fought—and won—in the courts as a vestige of illegal segregation and institutionalized discrimination.

In the 1970s, there was no dispute as to (1) whether minorities were, in fact, underrepresented in higher education, or (2) whether that underrepresentation was attributable to patterns of discrimination and segregation. The general consensus was that the persistent pattern of low employment of minorities at white institutions was a past legacy of blocked opportunities. When these opportunities were unblocked, minority employment grew.

By the 1990s, things changed.[3] There was a ten-year period of retrenchment in affirmative action that many see as causally re-

---

[2]Reginald Wilson, "The Participation of African Americans in American Higher Education," in Justiz et al. (Eds.) *Minorities in Higher Education* (1994).

[3]African American full-time instructional faculty at american colleges and universities totaled 19,227 in the fall of 1985 according to EEOC counts. By 1993, the number reached 25,658. The black share of all faculty, however, only inched up from 4.1 percent to 4.7 percent in the decade, according to the *Digest of Educational Statistics,* 1989 and 1997.

lated to the "Reagan revolution" and the concomitant decline in civil rights enforcement. Now there is dispute both as to whether there is a problem—are minorities really underrepresented on faculties?—and whether we need to be concerned about the problem if, in fact, it exists.

The dispute over the existence of a problem arises because different indicators of minority representation yield alternative pictures of minority exclusion on American college campuses. When non-native-born faculty and/or Asian faculty are included in calculations, there often is the appearance not of underrepresentation but of *overrepresentation.*

The controversy over whether we really need to be worried about underrepresentation—if it exists—involves a renewed sense that perhaps minorities are not qualified to teach this country's youth and future leaders, that they do not deserve these coveted positions. Of course, we would not demand that institutions hire unqualified minorities!

Both of these disputes rest on empirical issues. Are minorities really underrepresented? If so, does lack of qualification explain their underrepresentation?

In this chapter we explore the first of these issues. In the chapters that follow we examine the competing explanations for the underrepresentation of minority faculty. Ultimately in Chapter 7 we empirically weigh the arguments for and against the view that the scarcity of minority faculty is due to the scarcity of qualified candidates.

THE NATURE OF UNDERREPRESENTATION

Figure 3.1 shows that in 1990, blacks, American Indians, and "other race" persons were underrepresented in faculty employment. According to the figure, Asians were *overrepresented* and whites were present in roughly the same percentage they represent in the base population. These figures, from the latest available census at the time of this writing, reveal a pattern of underrepresentation initially addressed by *Adams* in 1973.

But what constitutes the base population? What do we mean by "minority," especially because Hispanics are not explicitly included?

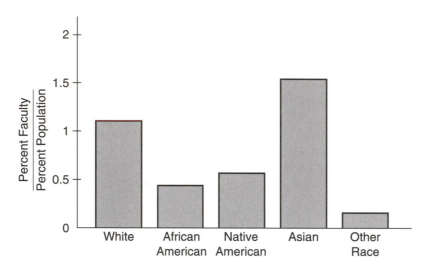

FIGURE 3.1   Underrepresentation of Faculty of Color

Source: Authors' computations from 1990 census data. See Midwest Higher Education Consortium (MHEC). *Minority Faculty Development Project: Final Report.* May 1995. Table D.6.

These two questions nag at all analyses of minority underrepresentation. The first deals with how we measure and define underrepresentation. The second deals with how we identify race and ethnicity.

Measuring Underrepresentation

What does *underrepresentation* mean? That is—compared to what? There are many defensible bases of comparison in common use. They range from those that restrict the comparisons to narrow subsets of faculty and general populations, to those that include broad categories of faculty and population. Typical analyses of underrepresentation are based on:

• Percentage of minority faculty compared to their percentage in the general population;
• Percentage of minority faculty compared to their percentage in the national pool of qualified individuals;

- Percentage of minority faculty compared to the expected availability ("fewer in a particular job group than would reasonably be expected by their availability");
- Percentage of minority faculty compared to their representation in the appropriate civilian labor force (which may be geographically determined).[4]

In each instance, the minority representation is measured by the ratio of the percentage of faculty who are minority to the percentage of the relevant population who are minority. The faculty numbers come from sources such as the EEOC or the U.S. Census Bureau.

What becomes clear from the analyses is that, no matter what comparator is used, African Americans, American Indians, and, to a lesser extent, Hispanics are consistently underrepresented as faculty of colleges and universities. It is the *degree* to which these groups are underrepresented that changes according to the basis of comparison.

African Americans, American Indians, and Hispanics are most acutely underrepresented in the fields of science, including physical and social sciences, and engineering. In these fields, the three minority groups account for 3.7 percent of full-time positions in U.S. institutions of higher education.[5]

According to the U.S. Department of Education, 33 percent of full-time regular instructional faculty in institutions of higher education are employed in science and engineering fields. Blacks, Hispanics, and American Indians, who account for about 6 percent of all faculty, comprise less than 3 percent of engineering faculty, 3.5 percent of natural science faculty, and 9 percent of social science faculty. Together, African Americans, Hispanics, and American Indians account for about 3.7 percent of science and engineering faculty. Thus, science and engineering fields are severely underrepresented by this subset of minority faculty.

Source: U.S. Department of Education, National Survey of Postsecondary Faculty (NSOPF); 1987–88, Table 22, April 1991.

---

[4]See Cooper and Smith (1990). The Department of Labor's Office of Federal Contract Compliance Programs (OFCCP) used the definition "having fewer minorities or women in a particular job group than would reasonably be expected by their availability." (41 CFR section 60-2.11, p. 118). It refers to "underutilization" and not "underrepresentation."

[5]U.S. Department of Education, National Survey of Postsecondary Faculty (NSOPF), 1987–88, Table 22, April 1991.

At the doctoral level in these fields, the underrepresentation of minorities—although still severe—is lower. Nationally, of all science and engineering Ph.D.'s employed in higher education, 4.7 percent are black, Native American, or Hispanic.[6]

The first percentage refers to all faculty in science and engineering fields. The second refers to faculty with Ph.D.'s in these fields. Surprisingly, the minority share of Ph.D. faculty is larger than the minority share of all science faculty.

This difference between the Ph.D. subset and the faculty as a whole is a small one; in both instances, the underrepresentation of blacks, Hispanics, and American Indians is phenomenal. The most important implication of the science/engineering faculty data is that it debunks the "not enough Ph.D.'s" explanation for minority underrepresentation. Were that the case, the Ph.D. subset would have a smaller rather than a larger percentage of minorities compared to the "all faculty" group.

Counting Minorities

Counting the numbers of minority faculty at a given institution can be fraught with confusion. Who is "minority"? Should a person of multiple ethnic heritage count as multiracial, or be counted in each of the defined groups which make up his or her heritage? What if the person's ethnic or racial heritage is not listed among the standard categories? These dilemmas are common to all analyses relating to minorities in the United States.[7]

Those conundrums aside, it is possible to isolate race and ethnicity using both census and EEOC data. It is important, however, in analyzing the data separately, to identify white non-Hispanics; black non-Hispanics; Asian non-Hispanics; American Indian non-Hispanics; other non-Hispanics, and Hispanics. This permits computation of mutually exclusive, collectively exhaustive sets of race and ethnicity labels.

Computations generally exclude persons who are not U.S. residents. More difficult, however, is the question of whether to in-

---

[6]Computations based on Table 1, Appendix F, from unpublished tabulations, 1991 Survey of Doctorate Recipients, National Research Council.

[7]See, for example, Office of Information and Regulatory Affairs, 1997. "Revisions to the Standards for the Classification of Federal Data on Race and Ethnicity." Washington, DC: Office of Management and Budget.

clude residents who are not citizens. In most analyses, faculty *with resident visas* are counted in whatever racial or ethnic category they fall, regardless of national origin.

Do these distinctions affect the conclusion that certain minority groups are underrepresented in higher education? To address this question, we compute representation ratios using two different data sets that have substantially different ways of measuring race, ethnicity, and faculty. The first uses EEOC data, based on institutional reporting, in which the institution categorizes and counts its faculty by race and ethnicity. The second computation uses census data in which both race/ethnicity and employment are self-reported by the individual.

We compiled EEOC statistics on minority faculty from a subset of states and compared them to our census data analyses. Both data sets reveal the same broad patterns, and we are confident about using the census data for both our discussion of minority underrepresentation and the analysis of its causes.

EEOC Counts

Using data compiled by the U.S. Equal Employment Opportunity Commission on full-time employed faculty, we have computed the percentages of faculty accounted for by race in various states.[8] Using the 1990 published census reports, we have computed the percentages of each state's population accounted for by each race.[9] The ratio of the percentage of faculty to the percentage of persons in the general population for each racial group is defined as the groups' faculty representation ratio. For example, in Illinois, Hispanics represent 7.8 percent of the population but only 1.6 percent of the full-time faculty. Thus, the Hispanic representation ratio in Illinois is only 0.21.

---

[8]Racial groupings obtained from the EEOC data are non-Hispanic whites, non-Hispanic blacks, Asians, American Indians, and Hispanics. Data are derived from 1991 EEO-6 Higher Education Staff Information, Table III.

[9]Population data include people of all ages and come from the U.S. Department of Commerce, Bureau of the Census, General Population Characteristics: Sex, Race, and Hispanic Origin, 1990. Thus, the comparison between the EEO-6 data, which refer to the fall term of the current academic year (1990–91), and the census, which refers to the count during the spring of the 1990, does not overlap precisely.

The general patterns are evident in Figure 3.2, which shows the severe underrepresentation of blacks, Hispanics, and American Indians across selected midwestern states.[10]

The broad pattern observed from the EEOC data is severe underrepresentation of African Americans and American Indians and various degrees of underrepresentation of Hispanics across selected midwestern states. Note, however, that the figures exclude part-

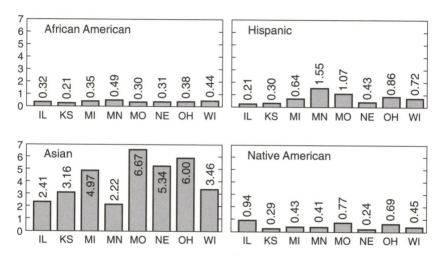

FIGURE 3.2   Faculty Representation Ratios in MHEC States

Source: Midwest Higher Education Consortium. *Minority Faculty Development Project: Final Report.* May 1995. Table D.1. Faculty data include full-time faculty only and are compiled by the Equal Employment Opportunity Commission from 1991 EEO-6 Higher Education Staff Information, Table III. Population data include people of all ages and come from the U.S. Department of Commerce, Bureau of the Census, General Population Characteristics: Sex, Race, and Hispanic Origin, 1990.

Reprinted by permission from *The Journal of Higher Education,* Vol. 70, No. 1 (Jan/Feb 1999). Copyright 1999 by Ohio State University Press. All rights reserved.

The faculty representation ratio is the percentage of total faculty accounted for by each race (from EEOC file) divided by the percentage of the population accounted for by each race (from the 1990 census data).

---

[10]The full details of the EEOC counts are provided in Table 3.2 at the end of this chapter.

time faculty. Such exclusion could overstate the degree of minority underrepresentation. Moreover, the use of general population figures as the basis of comparison is likely to exaggerate the degree of underrepresentation. The measure is likely to show more severe underrepresentation in populations with large numbers of younger minorities. The computations from the Census Public Use Micro Sample (PUMS) are designed to address this concern.

Census Data

The 1990 Census Public Use Micro Sample (PUMS) represents a sampling of all long census returns, which provide information on industry and occupation for employed persons.[11] We identified "faculty" as individuals, ages twenty-four to seventy, with occupation listed as "postsecondary teacher," an industry classification of "college or university" and who are not attending school. This does not exclude part-time employment as does the EEOC data.

Census Analysis

The Public Use Micro Sample (PUMS) tapes for the United States and for specific MHEC states were utilized to analyze national and regional trends and patterns of minority faculty representation in higher education. The U.S. sample constituted a 1 percent sample of all returns from the 1990 census. A 3 percent random sample was taken of the U.S. sample base to compute representation ratios and to perform an econometric analysis. All persons over twenty-four and under seventy years of age who held master's or Ph.D. degrees were separately identified in the U.S. sample base. This subgroup was used in calculating predictions of faculty earnings and in estimating determinants of faculty representation ratios. Finally, 5 percent state-based samples were combined to estimate representation ratios and to perform analysis of higher education patterns in MHEC states.

---

[11]The census analysis in the accompanying box uses the full 5 percent sample for states but a 3 percent sample of the 5 percent sample for the entire United States.

Our census data (PUMS) computations involve a more conservative measure of representation[12] and still show the same patterns of underrepresentation revealed by the EEOC data. In the selected midwestern states, as well as in the nation as a whole, African Americans and American Indians are severely underrepresented.[13] A breakdown by state likewise shows the same *patterns* of underrepresentation evident in the EEO data, though the *degree* of minority representation is consistently higher using the census data because of the more conservative measure used. Using Michigan as an example, the EEOC-derived representation ratio for African Americans in Michigan is 0.35, and the census-derived ratio is 0.36. Figure 3.3 depicts faculty representation ratios for selected midwestern states using these census data.

Despite vast differences in how the representation ratios are computed, the basic story remains the same. There is substantial underrepresentation of African Americans and American Indians, significant underrepresentation of Latinos in certain states, and no apparent underrepresentation among Asian/Pacific Islanders.

Figure 3.4 compares minority faculty representation in the selected midwestern states with the United States as a whole using census data. The figure reveals that in the midwestern states faculty representation for African Americans and American Indians is lower than the national average. Asian/Pacific Islander and Hispanic representation is above the national average. Hispanic males have the lowest representation of any group.

---

[12]The representation ratio used here is the ratio of the percentage of faculty accounted for by a specific racial group to the percentage of persons ages twenty-four to seventy in the general population accounted for by that group. Thus, this ratio more broadly covers faculty but more narrowly defines the comparison population group. It, therefore, can be considered a more conservative measure of minority faculty representation.

[13]The representation ratios for African Americans and American Indians in MHEC member states are 0.39 and 0.50 as compared to 0.45 and 0.57 in the rest of the nation. These calculations are presented in Table 3.2. Note that we have performed the calculations for both race and race/ethnicity: (a) whites, blacks, American Indians, Asians, other races; and (b) white non-Hispanics, black non-Hispanics, American Indian non-Hispanics, Asian/Pacific Islander non-Hispanics, other race/non-Hispanics, and Hispanics.

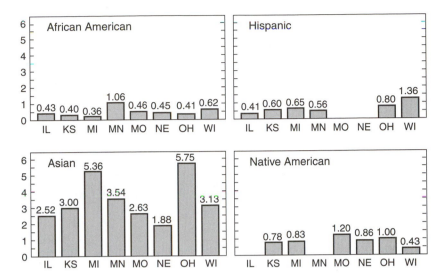

FIGURE 3.3 **Faculty Representation Ratios Using Census Data**

Source: Authors' computations from 1990 census data. See Midwest Higher Education Consortium. *Minority Faculty Development Project: Final Report.* May 1995. Table D.1.

PATTERNS OF UNDERREPRESENTATION

The advantage of the census data is that it permits examination of underrepresentation by age, gender, and nationality. Table 3.1 (page 79) provides a rare glimpse of the details of the minority faculty representation by various subgroups.

Minority Representation at Various Ages and Career Levels

Table 3.1 (page 79) shows that white males are substantially overrepresented among faculty thirty-four to forty-three years old. The census data show that in the general population white males account for 75.2 percent of all thirty-four- to forty-three-year-old men

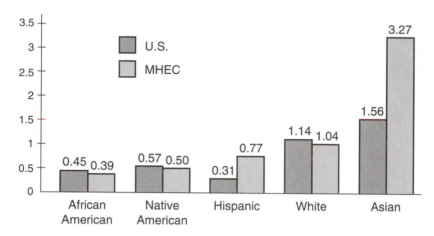

FIGURE 3.4   Faculty Representation Ratios, U.S. versus MHEC States

Source: Authors' computations from 1990 census data. See Midwest Higher Education Consortium (MHEC). *Minority Faculty Development Project: Final Report.* May 1995. Table D.4 (PUMS, 1990).

Reprinted by permission from *The Journal of Higher Education,* Vol. 70, No. 1 (Jan/ Feb 1999). Copyright 1999 by Ohio State University Press. All rights reserved.

with M.A. or Ph.D. degrees who had income in 1989, but represent 88.9 percent of all individuals identified as "faculty" (i.e., postsecondary teachers employed in colleges or universities) and their representation ratio is 1.18.

For blacks, American Indians, Asians, and Hispanics ages thirty-four to forty-three, the representation ratios are 0.53, 0.29, 0.85, and 0.20, respectively. They are severely underrepresented among the age group that commonly begins to move into tenured slots or mid-level positions in academia.

Among younger, entry-level faculty, ages twenty-four to thirty-three, Hispanic underrepresentation is less severe than for other age groups. Also, at the entry level—although their numbers are small—American Indians make up a larger percentage of faculty than their percentage in the general population (i.e., among all persons with advanced degrees and income in 1989).

Asians are overrepresented among the younger faculty. They are 1.9 times as likely to be faculty as they are to be in the general population. Asians also appear to be overrepresented for ages fifty-four to sixty-three—the group nearing retirement, as well as in the presumably "ready-to-retire" group ages sixty-four to seventy.

Figure 3.5 graphically displays the patterns of these variations by age group. The figure shows that all minorities are underrepresented in the mid-career age groups, and that there is a sharp drop in representation ratios for American Indians, Asians, and Hispanics from early career to mid-career. Black representation is low at the youngest age groups and rises slightly at mid-career.

One conclusion to be drawn from the graph is that there are not enough minorities at the mid-career level to improve their

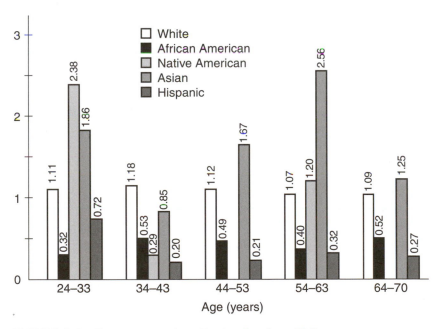

FIGURE 3.5   Representation Ratios by Age, U.S.

Source: Authors' computations from 1990 census data. See Midwest Higher Education Consortium (MHEC). *Minority Faculty Development Project: Final Report.* May 1995. Table D.9.

representation in top academic positions anytime soon, although the entry of Hispanics and Asians among the youngest group could mean greater representation in top academic positions twenty to thirty years from now. However, the graph now shows a drop-off in minority faculty representation from the younger, entry level to the mid-career level, and optimism for even the long term rests on the assumption—perhaps unrealistic—that this pattern of early drop-off will change in the short term.

Another important observation drawn from Figure 3.5 is that the representation ratios for blacks differ little from age group to age group. There is no suggestion that black representation is improving at any of the career levels. To the contrary, the small differences from age group to age group suggest that earlier efforts to increase African American presence on college campuses may have played themselves out. The slightly smaller representation ratios for blacks in the youngest groups signal not continued improvement and upward mobility but possible deterioration in the years to come.

Table 3.1 (page 79) reveals that whites are not being displaced by any minority group. Their representation rates remain above 1 at every age group. Although Asian faculty representation seems impressive at the two age extremes, their presence does not coincide with any underrepresentation of whites. If anything, the Asian overrepresentation coincides with continued and persistent black and Hispanic underrepresentation.

Minority Group Representation Differentiated by Gender

The statistics in Table 3.1 (page 79) show substantial differences between the presence of minority men and minority women on the faculties of colleges and universities. Figure 3.6 illustrates these patterns.

Among American Indians and Latinos, females are better represented than males. Latinas have a representation ratio 50 percent higher than their male counterparts; American Indian women have a representation ratio double that of American Indian men.[14]

---

[14]The representation rates are 0.24 and 0.36, respectively, for Hispanic males and females. They are 0.43 and 0.86, respectively, among American Indians. (See Table 3.1 on page 79.)

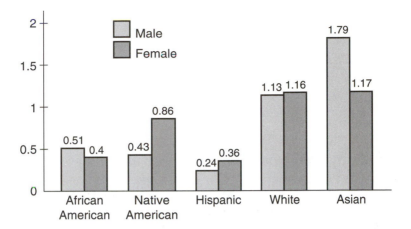

**FIGURE 3.6   U.S. Faculty Representation Ratios
by Gender**

Source: Authors' computations from 1990 census data. See Midwest Higher
Education Consortium (MHEC). *Minority Faculty Development Project: Final
Report.* May 1995. Table D.9.

The gender balance goes in the other direction for blacks and
Asians. Black men are about 25 percent better represented than are
black females, and for Asians, the male representation ratios are
about 50 percent higher than the female ratio.[15]

The numbers are particularly sobering when one remembers
that the denominator in the representation ratio denotes persons
with master's or Ph.D. degrees. Therefore, in addition to the fact
that there are few minorities with advanced degrees to begin with,
their chances of working as faculty in higher education are profoundly affected by gender as well as race/ethnicity.

Considering National Origin

A frequent complaint about analyses of race and ethnicity is that
they fail to distinguish between U.S.-born citizens, foreign-born

---

[15]Black female and black male representation ratios are 0.40 and 0.51, respectively;
Asian representation ratios for females and males are 1.17 and 1.79, respectively.

citizens, and immigrants. The representation ratios in Table 3.1 (page 79) do differentiate between native- versus foreign-born and, among the foreign-born, further distinguish recent immigrants from those who immigrated before the late 1980s. Figure 3.7 shows these patterns.

The figure shows the expected underrepresentation of native-born black, Hispanic, and American Indian faculty, a picture not materially affected by considerations of national origin.[16] The native-versus foreign-born analysis is most interesting in connection with Asian faculty. Although in other analyses "Asians" appear to be statistically "overrepresented," when we distinguish Americans of Asian ethnicity from Asian immigrants, we find that Asian Americans are *appropriately* represented—not overrepresented—on faculties.[17]

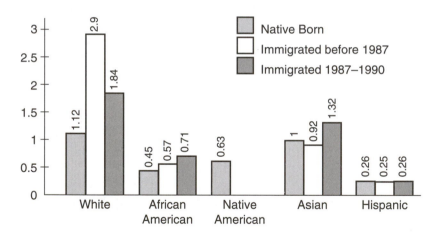

FIGURE 3.7   U.S. Faculty Representation Ratios by Immigration History

Source: Table 3.1.

---

[16]The native-born black, Hispanic, and American Indian faculty representation ratios are 0.45, 0.63, and 0.26. The foreign-born faculty representation ratios for blacks and Hispanics are 0.57 and 0.28.

[17]Representation ratios for native-born and foreign-born Asians are 1.0 and 1.3, respectively.

Table 3.1 (page 79) reveals, moreover, that the greatest overrepresentation rests among the white foreign-born who are almost three times as likely to be faculty as they are to be in the base population. Black and Hispanic foreign-born are underrepresented among faculty. The foreign-born Asian representation is lower than the foreign-born white representation.

Table 3.1 (page 79) distinguishes not only between native-born and foreign-born, it captures information for recent immigrants (since 1987) versus longer-term immigrants. The data confirm that whites are overrepresented among both recent and longer-term immigrants[18] and that the representation ratios of white, foreign-born faculty exceed the representation ratios of white, native-born faculty.

The low representation ratios are virtually the same for Latino immigrants who arrived before 1987 (0.26) and those who arrived later (0.25). For black immigrants the representation ratio is higher for earlier rather than more recent arrivals (0.71 and 0.57, respectively). A similar pattern is found among Asian immigrants: 1.32 versus 0.92, respectively.

The conclusion, then, is that native-born minorities—rather than native-born whites—bear the brunt of any displacement attributable to foreign-born faculty. The image of large numbers of foreign-born minorities replacing white males is probably inaccurate. Whites still dominate among foreign-born faculty as they do among native-born faculty. Whites also dominate among both males and females, with white females slightly better represented than white males. No matter how one slices it, black, Hispanic, and Native American underrepresentation does not disappear.

EXPLAINING THE UNDERREPRESENTATION

What explains the persistent pattern of minority faculty underrepresentation in higher education? There are four conventional explanations:

---

[18]The white representation ratio is 1.84 among highly educated immigrants who came before 1987, and 2.9 among recent immigrants.

- *"Chilly climate." This explanation ascribes the underrepresentation of minorities in higher education to a white-male-dominated institutional culture that undervalues the contributions and/or presence of women and people of color.*

- *Turnover. The problem, in this view, is not an inability to recruit minority faculty but, rather, the failure of institutions to promote and retain them. This theory often relates the turnover to inadequate mentoring programs, the nature of the tenure and promotion process, and other institutional conditions that serve to neglect or even thwart minority faculty development.*

- *"Pipeline." This view assumes that minorities are poorly represented among faculty because 1) there are too few qualified minority candidates; and 2) this dearth of qualified minority candidates is attributable to losses of potentially qualified candidates along the "pipeline" from secondary school to completion of a doctorate.*

- *Market forces. Related to the "pipeline" explanation, this argument proposes that faculty supply is a combined function of Ph.D. production and the weakness of academic wages relative to wages in competing occupations. Explicitly or implicitly, economists argue that increased wages in other sectors of the economy drive talented minorities out of the academy.*[19]

The chapters that follow address, in one way or another, each of these explanations for minority faculty underrepresentation.

[19]Richard Freeman, *The Overeducated American*. New York: Academic Press, 1976; Richard Freeman and David Breneman, *Forecasting the Ph.D. Labor Market*. Washington, DC: National Board on Graduate Education, 1974.

TABLE 3.1   U.S. Faculty Representation Ratios by Race/Ethnicity

	White	Black	American Indian	Asian	Hispanic
			Representation Ratios		
AGE 24–33	1.11	0.32	2.38	1.86	0.72
% of Faculty	78.8%	3.8%	1.9%	6.7%	8.8%
% of Total	71.4%	11.9%	0.8%	3.6%	12.3%
AGE 34–43	1.18	0.53	0.29	0.85	0.20
% of Faculty	88.9%	5.7%	0.2%	3.4%	1.8%
% of Total	75.2%	10.8%	0.7%	4.0%	9.2%
AGE 44–53	1.12	0.49	0.00	1.67	0.21
% of Faculty	87.5%	4.9%	0.0%	6.0%	1.6%
% of Total	78.0%	9.9%	0.7%	3.6%	7.6%
AGE 54–63	1.07	0.40	1.20	2.56	0.32
% of Faculty	86.4%	3.8%	0.6%	6.9%	2.2%
% of Total	80.6%	9.4%	0.5%	2.7%	6.8%
AGE 64–70	1.09	0.52	0.00	1.25	0.27
% of Faculty	91.8%	4.4%	0.0%	2.5%	1.3%
% of Total	84.2%	8.4%	0.4%	2.0%	4.9%
MALE	1.13	0.51	0.43	1.79	0.24
% of Faculty	86.4%	5.0%	0.3%	5.9%	2.3%
% of Total	76.6%	9.9%	0.7%	3.3%	9.4%
FEMALE	1.16	0.40	0.86	1.17	0.36
% of Faculty	87.8%	4.5%	0.6%	4.1%	3.1%
% of Total	75.8%	11.2%	0.7%	3.5%	8.7%
IMMIGRATED 1987–1990	2.90	0.57	0.00	0.92	0.25
% of Faculty	56.8%	2.7%	0.0%	29.7%	10.8%
% of Total	19.6%	4.7%	0.2%	32.2%	43.1%
IMMIGRATED BEFORE 1987	1.84	0.71	0.00	1.32	0.26
% of Faculty	57.0%	3.2%	0.0%	29.0%	10.8%
% of Total	30.9%	4.5%	0.2%	21.9%	42.3%
NATIVE BORN	1.12	0.45	0.63	1.00	0.26
% Faculty	92.5%	5.0%	0.5%	0.8%	1.3%
% Total	82.3%	11.1%	0.8%	0.8%	5.0%
FOREIGN BORN	1.90	0.57	0.00	1.30	0.28
% Faculty	53.5%	3.4%	0.0%	31.8%	11.3%
% Total	28.2%	6.0%	0.1%	24.4%	41.0%

Source: Authors' computations from 1990 census data. See Midwest Higher Education Consortium (MHEC). *Minority Faculty Development Project: Final Report.* May 1995. 1% PUMS 1990 Sample. MA and Ph.D. only.

The faculty representation ratio is the percentage of total faculty among MA's and Ph.D.'s, ages 24–70, within each race divided by the percentage of total faculty among MA's and Ph.D.'s, ages 24–70, in the United States.

TABLE 3.2   Faculty Representation Ratios by State (EEOC and Census Data)

	Non-Hispanic White	Non-Hispanic Black	Hispanic	Asian	American Indian
Illinois	**1.17**	**0.32**	**0.21**	**2.41**	**0.94**
% of Faculty (EEOC)	87.5%	4.7%	1.6%	6.0%	0.2%
% of Faculty (1990 Census)	74.9%	14.7%	7.8%	2.5%	0.2%
Kansas	**1.06**	**0.21**	**0.30**	**3.16**	**0.29**
% of Faculty (EEOC)	93.4%	1.2%	1.1%	4.0%	0.3%
% of Faculty (1990 Census)	88.5%	5.7%	3.7%	1.3%	0.9%
Michigan	**1.07**	**0.35**	**0.64**	**4.97**	**0.43**
% of Faculty (EEOC)	87.9%	4.9%	1.4%	5.6%	0.3%
% of Faculty (1990 Census)	82.4%	13.8%	2.1%	1.1%	0.6%
Minnesota	**0.99**	**0.49**	**1.55**	**2.22**	**0.41**
% of Faculty (EEOC)	93.4%	1.0%	1.1%	4.0%	0.5%
% of Faculty (1990 Census)	94.2%	2.1%	0.7%	1.8%	1.1%
Missouri	**1.03**	**0.3**	**1.07**	**6.67**	**0.77**
% of Faculty (EEOC)	89.9%	3.2%	1.2%	5.4%	0.3%
% of Faculty (1990 Census)	87.0%	10.7%	1.2%	0.8%	0.4%
Nebraska	**1.01**	**0.31**	**0.43**	**5.34**	**0.24**
% of Faculty (EEOC)	93.5%	1.1%	1.0%	4.2%	0.2%
% of Faculty (1990 Census)	92.6%	3.6%	2.3%	0.8%	0.8%
Ohio	**1.03**	**0.38**	**0.86**	**6.00**	**0.69**
% of Faculty (EEOC)	89.7%	4.0%	1.1%	5.0%	0.1%
% of Faculty (1990 Census)	87.1%	10.6%	1.3%	0.8%	0.2%
Wisconsin	**1.01**	**0.44**	**0.72**	**3.46**	**0.45**
% of Faculty (EEOC)	92.3%	2.2%	1.3%	3.8%	0.4%
% of Faculty (1990 Census)	91.3%	4.9%	1.8%	1.1%	0.8%
Indiana	**1.01**	**0.25**	**0.67**	**8.50**	**0.71**
% of Faculty (EEOC)	90.9%	1.9%	1.2%	5.8%	0.2%
% of Faculty (1990 Census)	89.6%	7.7%	1.8%	0.7%	0.2%
Iowa	**0.96**	**0.81**	**1.05**	**5.11**	**0.89**
% of Faculty (EEOC)	92.5%	1.4%	1.2%	4.7%	0.2%
% of Faculty (1990 Census)	96.0%	1.7%	1.1%	0.9%	0.3%
North Dakota	**0.97**	**0.48**	**0.92**	**7.20**	**0.99**
% of Faculty (EEOC)	91.2%	0.3%	0.6%	3.9%	4.0%
% of Faculty (1990 Census)	94.2%	0.5%	0.7%	0.55	4.1%

TABLE 3.2 *Continued*

South Dakota	1.03	0.71	1.18	7.53	0.20
% of Faculty (EEOC)	94.2%	0.3%	0.7%	3.4%	1.4%
% of Faculty (1990 Census)	91.2%	0.5%	0.6%	0.4%	7.3%

Source: Midwest Higher Education Consortium (MHEC). *Minority Faculty Development Project: Final Report.* May 1995. Table D.1.

The faculty representation ratio is the percentage of total faculty accounted for by each race (by EEOC data) divided by the percentage of the population accounted for by each race (from the U.S. census data). Faculty data include full-time faculty only and are compiled by the Equal Opportunity Commission from 1991 EEO-6 Higher Education Staff Information, Table III. Population data include people of all ages and come from the U.S. Department of Commerce, Bureau of the Census, General Population Characteristics: Sex, Race, and Hispanic Origin, 1990.

4

A CHILL IN THE AIR
In the Words of Faculty of Color

The literature and the statistics lead to the conclusion that faculty of color in predominantly white institutions continue to experience exclusion, isolation, alienation, and devaluation. The result is an uncomfortable work environment that undermines the productivity and satisfaction of minorities attempting to pursue academic careers, or serves to discourage their entry into academic life entirely.

This chapter presents the real-world experiences of individual faculty of color, obtained through interviews and focus groups we conducted. Although we will first briefly revisit the literature, describe our interview protocol design, and give an overview of the responses we obtained, the majority of this chapter is devoted to direct quotations from the faculty of color we interviewed, describing in their own words many of those things that make up what we and other scholars have come to call the "chilly climate."

REVISITING THE LITERATURE

Many writers have described the inhospitable environments faculty of color face. One view of what constitutes "chilly climate"

> [*Campus climate is a*] *term used to describe the culture, habits, decisions, practices, and policies that make up campus life. The degree to which the climate is hospitable determines the "comfort factor" for African Americans and other nonwhite persons on campus.*
>
> Harvey, (1991, p. 128)

comes from a 1990 study involving seventy-eight University of Wisconsin System faculty. The report, authored by Jeri Spann, summarizes respondents'—or panelists as they were called—views on campus climate:

> *Panelists defined climate as the quality of respect and support accorded to women and minorities on individual campuses and in individual departments. [Panelists] believed that climates were created by institutions and could be measured in specific ways...by the number of women and minority faculty members at junior and senior levels...by the social distance between majority and minority group faculty and administrators...by the equitability of work assignments.*
>
> *Panelists agreed that the most serious and pervasive environmental problems were subtle ethnic and gender biases that "chill the air" and act as critical influences in teaching, research and service evaluations...Dealing with bias is like peeling an onion. We've dealt with the gross outer layers; now we are trying to peel back a much more complex and difficult layer. Panelists agreed that more often than not, it was subtle bias, passing as objective decision-making, that had to be uncovered and addressed.[1]*

It appears—from much of the literature, as well as from our own interviews—that at every level of academia a person of color is treated, at best, as "a guest in someone else's house." It seems that even when white faculty and administrators greet minority faculty with apparent cordiality, they project the underlying attitude that they are making "others" feel welcome in "their" space.

Ron Wakabayashi, national director of the Japanese American Citizen's League, expressed this sense of exclusion very well. He said, "We feel that we're a guest in someone else's house, that we can never relax and put our feet up on the table" (quoted by Lee Daniels, 1991, p. 5). Daniels points out that guests are not family, whose foibles and mistakes are tolerated. On the contrary, guests honor their hosts' customs without question, keep out of certain rooms of the house, and must always be on their best behavior.

---

[1]J. Spann, *Retaining and Promoting Minority Faculty Members: Problems And Possibilities.* Madison: The University of Wisconsin System, 1990, p. 1.

Other faculty of color fare worse than "guests" and—according to some of our colleagues—this image is too kind, because it describes a situation in which faculty of color are welcome but with limitations. Many other faculty of color have experienced open or thinly veiled hostility in their academic environments, and the guest metaphor does not apply to the toxic environments they and many other faculty of color experience. The guest metaphor does serve to explain the discomfort faculty of color feel even when a predominantly white college is "welcoming" rather than openly hostile, and we find it to be an apt analogy for the more subtle forms of "chilly climate."

Experiences of faculty of color in academe are filled with the bitter and the sweet. This chapter is devoted to an examination of the bitter—to developing an understanding, through our interview respondents, of those "facts of life" that appear to impose unique or more substantial hardships for faculty of color than for their white colleagues. For those who wish to change the status quo—to provide a warmer, more welcoming climate for faculty of color—such an understanding is critical.

DESCRIPTION OF THE STUDY

We conducted individual interviews with 55 faculty of color, and focus group interviews with nine more (in two focus groups), to learn about the workplace perceptions of faculty of color in midwestern college and university settings.

The 64 faculty participating in interviews included 11 Asians (7 male, 4 female), 28 African Americans (13 male, 15 female), 11 American Indians (7 male, 4 female), and 14 Latinos (6 male, 8 female).

Most of the respondents (44) held tenured positions. Some also held high-level administrative positions in their departments or colleges, and senior-level positions in university administration. Their average age was 46 years old. Twelve professors were in the biological and physical sciences.

The sample included faculty from institutions in seven Midwestern Higher Education Commission (MHEC) states (Illinois, Kansas, Michigan, Minnesota, Missouri, Nebraska, and Ohio). Potential respondents were identified by members of the MHEC state commissioners, representatives from the Minority Faculty Development

Project (MFDP) steering committee, and the MFDP panel of scholars (faculty members involved in research related to minority faculty recruitment and retention). They supplied a list of possible interviewees who were willing to share some of their experiences. Additional names were supplied by some of the respondents on completion of their interviews.

The interview protocol was developed by a research team headed by Caroline Turner (coauthor of this book). Responses were tape recorded, transcribed, and analyzed with the assistance of a qualitative computer software program named Nonnumerical Unstructured Data: Indexing, Searching, and Theorizing (NUD*IST). Emergent themes from each interview were coded and named by category (using categories generated primarily from the interview protocol). Interviews solicited participant views on their reasons for pursuing an academic career, the pathways that led them to their current position, their professional development experiences, their experiences as faculty members, their general experiences in the academic workplace, their future plans and whether they expected to leave academia, and strategies for improving recruitment and retention of faculty of color. Interviews elicited perceptions and assessments of institutional practices associated with recruitment and retention of faculty of color.

OVERVIEW OF THE RESPONSES

Our interviews sought the views of minority faculty, with the ultimate purpose of helping educators and policy makers understand those factors in the academic experience that influence minority faculty representation—both positively and negatively. Much of what we learned from our respondents is consistent with the literature, although unlike ours, few studies reported in the literature focus solely on faculty of color in midwestern institutions or examine the experiences of minority faculty members who are tenured.

Interviews elicited perceptions and assessments of institutional practices associated with recruitment and retention of faculty of color. Although a few respondents report having not encountered racial and ethnic discrimination, most say that they continue to be plagued by racial and ethnic biases in the process of performing their duties as faculty members.

Though most of the faculty interviewed say they plan to stay in academe, they identify racial and ethnic bias as the most troubling challenge they face in the academic workplace. Issues commonly cited involve feelings of isolation, lack of information about tenure and promotion, unsupportive work environments, gender bias, language/accent bias barriers, lack of mentorship, and lack of support from superiors. Although many respondents acknowledge that pursuing a successful academic career involves struggles for everyone regardless of race or ethnicity, they believe that faculty of color are burdened with additional challenges not experienced by white colleagues.

Whether already tenured or on a tenure track, most of the faculty of color we interviewed cite firsthand experiences of racial and ethnic bias in the workplace. Their anecdotes and observations reveal the conditions—manifesting racial and ethnic bias—that these faculty of color commonly find troubling and burdensome. Major concerns, repeatedly cited, include:

1. denial of tenure or promotion due to race/ethnicity
2. being expected to work harder than whites
3. having color/ethnicity given more attention than credentials
4. being treated as a token
5. lack of support or validation of research on minority issues
6. being expected to handle minority affairs
7. having too few minorities on campus

The faculty quotations that make up the balance of this chapter elaborate and capture the essence of these problems, and we have organized their comments by these seven areas. For each quote we identify the gender, race/ethnicity, tenure status, academic discipline, and administrative rank, if relevant, of the speaker.[2]

---

[2]The identifiers are broad to protect the anonymity of study participants. We also, unfortunately, cannot reveal the high-level administrative positions many of our respondents hold. Because so few faculty of color occupy such positions, to identify their positions more specifically would be to reveal their identities. We do, however, distinguish among department-, college-, and university-level administrators to capture the unique perspectives that administrators at different levels bring to the discussion. For example, a "department-level administrator" might indicate chair or associate chair; "college-level administrator," a dean or an associate dean; and "university-level administrator" might be a vice president or a provost.

The seven problem areas are common to all of the racial/ethnic groups we interviewed. However, we also identified certain themes that appear to be of special significance to each particular group. These themes and related faculty quotes are presented by ethnic group in the last part of this chapter. We feel that this special focus is important, not only to better understand the particular experience of each group, but to add dimension to our overall understanding of bias in academia. For example, we know from the quantitative data that Asians are relatively well represented in academia and do not suffer the problem of underrepresentation evident for other racial/ethnic minorities. Nevertheless, our Asian respondents describe negative treatment related to stereotyping—for instance, being ghettoized in science and engineering and excluded from administrative positions—and they recount many of the same "climate" problems other minorities face. The experience of Asian Americans serves to underscore the idea that for minorities to be full participants in the academic world there must be a change, not only in the numbers, but in the climate as well.

CHILLY CLIMATE: WHAT OUR RESPONDENTS HAVE TO SAY

We are not succeeding and I think it's because we are still looking at this process [recruitment and retention of faculty of color] as a sorting and weeding, rather than an affirming and building.

Male African American tenured humanities college-level administrator

We have included the many quotes that appear in the following pages because we feel it is our respondents' words that best convey the real meaning of "chilly climate." As a body, the number of quotes addressing the same underlying concerns gives some sense of the universality of the experience. Taken one by one, the quotes provide a glimpse into the day-to-day reality—unique, personal, and varied—of what faculty of color experience.

As noted, we have grouped quotes according to what we identified as dominant issues, and from time to time we offer comments or a quote from the literature. Other than that, in the following pages we leave our respondents to speak for themselves.

Denial of Tenure or Promotion Due to Race/Ethnicity

Promotion and tenure processes are especially problematic for faculty of color. Many report clearly perceiving—and in some instances being told outright—that they did not fit "the profile" for promotion. Some report that, having been passed over for promotion, they were advised to relocate to other institutions where promotion for faculty of their ethnic/racial group was more likely.

> First, there were no women's names floating around. But here I was a woman and an Asian American and I felt that if I were a white male, my name would have been out there.
>
> Female Asian American tenured sciences department-level administrator

> That whole year I had more publications, more presentations, and community work than any of the faculty that I supervise…We found out who was promoted through the student newspaper, and I looked and I wasn't promoted. In the student newspaper of all things. No one had the decency to call…
>
> Male African American tenured humanities college-level administrator

> And I've heard some anecdotal things with one of my friends that was told very straight-in-the-face, you might say…He was going for a provost position and the president of that place said, well you know, you should try this other place. There are more Asians there…
>
> Male Asian American tenured sciences university-level administrator

> I was denied on the fact that I wasn't here long enough. And one of the [white] faculty had been here one year less than I had. They were granted promotion…So the next year I applied for promotion again and was denied.
>
> Female African American untenured social sciences

Issues regarding tenure and promotion are articulated by our study respondents as well as in much of the literature reviewed elsewhere in this book. A few works highlight some of the inherent complexity of promotion and tenure issues. "Academic Acrimony:

Minority Professors Claim Racism Plays Role in Obtaining Tenure,"
by Itabari Njeri (1989), discusses several tenure cases brought forth
by faculty of color, and concludes:

> *The orthodox, i.e. the white interpretation of the world, is the ob-
> jective one, and the black person's interpretation is political. And
> we haven't reached the stage in this society yet where there's any-
> thing like an objective perspective on racial phenomena. (p. 4)*

The focus of Njeri's article is the particularly dramatic case of
racial discrimination in the tenure process: the racial discrimination case of *Clark v. Claremont University Center and Graduate School*.
This tenure denial case was tried in a California court, which
awarded the plaintiff $1.4 million. The state court of appeals up-
held the verdict. Leap (1995) also writing about the case, calls it
"one of the most flagrant and costly examples of intentional discrimination" (p. 124). Such tenure discrimination suits strongly reinforce our view that the tenure process as it applies to faculty of
color is in dire need of reexamination.

Being Expected to Work Harder Than Whites

Added to this burden of being passed over for promotion is the
sense of being expected to work harder than whites, the perception
that faculty of color must be twice as good just to be equal. Being
in the "spotlight," faculty of color feel they are under constant
scrutiny—that they must always be at their best and must constantly exceed what whites do in comparable situations. Faculty of
color believe that meeting the "normal" expectations may somehow be construed as a lack of drive.

> The competence of minority faculty is more apt to be ques-
> tioned and challenged. It makes it more difficult.
>
> Male African American tenured social sciences college-level administrator

> Rightly or wrongly, many of my nonminority colleagues…are
> never 100 percent sure that a minority person is here because
> they are good at what they do or because of affirmative action.
>
> Male American Indian tenured social sciences
> department-level administrator

There is a common sentiment that the minority faculty member "kicks into high gear," especially when in pursuit of tenure. This means that even when the burden becomes nearly unbearable, faculty of color must press on in order not to be judged unfavorably.

> I am expected to teach and do research as well as represent a whole ethnic group, something that is not expected of white faculty members.

Female Latina tenured social sciences

> We have to work twenty times harder than anyone else...if you entered [the faculty ranks] as an African American, regardless of what I'd done my research on, I'm expected to know the answers to all the [racial] problems..."

Female African American tenured humanities

Having Color/Ethnicity Given More Attention Than Credentials

Being very conspicuous adds to the burdens described by interviewees. This situation creates great discomfort for minority faculty because they feel diminished in their professional capacities. They want to be recognized first for their academic credentials.

> I'm the department chair in the [science] department and I meet with a lot of people who don't know me—you know, prospective students and their parents. And I know that their first reaction to me is that I'm an Asian American woman, not that I'm a scientist or that I'm competent...

Female Asian American tenured sciences department-level administrator

> When I first came here, I remember that I was being introduced at the college faculty meeting the first day and my chair introduced me and didn't say anything about my qualifications or my background or my research interests. She said, she's come in as chair of the [minority affairs committee]. Now that's an administrative position. I'm a faculty member... The first years were tough and I would not let myself feel these experiences,

but now in retrospect I can see that I went through an extreme
amount of pressure.

                    Female Asian American tenured social sciences

It's like you get this look and all of a sudden you think to your-
self, that's right, I'm black. That's right, I'm a person of color.
And so, they're not seeing me the way I see myself. They see
that [color] first and then get their little shock...

                    Female African American untenured humanities

Mainstream students look at minority professors in a different
light...not looking like a mainstream instructor naturally tends
to work against you.

                    Male American Indian tenured humanities

Although our study did not look at this specifically, we believe
that it is safe to assume that a great many students at predominantly white institutions have had few, if any, classroom experiences with teachers of color. One male African American tenured
in the social sciences states: "I'm probably the first teacher of color
they've ever had." This may be part of the problem that faculty of
color describe with regard to negative student interactions. (This
problem appears to be of particular concern to female faculty of
color and is elaborated further in this chapter in the section called
"Manifestations of Interlocking Race and Gender Bias."

Regarding my reception by students, we work with paradigms
and world views that are so tuned into linear models that students have difficulty accepting why we have to understand different cultures. Students wonder, "When is he going to get off
cultural diversity? When is he going to present the facts?"

        Male American Indian tenured social sciences college-level administrator

Being Treated as a Token

Webster's New World Dictionary describes tokenism as a "show of ac-
commodation to a demand, principle, etc. by small, often merely
formal concessions to it" (Guralnik, 1970, p. 1495). Study participants indicate that they do not want to be seen as "merely formal

concessions" for whom standards were lowered in the hiring or promotion process.

> Whenever [university name] tenures a person of color, they like to highlight the fact that this is a person of color who's been tenured or hired just to say, "Here, we're making progress." [When I was tenured] a press release went out that I thought highlighted my being [Asian] much more than was at all relevant...I didn't like being displayed in that way."
>
> Male Asian American tenured social sciences

> It's just like when they trot me out for the minority students and then they trot me back in. It's the same notion, they trot me out when they need attention...and then they trot me back in when they no longer need me.
>
> Female American Indian untenured social sciences

> ...it was clear to me that in many of the searches being an Asian did not help and that in some of the cases I felt that I was put in there just to make the slate look like it was well rounded and there was no particular intention of choosing the person.
>
> Male Asian tenured sciences university-level administrator

> I think that one of the challenges is to prove that you don't have your job because you were an affirmative action hire, that you're not a token.
>
> Male American Indian untenured social sciences
university-level administrator

> ...one person really got mad at me...He was resentful that I was hired...he thought it was solely on my race.
>
> Male Asian American tenured social sciences

> You feel like a token. I always feel like that. The token Indian.
>
> Male American Indian untenured social sciences

> Being Hispanic wasn't necessarily a plus for me, but a plus for the department...That made the department look good in front of the dean...You know, "We have a Hispanic and not a

lot of other departments do. We don't have affirmative action down our throats. We can hire another white male now because we have a Hispanic." Those kinds of things have come up.

Male Latino untenured social sciences

Lack of Support or Validation of Research on Minority Issues

Many faculty of color interviewed for this study have research interests that do not focus on issues of racial and ethnic concerns. However, individuals who examine such issues believe that their research is devalued and discounted:

> We must have more diversity in scholarship. Indians get censored even before we get in print. More outlets are needed to publish articles on minority concerns. An editor I know implied that research on Indians is second rate. Tribal sovereignty is not an interest of mainstream publications, but outlets to publish articles about minority concerns are growing and growing with respect to respectability.

Male American Indian tenured social sciences college-level administrator

In many instances, teaching interests are also coupled with research interests. This respondent articulates how her classroom evaluations are affected by the types of courses she teaches.

> Dealing with sensitive topics such as multiculturalism and racism, I have a bimodal distribution in my evaluations…students have been very, very critical of minority faculty in course-instructor evaluations. This is [names a state]. This is a very restricted environment…[Institution administrators] need to warn faculty that this may happen but also encourage faculty by saying that this is a valuable course and you are a valuable resource for us.

Female Asian American tenured social sciences

Being Expected to Handle Minority Affairs

Issues of pedagogy and cultural diversity and gender are not the province of just women or just faculty of color. I think that happens too often and that puts the faculty of color person or woman on the spot, to kind of convince or persuade—be this change agent...The faculty members feel the added pressure, but are caught in a "Catch-22" because minority issues are also important to them.

> Female American Indian tenured social sciences

It's time consuming...almost every committee wants you to be on it. It gives you opportunities at the same time.

> Female Latina tenured social sciences

Minority faculty have responsibility for minority students and for minority issues.

> Female African American tenured social sciences
> department-level administrator

Nowhere does it state that I was supposed to be the healer of black people on campus.

> Female African American tenured humanities

...it was frustrating, too, because anything that had to do with diversity, people dumped it on my lap...and that's just too much work for one person, and diversity should be everybody's job.

> Male African American tenured social sciences

You're required to be an Indian expert at everything. I went to one class to talk about.... After we were done, students had all kinds of questions about gaming. I don't know anything about gaming.

> Male American Indian untenured social sciences

People in college or university administrative positions are commonly expected to speak using the institutional "we." Our respondents describe the dilemma of being called on to do so within a predominantly white campus environment. No matter what faculty members of color decide to do in these instances, they are placed in uncomfortable positions.

I think that the University...wants a cadre of predictable ser-
viceable people in positions that can somehow justify the University public relations commitment to diversity and to
educational opportunity and at the same time it's winnowing
out and not being particularly active in recruiting the kind of
critical mass that would really change the atmosphere...Faculty
of color, many times, are caught between constituencies...being
asked by the institution to advocate for the administration and
to be spokespersons for their [racial/ethnic] group... [a danger
is that] you can be seen as a loose cannon by the administration if you take positions that are counter to their goals or you
are seen as a sell out by students because you are speaking for
the administration...so that's another thing I think is really difficult [for faculty of color]...

Female American Indian tenured social sciences

Basically it means that faculty of color are called upon to take
a role on campus having to do with students of color. For example, we are called upon to mediate between the students and
the administration...This is an aspect that I don't think my
other colleagues are naturally called upon to do. Faculty of
color have this additional layer of responsibility.

Male Asian American tenured social sciences

One of my mentors said to me, "Well, academic administration
is going to have to be done and it might as well be done by
good people, and that's why I think you should be in it"...I was
to speak at an Asian American conference and this young professor came and just could not understand how a faculty member could become one of them.

Male Asian American tenured sciences university-level administrator

In addition to the dual pressures described previously, another
administrator comments on the "wasteland" that some administrative faculty endure.

This position was attractive because it put me at the center of
academic affairs...there has been a tendency to shunt really
good people off in minority affairs positions and burn up their

talent or to isolate them and not really provide much resource redeployment in the interests of their functions.

> Male African American tenured social sciences
> university-level administrator

Padilla (1994) refers to being expected to handle minority affairs as "cultural taxation." This is "the obligation to show good citizenship toward the institution by serving its needs for ethnic representation on committees, or to demonstrate knowledge and commitment to a cultural group, which may even bring accolades to the institution but which is not usually rewarded by the institution on whose behalf the service was performed" (p. 26).

Having Too Few Minorities on Campus

Being one of only a few—if not the only—minority faculty on a campus presents problems, according to the respondents. Although most of those interviewed adapted to this situation, some said that it presents special problems:

> I've gotten tired of going to faculty meetings and being the only African American there.
>
> Male African American tenured sciences

> Every place I've been they've talked about the fact that there are not enough minorities to provide any faculty balance. As far as I can tell that's all over the United States. I don't think the Midwest is any exception.
>
> Female African American tenured sciences

> The faculty of color numbers ought to increase because of the reason of channeling students through them as mentees... We have not increased proportionately with the student increase.
>
> Male Latino untenured humanities

One respondent said that the small numbers of minority faculty at many institutions perpetuates the notion that minorities cannot achieve as highly as whites in academia:

And I think that the paucity of black professors and administrators in these kinds of settings reinforces the presumption people have that we're out of place and it leads to all kinds of ironic, comical and downright restrictions on life chances for blacks and other minorities in these kinds of settings. It often leads to a good deal of anger and frustration for many people.

> Male African American tenured social sciences
> university-level administrator

THEMES OF SPECIAL SIGNIFICANCE TO EACH OF OUR GROUPS

Race-based bias was a matter of concern expressed within all of the minority groupings interviewed in this study. At the same time a number of issues that surfaced were of special concern to specific groups. Reporting these comments within each racial/ethnic category is not meant to imply that others do not face such issues. According to our study findings, however, these are themes emerging from specific groups of faculty interviewed.

American Indians

One of the major concerns of American Indians was identity. It is often difficult for them to maintain ties to their own Indian community while at the same time being part of an often culturally incompatible academic community.

> I think that American Indian people particularly have the problem of identity to deal with. All American Indian people have it, whether they're traditional, whether they're full blood, whether they're mixed blood, whatever their background. Identity is a very complicated factor in their personal and their professional life.
>
> Female American Indian tenured social sciences

> The role of the university is not to make you comfortable as an Indian; the role of the university is to strip the Indian away from you...
>
> Male American Indian tenured social sciences college-level administrator

I would say that over the years, the biggest challenge that I've had to face as an Indian faculty member is that I've had to make sure that I don't act in such a way that the Indians in the community feel that I'm trying to "put on the dog," or feel that I'm better than they are...I have to remind myself of that periodically. As long as you do, you can steer clear of the pitfalls of that.

Male American Indian tenured
social sciences department-level administrator

The struggle between maintaining American Indian identity and assimilating into the university culture is further highlighted by the two contrasting approaches to the problem as presented in the following quotes.

I've done my best to make this system more accessible. I don't think that it robs us of our culture. It does lead us away from our past, but education does that for all people and the real challenge to American Indians today is to live in [an] evolving culture and contribute to its evolution, rather than struggle to maintain its history.

Male American Indian tenured social sciences
university-level administrator

[It's]'s what you want...I would never go any place where there aren't American Indian students. That's one thing I would not do. I learned my lesson when I went to.... But some American Indians just simply want to do research and want to write that book and it doesn't really matter where they are. They could teach at [prominent private university], that's fine. Personally, I would not want to teach [there] because of the simple reason there aren't any Indians there.

Female American Indian untenured social sciences

Asian Americans

Three issues were especially important to Asian Americans: the presence of a glass ceiling, perceptions of language barriers, and absorbing the difficulties in silence.

A number of Asian faculty members expressed concern for what might be termed a *glass ceiling* beyond which they were not able to pass. A second concern revolved around language. It was not that they necessarily felt that they had a problem with the language. Rather, the concern was that others often

> *Quantitative data reveal a concentration of Asian faculty in science and engineering and a lack of representation in administrative ranks. Don Nakanishi in "Asian Pacific Americans in Higher Education: Faculty and Administrative Representation and Tenure" addressed this issue, observing that the image of Asian Pacific Americans as "successful" serves to hide their underrepresentation in college faculties and key administrative positions.*

perceived them as not being able to adequately speak or fully comprehend English. Being expected to work hard while absorbing the difficulties in silence was felt as an additional burden.

> ...as you know, there are very few Asians, especially in academic administration. Part of the reason for that is [the belief] that Asians are not managers, are not administrators. They are good faculty members, but that's all they can do...Nonverbal skills are fine, but we don't expect any Asian to have any verbal skills or be able to write memos that command the respect of the faculty.
>
> Male Asian American tenured sciences university-level administrator

> People ask me why I speak English so well...They've already superimposed on me that I don't belong here...I used to think it was a harmless little question but now I feel that the message that I've received is that I don't belong, I don't look like I belong.
>
> Female Asian American tenured sciences department-level administrator

This observation is reminiscent of the introductory comments made by Ronald Takaki in *A Different Mirror: A History of Multicultural America*. Such encounters may appear inconsequential—"I used to think it was a harmless little question"—but these seemingly harmless questions perpetuate and reinforce patterns of marginalization or exclusion, whether they take place within an academic setting or elsewhere. The tendency to dismiss such incidents as unimportant and view the respondent as "overly sensitive" must be resisted. Takaki (1993) articulately expresses the import of such exchanges:

> *I had flown from San Francisco to Norfolk and was riding in a taxi to my hotel to attend a conference on multiculturalism...My driver and I chatted about the weather and the tourists...The rearview mirror reflected a white man in his forties. "How long have you been in this country?" he asked "All my life," I replied, wincing. "I was born in the United States." "I was wondering because your English is excellent!"...Somehow I did not look "American" to him; my eyes and complexion looked foreign... Questions like the one my taxi driver asked are always jarring, but I could understand why he could not see me as American. He had a narrow but widely shared sense of the past—a history that has viewed American as European in ancestry. (pp. 1–2)*

Such comments can even be more destructive when they occur in the academic setting in which one's professional status and reason for belonging have purportedly been established.

> I guess essentially I work hard, I don't make waves. I wouldn't even dare to do this kind of thing [write about minority faculty experiences]...If I were not a minority person, I probably would speak out, but I hesitate to do that.
>
> Male Asian American tenured sciences

> ...when minority people are more vocal, then there are less chances [opportunities]. So, over the years I've kept myself blind and didn't scream about it, and so things have gone on ...what keeps me here at the present position is maybe my ego...I don't leave a place considering it a defeat. I always feel I leave a place only after I have succeeded in my efforts...I've always told people, "Never quit!"...prove to yourself that you have won, and then you can say "Bye."
>
> Male Asian American tenured sciences

These comments provide contradictions to the "model minority" myths and stereotypes. They also bring to mind the thought that racism can be silencing in very different ways. African Americans are expected to be angry and violent whereas Asian Americans are expected to be quiet and polite. Both sets of racist expectations are silencing.

Latinos

Two issues that prompted a number of comments specifically from Latinos were cultural isolation and overwork.

> This is something that has been a struggle since I came to this country from Puerto Rico…there was a lot of prejudice…people at first…start laughing at your accent …It's just the stereotype that's always been in the U.S.A. They put all of the Hispanics in the same spot. "None of you work," or "All of you are on welfare and you're not going to get off of welfare."…We need more Hispanics…Our students…don't have an image of Hispanic faculty, administrators…
>
> Female Latina untenured social sciences

> One situation that is particularly challenging for me is the language. You are hesitant to participate. Some colleagues become impatient with you…Sometimes I just keep quiet…lack of a [perfect] command of English can be seen as if you were not good enough in your field…They don't have any Latinos here. You feel isolated in terms of your culture. You don't have the other people that listen to your music, eat your food…
>
> Female Latina tenured social sciences

> Dilemma—the expectations that I know everything, expertise in everything that happens—race relations is one…
>
> Female Latina tenured social sciences college-level administrator

> There is a lot of service—committees where I'm representing the whole institution at various things…not just within the department but university-wide committees…This year service seems to be eating away my time. At every level, they don't realize that each is asking for a lot…It is hard to say no, especially on minority issues, when there are so few people…I realize how few people are available [to address these issues]…I sit on

53 doctoral committees. Doctoral students take a lot of time for the dissertation process. I turned down being chair of one doctoral student's committee and she nearly cried. She was a good student studying multicultural issues, but I can't chair these committees. I'll wind up spending all my time correcting dissertations and not doing my own writing.

Female Latina untenured social sciences

A good friend said to me that when you're a minority, you're going to have to be better than everybody else and, whatever you do, you have to take great care, you're going to have to be sure that you're very meticulous, that you do your best, that there are no questions about anything that you do...

Male Latino tenured social sciences

African Americans

The concern most frequently mentioned by African Americans is being simultaneously hypervisible and invisible. Participants express frustration at being at once very visible because of color and advocacy of cultural diversity, and at the same time being overlooked for not fitting others' view of the "norm."

Coming on campus, it was perceived that you got the job because you're a minority... You're not perceived as having something to offer. It's like—you've

Patricia J. Williams, a lawyer and a professor of commercial law, sheds light on this situation for African Americans as she describes her days as a graduate student and a junior faculty member:

My abiding recollection of being a student at Harvard Law School is the sense of being invisible...Law school for me was like being on another planet, full of alienated creatures with whom I could make little connection... When I became a law professor, I found myself on yet another planet: a planet with a sun as strong as a spotlight and an atmosphere so thin that my slightest murmur would travel for miles...I know that my feelings of exaggerated visibility and invisibility are the product of my not being part of the larger cultural picture.

Williams (1991, pp. 55–56)

had a good day if you do something well, you're not quite as good at things, not as deserving of some of the rewards.

> Female African American tenured social sciences
> college-level administrator

I wonder, when I go into those kinds of meetings, when candidates are coming in, if my fellow colleagues look at me in terms of their equals or is this just another project—a minority development project—and so it's to get numbers, it's to get minorities...

> Female African American untenured social sciences

One of the things I've gotten tired of is going to faculty meetings and being the only African American there...I was saying that we needed to bring in more African Americans but no one really was taking it seriously...It is extremely difficult to work in that environment...I am looking to leave...if they don't bring on another African American.

> Male African American tenured sciences

Respondents discuss their "invisibility" in the following ways.

I don't feel like a part of the department. I have been alienated from my department for a number of years...It is not an environment that's nurturing for me.

> Male African American tenured social sciences college-level administrator

The college was very chilly. There's the typical thing that happens when people don't feel you came through the ranks. They thought that it was a top-down move to get me in this campus...A lot of faculty didn't feel like they had voted for me. So, the first year was hands-off. There were a lot of people who just didn't know what to make of me...So, I got jerked around a lot, swept aside...

> Female African American untenured sciences

A lot of times, when I expressed dissatisfaction at the hiring rate—that, I think, appalling hiring level of people of color, the conditions and the atmosphere for minorities at the school—people look at me with a puzzled look and say, "Well, I thought you were happy. We didn't know you felt like that." So it's almost as if they've been looking at me as an honorary white person, or honorary European, if you will. And all the while I thought I was expressing me as a unique African American individual there.

Male African American tenured social sciences

MANIFESTATIONS OF INTERLOCKING RACE AND GENDER BIAS

Fourteen female faculty members—nearly one-half the total number of female respondents—describe instances of gender as well as racial bias in their academic workplaces. The interlocking effects of gender and race compound the pressures of the academic workplace for these professors. They perceive that their success as faculty members is hampered by their being both minority and female. One Latina (untenured, social sciences) states: "Women of color leave at a higher rate from this institution. They have a higher leave rate and are less likely to get tenure." Two male informants state that they have witnessed such sex bias.

According to Hu-DeHart, there is serious minority faculty underrepresentation, but "men have progressed considerably farther than women, for the simple fact that they are, after all, men in an institution designed for men."[3] Hu-DeHart goes on to state that colleges and universities are more flexible when it comes to the work needs of men, less flexible in providing for the needs of female professors. Women may experience more role conflict between career and family responsibilities, which increases the burden of the female academic. The observations provided here suggest that such situations continue to exist for contemporary female faculty members, compounding the stress factors for female faculty of color. Four themes emerge from these data:

1. feeling isolated and underrespected
2. being underemployed and overused by departments and institutions

---

[3]E. Hu-DeHart, Women, minorities, and academic freedom. In C. Kaplan and E. Schrecker (Eds.), *Regulating the Intellectuals: Perspectives on Academic Freedom in the 1980's*. New York: Praeger, 1983, p. 142.

3. being torn between family and career
4. being challenged by students

Feeling Isolated and Underrespected

I have to think about the fact that black females or any female in the field of [name], which has been predominantly a white male profession, has a problem. Many females in the college that are white complain about the fact that up until recently, like last year, we had never had a full professor in [department name]. It's changing, but it's not changing fast. And then you add to that being the black female who has to be superwoman.

Female African American untenured sciences

I got a sense at times like, "Shut your mouth. We don't want to hear it. You're a woman." So I think there is some [negative] climate on this campus, and not just toward minorities because I hear it from the white females [as well]…how they don't get promotions like the guys. And I don't think that's just unique to this campus, I think that's kind of epidemic across the United States.

Female African American untenured social sciences

I had one of the female faculty say to me, "I'm the only woman in this department and they go off on Thursdays to golf and they make decisions about things that affect the department when they're golfing and because I'm not there, I find out about it later."

Female African American untenured social sciences

I felt really isolated—more isolated than normal Indians do, more marginalized than I normally even feel. And it was like a double whammy, the only minority and the only woman. For instance, when the secretaries had to go to the restroom, they'd come and get me to watch the phones. They never went and got the new male faculty person. They never got him to watch the phones.

Female American Indian untenured social sciences

This one dean—I don't know what he was dean of, but he was writing down all the federal slots that I would fit in as far as hiring, you know, equal opportunity. And he said, "Okay, you're a woman, you're over fifty-five, you're an American Indian," and then he looked at me and grinned. He said, "Do you have a handicap?" You know, these schools do have to fulfill these guidelines and in getting me they can check a lot of boxes.

Female American Indian untenured social sciences

...our [name] position opened up and there were a lot of names—and so it was clear that an active [internal] person would be named. I would hear on the grapevine, "so-and-so's" name—and this other administrator's name came up a lot. I worked with this person, well, I thought [that] I was more qualified than this person. I never heard my name brought up. Nobody ever came to ask me if I was interested...I felt that if I were a white male, my name would have been out there. I mean I am sure of that. But it never was and, you know...there is no question in my mind that race and gender influenced that.

Female Asian American tenured sciences department-level administrator

For new faculty if I were a minority or woman I would say that you need to be a little more careful whenever you speak. You have to make sure you understand the overall climate, political climate, something like that. Don't get involved too early, make sure you understand the overall situation. Then start to take your stand. Don't take your stand too early. That could damage your tenureship.

Male Asian American tenured sciences

I served on a hiring committee, I'm the only minority, it's a university regulation to put a minority in there. So, I've served on several...there was one time that there was quite a bit of hatred toward a woman. Because of that I think the person was not considered for the job. The woman's husband was favored for a position. Both of them had been faculty members and both had degrees from [elite private research university]. Afterwards one committee member complained that the man didn't get to talk very much because his wife talked so much. I felt that he [the committee member] was being biased against the woman.

Male Asian American tenured sciences

In this case, it was also interesting that each potential faculty member was not interviewed individually.

Despite shared gender discrimination, however, women faculty of color cannot always expect support from their white female colleagues. There is also a sense that white women have fared and are faring better than are women or men of color.

I think the white women feel very competitive toward me. I think they feel threatened by me...the women faculty are all white women and, even though I'm a feminist and they're also feminists, I have not been accepted...The resources of the university are so limited so they can literally dole out the resources. Who do you give it to? You give it to a sister from your own group. It makes sense to me.

Female Asian American tenured social sciences

Even the white females they've hired still have a problem with minority students and minority perspectives. This is particularly true in [discipline]. It is really dominated by Western European notions.

Female American Indian untenured social sciences

Being Underemployed and Overused by Departments and Institutions

I mean, I am a female and African American. Needless to say, I got used...I was doing a lot of things in terms of serving on this board, serving on that board, being faculty adviser for one of the professional fraternities...In retrospect, since I didn't get tenure, neither the department chair or dean said, "Okay, well, this is what you're lacking"...I basically had to find my own avenues.

Female African American untenured humanities

...for a long time—this is hard to believe—for a long time I was the only woman of color on this faculty—for years. It meant that I was a twofer, I was asked to be on every committee imaginable…This campus is very, very white. Almost all of the Indian faculty have been men.

Female American Indian tenured social sciences

The university is using and abusing people to teach courses, do administration, committee work but they have less authority, status, and not any hope of acquiring a permanent position. They will have low self-esteem as a result. This may affect women and minorities more. This is a tough area to study—marginality.

Female Latina untenured social sciences

When you are one of three or four Latinas and being a woman, almost every committee wants you to be on it. It gives you opportunities at the same time. I think you are expected to do a lot of things not expected of other faculty.

Female Latina tenured social sciences

These quotes bring attention to the apparent contradiction and actual "double whammy" faced by women of color. On the one hand, there is too little opportunity and support for the work that is valued (research); on the other hand, there is too much demand for the work that's not valued (committee work, student club advisor, etc.), which takes time away from research and does not even lead to prestigious positions related to committee service (i.e., administration).

Being Torn Between Family and Career

I know that there are lots of values that are indirect, that sometimes get in the way of the careerist profile. Family for example. My family is very important to me. My family is more important to me than my career. That is not the position that will, at least on the surface, get one to the top in the conventional academic setting…

Female American Indian tenured social sciences

We became parents after seventeen years of marriage. Although the university—I mean, that's one of the nice things about being an academic—to have some flexibility, you know, in your schedule. But I think I underestimated the pull [between family and career] from both sides.

Female Asian American tenured social sciences

Being Challenged by Students

Let's put it like this, if a white male professor says something that's wrong in class, my observation is that even if the students perceive that it's wrong, they may say something outside of class, but they hesitate to challenge a 50+ white male professor. They feel quite comfortable challenging an African American woman in class, and I find that...I just think it's society and the way that they're brought up and the way that they perceive people.

Female African American untenured social sciences

I think gender is an issue for some students. Some students want to be more familiar with a woman. Some students don't trust the authority of a woman [or person of color] in the classroom.

Female American Indian tenured social sciences

Regarding interaction with students, there's a different expectation for us when we walk in as a minority; they automatically assume that we know less than our colleagues in the same department...it doesn't matter whether it's undergraduate level or graduate level...They challenge females more...So, I wear dark, tailored suits and I am very well prepared. They don't hire us unless we're prepared anyway but students think we are here because of our color.

Female African American untenured social sciences

A FINE BALANCE

Before ending the interview, study participants were invited to offer any additional comments they wished to make. One respondent directed words of caution to present and prospective faculty of color regarding expectations of support from others.

Yes, my department has been very supportive but they all have their self-interest at heart and on their mind. So the chair says he will protect me from committee work but does assign me to committees he wants me to do. He will protect me from others, however [my mentor] gave me this advice…He said, "Do not think for a moment that any other person has your best interest in mind." He said any other person, that means no one. So you have to set boundaries without looking like a trouble maker or someone not willing to do the work. You have to challenge and say no, push for what you need. It's a fine balance.

Female Latina untenured social sciences

CONCLUSION: WHY WE MUST LISTEN

People were saying that everything was an isolated incident—an isolated incident. But you started to see isolated incidents [at various colleges and universities] and so now we have thousands of isolated incidents…

From the video Racism 101; comment by a male African American student

Listening to this African American student describe the pattern of racial incidents occurring on major college and university campuses, we are reminded of the disbelief that occurs when discriminatory situations are described by people of color. Even though these experiences are documented over and over again in the literature, assertions that "it was only an isolated incident" or "that it is only anecdotal evidence" abound. It appears that the voices of faculty of color are largely ignored, and that what they have to say is deemed inherently unreliable.

Why? Is failure to understand something a reason to discredit it? Or is there a refusal to understand and credit it because of investment in the status quo?

Scheurich and Young (1997) define institutional racism as existing "when institutions or organizations, including educational ones, have standard operating procedures (intended or unintended) that hurt members of one or more races in relation to members of the dominant race" (p. 5). The chilly, unreceptive climates described by our respondents and throughout the literature are manifestations of such institutional racism.

In our view, testimony provided by faculty of color is especially valuable because it comes from unique, authentic, and revealing vantage points. Our study clearly shows that faculty of color perceive subtle and persistent racism that others apparently have a stake in ignoring or explaining away. We need to credit the knowledge shared by our respondents rather than maintaining the ignorance of privilege and the privilege of ignorance. Olson (1996) tells us that "we can address prejudice only when we make ourselves open to the truth of other people's experience and when we join hands to eliminate it" (p. 30).

This chapter has provided many illustrations of what faculty of color find discouraging in their professional settings. Chapter 6 provides some understanding of the "sweetness" of the experience that allows them to overcome the bitter.

5

MINORITY FACULTY HIRING: EQUALITY OF OPPORTUNITY?

In the 1990s, affirmative action came under severe attack. Conventional race-based scholarships and preferential admission programs received increasing judicial scrutiny, and even voluntary initiatives to enhance campus diversity were viewed with mounting hostility. In many respects affirmative action all but died on many campuses across the nation.

The '90s trends aside, affirmative action in faculty hiring was never robust. With or without legal challenges to "reverse discrimination," many departments within colleges and universities always voiced great skepticism about affirmative action, both as to its utility and its appropriateness in hiring faculty. In many colleges

Support for the claim that MHEC states disproportionally produce Ph.D.'s comes from the National Research Council's (NRC) 1991 Survey of Doctorate Recipients. Of the 45,121 employed doctorates in arts and science fields who received their degrees between 1980 and 1990, 41 percent received their degrees from institutions in MHEC states. According to the U.S. Census, these states accounted for 24 percent of the nation's population. Moreover, of all U.S. doctorates in the arts and sciences awarded to minorities between 1980 and 1990, 33 percent were awarded by MHEC states, although the region only accounted for 16 percent of the nation's minority population. The numbers are even more pronounced for African Americans. Of the 1,328 employed black Americans in 1991 who received their Ph.D.'s in the arts and sciences between 1980 and 1990, 591 or 44.5 percent received their degrees from MHEC institutions. The region, however, accounts for only 19 percent of the nation's black population.

and universities, it is at the department level that most important policy decisions about hiring and firing are made. Department heads and senior faculty decide what constitutes "quality," how "scholarly productivity" is measured, how publications and research are credited, and what areas of intellectual endeavor are most worthy of hiring and promotion. Courts tend not to interfere with faculty peer review and evaluation. Academics are the "experts" and courts are loath to second-guess their opinions.[1]

We sought to learn whether and how affirmative action affects hiring decisions—and to determine its effectiveness in increasing minority hiring—through a survey of institutions in selected midwestern states. We surveyed more than 700 midwestern colleges and universities to obtain information about their minority faculty development programs.[2] Of the 700 institutions contacted, 486 responded. As a by-product of that survey, we were able to measure the flow of minority faculty at the responding institutions.

Our survey examined minority faculty development programs in institutions of the member states of the Midwestern Higher Education Commission (MHEC). We believe that the midwestern experience is relevant to institutions throughout the country, and that the lessons are valuable to any institution seriously interested in increasing minority faculty hiring. We believe this is true for several reasons.

First, the institutions in the MHEC states—Illinois, Kansas, Michigan, Minnesota, Missouri, Nebraska, Ohio, and Wisconsin—

---

[1]In 1974, the Supreme Court found that "of all fields, which the federal courts should hesitate to invade and take over, education and faculty appointments at a University level are probably the least suited for federal court supervision." [*Faro v. New York University*, 502 F.2d 1229 (2d. Cir.)]. For a discussion of "judicial deference" to academe, see S. G. Mezey, *In Pursuit of Equality: Women, Public Policy, and the Courts*. New York: St. Martin's Press, 1992, pp. 182–83, 191.

[2]We debated intensely over the difficulties we might introduce should we design our questionnaire specifically for the purpose of investigating affirmative action. At the very time we were conducting the research, several prominent court challenges to affirmative action emerged. We chose an oblique approach to our ultimate question by focusing our inquiry on "faculty development programs."

have disproportionately high minority student enrollments.[3] Second, these institutions produce a disproportionate number of the nation's doctorates, as well as doctorates to minority scholars in the arts and sciences.[4] Finally, the Midwest has pioneered a number of initiatives designed specifically to increase minority faculty and minority doctorates.[5]

Although, as with any survey, we must be cautious about generalizing beyond the intended sample, many of the institutions in our sample are viewed as peers of major institutions in other regions and are closely watched and emulated by others throughout the nation.

> *Every place I've been they've talked about the fact that there are not enough minorities to provide any faculty balance. As far as I can tell that's all over the United States. I don't think the Midwest is any exception.*
>
> Female African American
> tenured sciences

Our survey showed that the average institution hired twelve white professors (including assistant, associate, and full professors) between 1991 and 1994 (the three years preceding our survey in the spring/summer of 1994). During that same period, the average

---

[3]That MHEC states disproportionately enroll minority students is seen easily by comparing the numbers of minority students enrolled in colleges and universities in these states and in the entire nation to the minority populations in these states and the entire nation. According to the Current Population Reports, the minority population in the MHEC states in 1994 equaled 8,394,000. The total U.S. minority population in that year was 67,606,000. Thus, the MHEC share of the minority population is 12.4 percent. According to the U.S. Statistical Abstracts, minority college enrollments in MHEC states and in the United States equaled 475,000 and 3,496,000, yielding a MHEC share of minority college enrollments of 13.6 percent.

[4]Figures shown are authors' calculations from National Research Council (NRC), Survey of Doctorate Recipients 1991, unpublished tabulations. Full results of these tabulations appear see MHEC, *Minority Faculty Development Project,* May 1995, Appendix F.

[5]An important example is the CIC consortium of twelve midwestern universities, which—with substantial support from the Mellon Foundation—provides minority doctoral fellowships.

institution hired slightly more than three minority faculty.[6] In other words, for every minority hired, four whites were hired.

Many of the 486 institutions did not hire any faculty at all during the three-year period. To compute the ratio of the number of minority faculty hired to the number of white faculty hired, we restricted our sample to the 256 institutions that hired at least one white faculty member. The resulting ratio is 0.33; that is, for every minority hired, three whites are hired.

We found that the rate of minority faculty hiring differs substantially among the various types of institution. At two-year colleges, minorities account for 12 percent of all faculty hiring. At four-year colleges, minorities constitute 52 percent of new hires, and at universities offering the Ph.D., 14 percent of faculty hired are minority. Professional schools and "other" institutions both had minority hiring rates of 11 percent. The vast majority of the two-year colleges and universities are public institutions, whereas most of the four-year colleges are private.

In this chapter we discuss the major findings of the survey, whose purpose was to examine the nature and extent of faculty development programs and attempt to isolate program characteristics linked to success in minority faculty hiring and retention. After summarizing what the survey revealed about faculty development programs—in general and specifically related to minorities—we examine three sets of hypothesized factors that may contribute to increased minority faculty hiring. Next we look at what our data show about the existence of any "revolving door" phenomenon for minority faculty, detailing the relationship between number of minority hires and the number of departures. Finally, we explore how the factors hypothesized to affect minority hiring actually relate to success in achieving high minority hiring rates.

FACULTY DEVELOPMENT PROGRAMS: IN GENERAL AND FOR MINORITIES

Unfortunately, we find that few of the MHEC institutions have organized programs for supporting minority faculty development. Al-

---

[6]Minority faculty were specified in the survey to be African American/Black, American Indian/Native American, Asian/Pacific American, and Hispanic/Latino/Chicano.

though 77 percent of the institutions we surveyed consider minority faculty retention a "high" or "very high" priority, most offer little in the way of structured support for minority faculty development.

Specifically, of those institutions responding to our survey:

- Slightly more than half (54 percent) of the institutions responding to the survey have an individual or unit responsible assigned to coordinate overall faculty development.
- Fewer than half (47 percent) have a centrally organized program of faculty development (i.e., faculty development activity that is primarily coordinated by one office or unit).
- Approximately the same proportion (46 percent) rely upon decentralized approaches to faculty development.
- One-third (33 percent) indicate that their current investment in faculty development is about the same as it was three years ago, whereas over half said that it is greater than it was three years ago, either "much greater" (16 percent) or "somewhat greater" (45 percent).

> *Over half the institutions (56 percent) indicate that new faculty orientation is available for minority faculty and 69 percent say it is available for all tenure-track faculty; 54 percent offer teaching skill workshops or seminars to minority faculty, and 69 percent make them available to all tenure-track faculty.*

What exactly is it that these institutions do under the rubric of faculty development? Many offer workshops and seminars. Most commonly, these are "orientation" or teaching skills workshops and seminars offered to new faculty, but these are not generally focused on the special needs of new minority faculty.

Out of an extensive array of faculty development services (including, for example, such things as released-time or special professional libraries), programs for instructional improvement are by far the most common: 59 percent of responding institutions have instructional improvement programs for minority faculty, and 71 percent have them for all tenure-track faculty.

The list of specific forms of faculty development that institutions fund is a long one. The most prevalent are:

- travel to conferences (available specifically for minority faculty at 68 percent of the institutions and for all tenure-track faculty at 83 percent of the institutions);

- purchase of special equipment, such as computers and software (57 percent for minority faculty and 72 percent for all tenure-track faculty);
- curriculum improvement (55 percent for minorities and 70 percent for all tenure-track faculty);
- faculty sabbaticals (52 percent for minorities and 73 percent for all tenure-track faculty).

These figures show that faculty development services are available to both minority and nonminority faculty.

To establish that none of these services is available *exclusively* to minority faculty, we performed a detailed analysis of each of thirty specific faculty development programs, services, and activities listed in our survey of MHEC institutions. The 487 respondents were queried about such services as workshops or seminars for developing research or teaching skills, faculty exchanges, tuition reimbursement, graduate research assistants, released time, annual goals setting, and professional or personal development plans for individual faculty members. We computed a variable that indicated whether programs or services available specifically to minority faculty were unavailable to other faculty generally.[7] In not a single instance was a service available to minority faculty that was not also available to other faculty. Indeed, our analysis also revealed that most services were generally available to tenure-track faculty but did not exist in similar forms specifically for minority faculty.

In short, minority faculty development programs do not appear to take away from majority programs or services. The immediate implication is that there appears to be very little "special treatment" of minority faculty in the form of travel money, purchase of equipment, curriculum improvements, or sabbaticals. Despite widespread perceptions to the contrary, minority faculty reap few material benefits unavailable to other faculty.

---

[7]The categories considered were tenure-track faculty, non-tenure-track faculty, female faculty, and minority faculty. The variable created was coded such that the respondent indicated a specific program or service was available to minority faculty, but the same respondent did not indicate the program or service was available to either tenure-track, non-tenure-track, or female faculty.

Unfortunately, mentoring, either within departments or campuswide, is one of the least used faculty development strategies for minority and general faculty alike.[8] Only 9 percent of the institutions report that mentoring financed by external funds is available to minority faculty and only 10 percent say it is available for all tenure-track faculty. Mentoring programs are arguably of even greater benefit to minority faculty than to others, and mentoring appears to be the strategy with the most significant payoff. Nevertheless, it is the support mechanism least available to minorities and nonminorities alike.

A 1994 tenure-track faculty study focusing on the experiences of women and people of color emphasizes the importance of mentors, and discusses the problem of unevenness:

> *While some departments and colleges have mentoring programs, they are neither across-the-board nor institutionalized. Faculty who work with mentors find them useful and helpful for professional development...New faculty report needing advice about many aspects of their work—the tenure process, publishing, teaching, office politics, and the like—and one person cannot necessarily supply advice to meet all the needs of a junior faculty member...The Center for Minority Faculty Development, which provides information and collegial support for people of color, was highlighted as an important resource by those who used it.*

Bensimon, Ward, and Tierney
(1994, p. 2)

There is a notable absence of innovation and investment in mechanisms to increase minority representation. Approximately 89 percent of the participating institutions report stable or increased funding over the previous three years for general faculty recruitment.

Although eighty-two percent report stable or increased funding for minority faculty recruitment, the vast majority (84 percent) do not augment departmental budgets to make funds specially available for hiring minority faculty. Of those institutions that do,

---

[8]Of responding institutions 31 percent report *departmental* mentoring programs for minority faculty and 39 percent for *all tenure-track* faculty; 22 percent have *campuswide* mentoring programs for minority faculty and 28 percent for *all tenure-track faculty.*

> *Rightly or wrongly, many of my nonminority colleagues…are never 100 percent sure that a minority person is here because they are good at what they do or because of affirmative action.*
>
> Male American Indian tenured
> social sciences department-level
> administrator

20 percent report that faculty hired through the use of such funds are poorly received or received with some reservations by colleagues in their departments. Despite the failure to provide special funds for minority faculty hiring, slightly more than half of the respondent institutions (51 percent) feel that funding earmarked for this purpose is moderately adequate (33 percent) or very adequate (19 percent).

It is not surprising that minority hiring does not receive special budget attention at most institutions, because it is often not a clear institutional goal. Almost two-thirds (62 percent) of the institutions do not have articulated goals for minority hiring over the next five years. Of those reporting goals, 51 percent say that the target is to increase minority faculty hiring by 10 percent, and 38 percent say that it is to increase minority faculty hiring by 10 percent to 50 percent. Thus, the significant hostility toward affirmative action goals in minority hiring seems unmatched by any substantial goals meriting the attack. What our data suggest is that affirmative action was nearly dead at the time of our study.

WHAT AFFECTS MINORITY FACULTY HIRING? HYPOTHESIZED DETERMINANTS

Table 5.1 shows the breakdown of twelve different factors that may contribute to increased minority faculty hiring. These factors are grouped into three broad categories:

- institutional and organizational support for minority faculty hiring and retention
- financial resources for hiring minority faculty
- perceptions about the causes of minority underrepresentation

The influence of these factors varies markedly by institutional type. When linked with information on minority faculty hires by type of

TABLE 5.1 **Determinants of Minority Faculty Hiring by Type of Institution**

	Type of Institution					
	2-year	4-year	Ph.D.	Prof.	Other	Total
Institutional/Organizational						
Percentage responding that diversity efforts are excellent	19.8	14.0	30.0	21.3	28.1	19.4
Percentage with minority faculty development office	3.4	4.5	16.0	4.3	6.3	5.4
Percentage indicating minority retention is a high priority	31.6	38.5	60.0	25.5	43.8	37.3
Percentage believing minority faculty hiring will increase	10.7	8.4	18.0	4.3	6.3	9.7
Financial Resources						
Percentage with high faculty development budgets	7.3	5.0	12.0	10.6	6.3	7.2
Percentage with high minority faculty development budgets	5.1	7.8	18.0	6.4	9.4	7.8
Percentage with increased funding for minority faculty development	20.9	23.5	36.0	23.4	31.3	24.3
Percentage with increased funding for minority faculty recruitment	45.2	41.9	68.0	36.2	43.8	15.4
Perceptions						
Percentage believing very adequate funding for minority faculty hiring	16.9	14.5	22.0	23.4	21.9	17.5
Percentage believing salary competition is cause of low minority hiring/retention	34.5	50.3	56.0	2.1	34.4	39.4
Percentage believing unqualified minorities is cause of low minority hiring/retention	41.8	31.8	28.0	6.4	37.5	33.0

institution, inferences can be drawn about which factors are most significant to increased minority hiring.

Institutional/Organizational Supports

Respondents were asked to rate their institution's faculty development services and general support for faculty. Although 20 percent give their institutions ratings of "excellent" in recognizing diversity, 47 percent give "good" ratings. In clarifying criteria for advancement, 23 percent give a rating of "excellent" and 45 percent give a rating of "good."

Institutional responses concerning retention efforts were mixed. Although close to 80 percent of the institutions rate the retention of minority faculty as either a high priority (38 percent) or a very high priority (39 percent), only 5 percent report that their institutions have special offices designated for minority faculty professional development. Although 93 percent of the responding institutions report that funding for faculty professional development has been either stable or increasing over the last three years, 58 percent report stable or increasing funding for minority faculty professional development. Forty-three percent of the institutions report that less than 1 percent of the budget is allocated to minority faculty professional development.

A few institutions in MHEC states have professional development efforts or programs directed at minority faculty recruitment and/or retention that they consider exemplary. Generally speaking, the institutions surveyed do not indicate the presence of extensive programs to improve minority faculty retention and recruitment. This may be due to financial constraints as well as the absence of institutionally assigned responsibilities for minority faculty recruitment and retention.

As Table 5.1 reveals, however, there is considerable variation across institutional types in response to the organizational/institutional questions. Ph.D.-granting institutions appear to dominate all others in the sample in: (1) diversity, (2) minority faculty development, (3) retention, and (4) hiring objectives. Figure 5.1 compares the responses to these four items between Ph.D.-granting and all institutions.

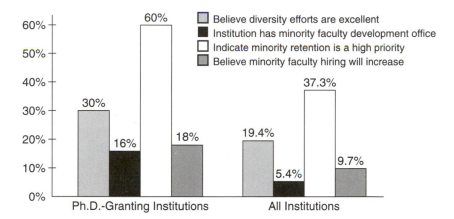

FIGURE 5.1 **Institutional Support in Ph.D.-Granting versus All Institutions**

Financial Resources

The Ph.D.-granting universities manifest their commitment to minority hiring and retention by committing financial resources, further distinguishing them from other institutions. Although only 7.8 percent of all institutions report *high* minority faculty development budgets,[9] 18 percent of Ph.D.-granting institutions have high minority faculty development budgets. The smallest minority faculty development budgets are among two-year colleges at 5.1 percent of total professional development funding.

To be sure, Ph.D.-granting institutions also have high total faculty development budgets—as measured by greater than 3 percent of the institution's total fiscal year budget.[10] But two-year colleges, with the smallest percentage allocated to minority faculty develop-

---

[9]Greater than 5 percent of total faculty professional development funding is allocated to minority faculty professional development.

[10]The modal value was 1 percent to 3 percent, with some institutions allocating less than 1 percent of their budgets to faculty development.

ment, rank second in the overall allocation to professional development. Ph.D.-granting institutions also show a three-year increase in funding for minority faculty development with more frequency than other institutions. Figure 5.2 reveals the differences between financial resources of Ph.D.-granting institutions and all institutions.

An even more pronounced difference between the Ph.D.-granting universities and other institutions involves salary augmentations for hiring minority faculty. Indeed, minority faculty salary augmentation within academic departments seems virtually unique to Ph.D.-granting universities. In these institutions departmental autonomy may be at once a threat to administrative pressures and a way to leverage direct allocations for units responsible for increasing minority representation in the institution.[11]

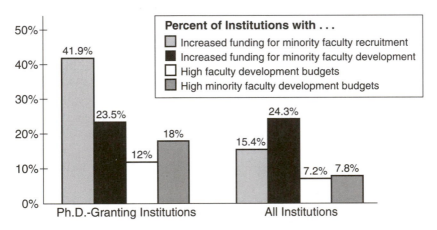

FIGURE 5.2   **Financial Resources at Ph.D.-Granting versus All Institutions**

---

[11]Only about 5 percent of 2-year colleges report using this type of minority-recruitment incentive. Professional schools are not too far behind, with a total of 6.4 percent reporting this form of financial incentive. Among four-year colleges the fraction reporting this incentive is 12.8 percent.

Perceptions

Sometimes what matters most is not what *is* but what appears to be. Perceptions often cloud reality in curious ways. The following question was asked of faculty in arts and humanities, in science, engineering and technology fields, the social sciences, and in professional and other fields.

> *For your institution, what are the obstacles you believe exist for recruitment and/or retention of minority, women, and nonminority [field stated] faculty?*

Respondents were asked to choose one or more of the following:

- undesirable location
- salary competition with other higher education institutions
- salary competition with industry
- lack of start-up funds or other inducements
- low representation (low numbers of minority faculty, students, and staff)
- insufficient numbers of qualified candidates

The response choices allowed for distinction between obstacles to recruitment and obstacles to retention, as well as whether they constitute obstacles for minorities, nonminorities, or both.

Officials at MHEC institutions identify three major obstacles to minority faculty recruitment: (1) a lack of qualified candidates, (2) generally low representation of minorities on campus, and (3) institutional salary competition among institutions. The most frequently reported obstacle to minority faculty recruitment is a lack of qualified candidates.[12]

The second most frequently reported obstacle to minority faculty recruitment is generally low representation of minorities on campus (i.e., low numbers of minority faculty, staff, and students).

---

[12]For all categories, the lack of qualified candidates is viewed as the primary problem by significant percentages: arts and humanities, 58 percent; science, engineering, and technology, 59 percent; social science, 49 percent; and professional, 48 percent (MHEC, *Minority Faculty Development Project: Final Report.* May 1995, p. 55, Figure 10).

Although second overall, this is cited as the number-one obstacle to recruitment in the social sciences.

A third obstacle identified by many respondents—and the one most commonly cited by the professional schools—is salary competition among institutions.

Salary competition is also viewed as a primary obstacle to *retaining* as well as recruiting minority faculty, as is low representation of minorities on campus.

Observations about the Hypothesized Determinants of Minority Hiring

Universities offering Ph.D.'s overwhelmingly have the characteristics positively associated with minority faculty hiring. These institutions are less likely than others to believe that hiring and retention problems are due to a lack of qualified minorities; they are more likely to believe that the problems are due to market competition. They are more likely to have both the funding and the organizational/institutional mechanisms for the hiring and retention of minority faculty.

On balance, then, we see that the Ph.D.-granting institutions— among which are the major state research universities of the Midwest, and several large urban universities with notable success in producing minority Ph.D.'s—tend to have both the institutional/ organizational commitment to hire and retain minority faculty and the financial incentives in place to make those commitments real. This reality, however, must be balanced by the fact that even among these often large and prestigious universities, the infrastructure for assuring the success of minority faculty is fragile. Despite the huge percentage of these institutions that value diversity and make minority retention a high priority, and despite the substantial sums undoubtedly spent on recruitment and hiring of minority faculty, the vast majority (84 percent) of Ph.D.-granting institutions still have no minority faculty development office. Even though they appear to shine in comparison to the rest of the institutions in terms of their stated priorities in retaining minority faculty, the Ph.D.-granting institutions still seem unsure about *how* to realize this goal, focusing instead on hiring and financial incentives to recruit minority faculty.

Clearly institution type, as well as institution size, may be strongly related to these hypothesized predictors of minority versus nonminority hiring. It is, therefore, important to adopt multivariate regression methods to isolate the independent influences of these predictors from size and type of institution.

ACHIEVING PARITY: EFFECTS OF HIRING VERSUS TURNOVER

In order for there to be appropriate representation of minorities on faculties, the ratio of minority faculty hires to nonminority hires must increase. This does not mean that the number of minority hires must be greater than the number of nonminority hires. It simply means that minorities must be hired in much larger proportions than they have been in order to change the present dismal underrepresentation of minority faculty on U.S. campuses.

Of course, if minorities leave academic employment at greater rates than nonminorities, minority hiring targets must be higher than what is necessary to achieve immediate parity simply to keep the existing proportions of minorities and nonminorities constant. If whites leave at greater rates, constant minority hiring will increase minority share.

As an illustration, suppose an institution had 1,000 faculty, of whom 50, or 5 percent, are minority. Suppose that 64 white assistant professors are hired. Suppose that 21 minority assistant professors are hired (or three whites for every minority assistant professor hired). Suppose, further, that 30 white assistant professors leave and nine minority assistant professors leave (or slightly more than three whites leave for every minority assistant professor who leaves.) This produces a ratio of 0.47 for white departures to hires. The ratio of minority departures to minority hires is 0.43. Over a very long period, minority representation will inch up because the white departure/hire ratio is slightly greater than that of minorities.

This illustration underscores the importance of knowing the ratio of departures to hires. Policy guiding the aggressiveness of hiring policies in combating minority underrepresentation hinges on the size of the disparity between minority and white departure/hire ratios.

The numbers in this example are the actual numbers from the survey results. These numbers—displayed in greater detail in Table 5.2—do not conform with the view that there is a significant

TABLE 5.2   Average Number MHEC Faculty Hired and Left in Last 3 Years by Institution Size

	Whites	Blacks	Asians	American Indians	Hispanics
Hired					
Professors					
LT 2,500	0.63	0.09	0.04	0.00	0.02
2,500–10,000	2.74	0.66	0.16	0.02	0.31
GT 10,000	12.48	1.80	1.72	0.06	0.67
Hired					
Assoc. Professors					
LT 2,500	1.37	0.21	0.07	0.02	0.04
2,500–10,000	2.95	0.41	0.31	0.10	0.15
GT 10,000	15.88	3.86	2.32	0.32	1.46
Hired					
Assist. Professors					
LT 2,500	6.99	0.66	0.68	0.07	0.34
2,500–10,000	21.19	1.82	2.38	0.27	1.06
GT 10,000	63.78	7.11	9.36	1.12	3.70
Left					
Professors					
LT 2,500	1.70	0.03	0.00	0.00	0.01
2,500–10,000	8.44	0.38	0.24	0.00	0.14
GT 10,000	35.96	1.20	1.36	0.05	0.20
Left					
Assoc. Professors					
LT 2,500	1.52	0.08	0.02	0.02	0.02
2,500–10,000	4.52	0.35	0.29	0.02	0.09
GT 10,000	26.57	1.45	1.73	0.19	1.09
Left					
Assist. Professors					
LT 2,500	3.06	0.23	0.12	0.02	0.10
2,500–10,000	10.33	0.84	0.90	0.14	0.48
GT 10,000	30.32	3.04	4.38	0.29	1.68

TABLE 5.2   *(Continued)*

	Whites	Blacks	Asians	American Indians	Hispanics
Ratio of Departing Faculty to Faculty Hired					
Professors					
LT 2,500	2.70	0.29	0.00	—	0.48
2,500–10,000	3.08	0.58	1.46	0.00	0.45
GT 10,000	2.88	0.67	0.79	0.95	0.30
Assoc. Professors					
LT 2,500	1.12	0.36	0.25	0.99	0.49
2,500–10,000	1.53	0.85	0.94	0.24	0.62
GT 10,000	1.67	0.38	0.75	0.60	0.75
Assist. Professors					
LT 2,500	0.44	0.35	0.17	0.26	0.30
2,500–10,000	0.49	0.46	0.38	0.51	0.45
GT 10,000	0.48	0.43	0.47	0.26	0.45

"revolving door" involving substantial loss of minorities hired. To the contrary—at least in our sample—minorities hired in every rank outnumber those who leave. The problem is that in order to increase minority representation, minority hiring needs to keep pace—must maintain or exceed current percentages—with nonminority hiring at every rank.

Our findings notwithstanding, there is a great deal of narrative data—including what was presented in Chapter 4—to suggest that minority faculty would tend to leave academia at higher rates than whites do. It is a commonly held belief that minority turnover is a significant roadblock to increased minority faculty representation, that because junior minority faculty fail to obtain tenure, or because talented minority faculty of all ranks are lured away by other institutions and industry, efforts to increase the numbers of minority faculty are thwarted by excessive outflow.

The statistics developed from our survey suggest that these conclusions may grossly oversimplify the nature of turnover. At the

A report on minority faculty retention and recruitment cites statistics from the University of Maryland indicating that of the fourteen African American faculty hired between 1982 and 1985, only one remains, and that of the eleven African American assistant professors hired during the period, only one (9 percent) was promoted to associate professor with tenure. This problem is termed the revolving door *effect by the authors of the University of Maryland report.*

Similar findings are cited in a report by the University of Minnesota, where a comprehensive effort began in 1988 to increase minority faculty representation. After five years, many new minority faculty were hired, but almost as many left. The University of Wisconsin also reported a revolving door phenomenon. Each year that university system hired impressive numbers of minority faculty, but large numbers of minority faculty also left those same years. About half as many minority faculty left the University of Wisconsin system as were hired.

lowest ranks, the ratio of whites who leave to whites hired is not much greater than the ratio of minorities who leave to the ratio of minorities hired. At the higher ranks—principally as a result of retirement and age differences—the numbers of whites who leave relative to the numbers of whites who are hired exceed the comparable ratio among minorities.

Table 5.2 shows these results. Whatever revolving door effect exists, it differs by racial group and tenure level. This table reports the responses to the survey question asking how many faculty of each race and each rank were hired in the last three years and how many left in the last three years. We have reported these responses by size of institution: enrollments under 2,500; 2,500 to 10,000; or more than 10,000 students. At the bottom of the table we compute the ratio of the average number leaving to the average number hired, by race and rank.

The ratio of departures to hires cannot reveal whether the individuals departing were the same individuals hired during the period. The ratio does show whether or not those who left were replaced by individuals of the same race/ethnicity. A high ratio indicates a low level of replacement; a low ratio shows that the new hires more than offset the departures. *Revolving door* is generally understood to mean that the departure/hire ratio is high, or that there are almost as many faculty within a cohort who leave as are hired.

Table 5.2 clearly shows that there is *less* of a revolving door for minorities than for whites. If there is any revolving door at all, it is slightly more pronounced for white faculty, whose leave/hire ratios within every rank and school size exceed those of minorities.[13] At the lower ranks, minority faculty turnover mirrors that of majority faculty, and at the higher ranks there is less turnover for minorities than whites. It seems that minority faculty underrepresentation cannot be blamed on turnover.[14]

The patterns just described do not isolate faculty gains and losses at individual institutions but represent overall gains and losses in the MHEC states. Table 5.2 could show an excess of minority hires over departures because some institutions in the region are hiring them away from other institutions in the region. Alternatively, it could indicate an overall gain of minority faculty in the region.

To determine gains and losses for individual institutions, we performed a different test. Some institutions had no hires and several losses of faculty; others had no losses and several hires. In the first instance, the cases would be all coded as zero; in the second, the cases would be coded as missing (due to division by zero). We computed, instead, the difference between hires and departures for each individual institution by rank and by race, and these computations are shown in Table 5.3.[15]

---

[13]For example, among the largest institutions with enrollments over 10,000, for every 100 white assistant professors hired, 48 left in the past three years. Yet, for every 100 black, Asian, American Indian, or Hispanic hires, there were 43, 47, 26, and 45 departures. These numbers are on the same order of magnitude as the leave/hire ratios among white faculty.

[14]The problem of turnover, however, may be important in and of itself, even if it is not the primary cause of the underrepresentation of minority faculty. Understanding the factors that contribute to turnover among minority faculty might result in an improvement in the overall climate of the university. Factors such as subtle discrimination, minority concentration in non-tenured or non-tenured-track positions, heavy concentration of ABD hires among minority faculty, concentration of many minority faculty in minority areas of scholarship and in education, and even disproportionate minority faculty promotion to administrative posts all thwart the goals of increasing minority faculty representation (Carter & O'Brien, 1993).

[15]Table 5.3 reports the results when these computations are performed with missing values excluded and when missing values are set equal to zero. Thus, if a respondent reported blank for the number of hires and 4 for the number of departures, then when missing values are excluded, this respondent would be dropped; when missing values are recoded to zero, this respondent's value would be computed as –4. Columns labeled (1) denote missing values excluded; those labeled (2) denote missing values replaced with zeros.

We conducted t-tests for the difference in the means of (H–L) between whites and minorities, where H = number of faculty hired in last three years and L = number of faculty left in the past three years. A two-tailed test significant at the 5 percent level is indicated by '**'.

TABLE 5.3 Mean Difference in Faculty Hires and Faculty Departures by Type of Institution

	2-Year College		4-Year College		University (w/Ph.D.)		Professional/ Other	
	(1)	(2)	(1)	(2)	(1)	(2)	(1)	(2)
Minority								
Total	1.4231	0.2373	2.283**	0.7374	10.1429	2.7843	1.5000	0.3038
Faculty	0.375**	0.0847**	2.0000	0.7654	12.8947	5.9608	0.4737	0.1266
Black								
Total	0.7407	0.1243	1.1186**	0.3911**	6.2500	2.1569	1.2500	0.3418
Faculty	0.2500**	0.0565**	0.5211**	0.2235**	5.1500	2.5098	0.3000	0.1139
Full Professor	0.1944	0.0395	0.0685**	0.0894**	0.7143	0.2941**	-0.1429	-0.0253**
Associate Professor	0.1250	0.0226	0.0811	0.0335	0.7727	0.4314	0.2381	0.0886
Assistant Professor	0.2432	0.0734	0.4878**	0.2570**	3.4828**	2.4118**	0.4400**	0.1519**
Indian								
Total	0.3333	0.0508	0.1500**	0.0670**	0.6471	0.2353	0.1667	0.0253
Faculty	0.0313**	0.0056**	0.1143**	0.0447**	0.4211	0.2353	0.0500	0.0127
Full Professor	0.0286	0.0056	0.0000**	0.0000**	0.0000	0.0000*	0.0000	0.0000**
Associate Professor	0.0313	0.0056	0.0270	0.0112	-0.0526	0.0196	0.0000	0.0000
Assistant Professor	0.0000	0.0000	0.0897**	0.0447**	0.5714**	0.2941**	0.0455**	0.0127**

Asian

Total	0.2963	0.0565	1.0357**	0.3352**	6.6250	1.9412	0.2500**	0.0506
Faculty	0.0938**	0.0226**	1.0448	0.3966**	5.4737	2.3922	0.1053	0.0253
Full Professor	0.0857	0.0169	-0.0141**	-0.0112**	0.4000	0.2549**	-0.0952**	-0.0253**
Associate Professor	0.0000	0.0000	0.0833	0.0335	0.3810	0.2157	-0.0455	-0.0127
Assistant Professor	0.1471	0.0395	0.9367**	0.4413**	5.0000**	2.9412**	0.7200**	0.2278**

Hispanic

Total	0.2593	0.0452	0.4655**	0.1620**	2.3125	0.9216	0.2500**	0.1139
Faculty	0.0000**	0.0000**	0.3188	0.1229**	2.0000	1.2549	0.2500	0.0633
Full Professor	0.0294	0.0056	0.0000**	0.0056	0.4211	0.2157**	0.0476	0.0127**
Associate Professor	0.0000	0.0000	0.0278	0.0112	0.3182	0.2353	0.0000	0.0000
Assistant Professor	0.0000	0.0056	0.3165**	0.1508**	1.2727**	0.9020**	0.1364**	0.0506**

Source: Appendix C, *MHEC Faculty Development Survey*, p. 7 (Q1), and p. 22 (Q34 and Q35).

**Significant at 5 percent level.

NOTE: (1) Missing values excluded (2) Missing values replaced by zero.

Definitions:

Faculty: full professors, associate professors, and assistant professors.

Total: full professors, associate professors, assistant professors, instructors, presidents, provosts, deans, and department chairs.

Racial difference in means from paired t-tests: (number of faculty hired in last three years) – (number of faculty left in past three years) by type of institution.

Table 5.3 confirms again that the proverbial revolving door does not account for low minority faculty representation. To summarize our analysis, we calculated the difference between faculty hires and departures for all minorities versus all whites. The differences are not statistically significant, except in two-year colleges where the gap between minority hires and departures exceeds that of whites. These results are based on combining faculty of all ranks.

When rank and racial/ethnic group are broken out, we find that for assistant professors there are also substantial minority hire/departure gaps in four-year colleges, Ph.D.-granting universities, and professional schools. At the higher ranks—particularly at the full professor level—even the suggestion of a distinctly minority revolving door disappears. At the top ranks, more whites leave than are hired, but minorities are hired and leave in the same numbers.[16]

If minority revolving door means that more minorities leave than are hired and that the excess of departures over hires is greater for minorities than for whites, Table 5.3 shows that there is no revolving door. If, however, revolving door means that nearly as many minorities leave as are hired, the table does show this to be the case in the middle and upper ranks and at four-year colleges and professional schools.[17] At all but the Ph.D.-granting universities—where much of the narrative data of the turnover problem originates—there are almost as many minority hires as departures. At the Ph.D.-granting universities, however, there are far more minorities hired than minorities who leave.

FACTORS CONTRIBUTING TO INCREASED MINORITY FACULTY HIRING

If minority underrepresentation on faculties is not due to high turnover, then the problem is one of underhiring. Among our hypothesized determinants of minority versus nonminority hiring, it

---

[16]MHEC, *Minority Faculty Development Project: Final Report.* May 1995, Table D.27.

[17]Note that whenever the difference is "close to zero" the average within-institution difference between hires and departures is zero, or the number of hires at an institution just equals the number of departures.

appears that *demand-side* effects (such as strong affirmative action efforts) rather than *supply-side* effects (e.g., the absence—or perceived absence—of qualified candidates) have the greatest influence on minority hiring.

This conclusion is based on a linear regression model in which the dependent variable was the ratio of minority faculty hired to white faculty hired in the past three years. The independent variables included:

- whether the institution was a two-year college, four-year college, Ph.D.-granting university, or a professional school
- whether the institution was public or private
- the size of the institution as measured by the number of students
- each of the hypothesized factors in Table 5.1

We find that once we control for size of institution, type of institution, and each of the hypothesized factors from Table 5.1, the only variables that emerge as statistically significant predictors of the ratio of minority hires to white hires across all ranks are the following affirmative action variables:

- the perception that minority hiring is adequate (-0.31, $p = .0014$)[18]
- increased funding for minority recruitment ($+0.20$, $p = .0128$)
- excellent diversity efforts ($+0.22$, $p = 0.0247$)
- high minority faculty development budgets ($+0.55$, $p < .0001$)

Figure 5.3 graphically shows that the impacts of the affirmative action factors are substantial. When there is significant financial support for hiring minority faculty, the relative hiring of minority

---

[18]The first number in parentheses denotes the change in the ratio of minority to white hiring. It is the coefficient from the regression equation. The second number in parentheses is the significance level of the coefficient. We report only those factors that are statistically significant at the 5 percent level or better. Because the overall minority/white hiring ratio is about 0.33, a coefficient value of -0.31 means that minority hiring would be virtually halted. A coefficient of $+0.20$ means that the minority hiring relative to white hiring would nearly double. A coefficient of $+0.55$ means that minority hiring would almost reach parity with white hiring.

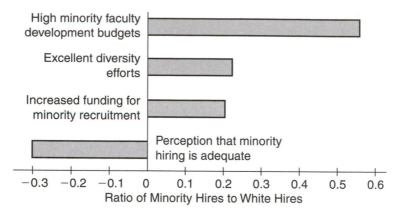

FIGURE 5.3   Effects of Affirmative Action on Minority Hiring

faculty increases. When the perception is that minority hiring is adequate (i.e., that "we're doing a good job"), minority faculty hiring drops. We consider several aspects of the affirmative action effect in turn.

Perceptions That Minority Hiring Is Adequate

Affirmative action is an institution putting its money where its mouth is and all efforts specifically allocating funds to hire minorities can be regarded as affirmative action efforts. In order to provide a meaningful context, our survey questions concerning perception followed a series of questions about funding that included:

- Does your institution make funds available for hiring minority faculty that augment departmental budgets? (17 percent yes)

Where appropriate:

- How are departments informed about this funding?
- In the past five years, how many times have the departments utilized this funding? (54 percent less than six times; 17 percent more than twenty times)
- How are minority faculty who are hired through these funds received by their colleagues in their departments? (40 percent

very well received; 40 percent well received; 20 percent received with reservation or poorly received)

- Are minority faculty hired with these funds given a different title than faculty hired through other means? (97 percent no)
- Do you feel the qualifications of minority faculty hired through this process are different than minority hired through other means? (91 percent no)
- How adequate do you feel the funds are at your institution for hiring minority faculty?

> very adequate, 19 percent
>
> moderately adequate, 33 percent
>
> somewhat adequate, 30 percent
>
> not at all adequate, 18 percent

We coded the variable "perception that minority hiring adequate" equal to 1 whenever the answer to the preceding question was "very adequate." This 19 percent of respondents, then, believe that existing funds—whether special funds for minorities or general funds for all faculty hiring—are very adequate for hiring minority faculty. Interestingly, there arises an extremely strong inverse relationship between believing that funds are very adequate and actually having minority funds available. The 17 percent of institutions with minority funding programs are very different from the 19 percent of institutions that believe their funding is adequate. They are located at two different extremes along the spectrum of affirmative action efforts. At one end are those that allocate little funds to affirmative action but that think they are doing a great job. At the other end are those that have specific allocations of funds for minority hiring but think they need to do more. In a sense, then, the adequacy question picks up both attitudes toward affirmative action and actual affirmative funding plans in place. The lesson here is that when an administration begins to feel satisfied with its minority hiring efforts, it may be time to look at the hard numbers anew.

Increases In Funding for Minority Recruitment

This factor measures whether the institution increased its funding for minority faculty for the past three years? The specific question was:

*For each area listed, how would you describe funding at your
institution for the past three years? (Please circle one response
for each area.)*

- professional development for all faculty
- professional development for minority faculty
- professional development for women faculty
- recruitment of all faculty
- recruitment of minority faculty
- recruitment of women faculty

Nearly half of all responding institutions (47 percent) report
that during the previous three years funding for the recruitment of
minority faculty increased. Other responses show funding to have
been stable (35 percent) or to have decreased (2 percent). There is
an unusually high percentage of "no response" or "not applicable"
(16 percent), and we determined that these institutions have a
much lower than average rate of hiring minority faculty than the
rest.

Because there is a strong correlation between increased funding
for recruitment of all faculty and increased funding for minority
faculty recruitment, it is difficult to know whether improvement in
minority hiring is the result of targeted funding or is simply a function of a rising tide lifting all ships.

Excellence of Diversity Efforts

The question here was:

*Overall, how do you believe your institution rates in providing
the following services or support for faculty? [Areas included]*

- understanding faculty needs
- providing orientation for new faculty
- securing funds for travel
- encouraging collegiality
- advocating faculty issues
- clarifying criteria for advancement
- recognizing achievements
- recognizing diversity

Possible responses included (1) excellent, (2) good, (3) fair, (4) poor, and (5) does not apply. The modal response (47 percent) is "good." The next most frequent response (29 percent) is "fair." Interestingly, none of the categories receives a majority or even a modal response of "excellent."

Institutional efforts to "recognize diversity" are rated "excellent" by about one-fifth of the respondents. Many administrators—the remaining 80 percent—then admit that there is room for improvement in the area of diversity as in other areas of faculty development.

"Recognizing diversity" is found to be influential in predicting higher minority hiring, suggesting that when *diversity is a high priority* at an institution—even when other factors such as collegiality and funding for travel are considered—this strength translates into positive minority hiring results.

The key, however, is to understand that believing diversity is excellent and recognizing diversity are very different ideas. The institutions with increased minority hiring *recognize diversity.* In other words, they value it and act to achieve it in the same way, for example, that valuing faculty participation in scholarly conferences translates to providing funds for travel.

High Budget for Minority Faculty Development

A high minority faculty *development* budget is the single most important factor to increased minority hiring. Its effect is greater than the combined effects of excellent diversity and increased funding for minority faculty *recruitment.*

The specific question was:

> *Approximately what percentage of your institution's total faculty professional development funding is allocated to minority faculty professional development?*

- less than 1 percent (43 percent)
- 1–5 percent (11 percent)
- 6–10 percent (4 percent)
- 11–25 percent (3 percent)
- 25–50 percent (1 percent)
- over 50 percent (1 percent)
- don't know (37 percent)

An allocation of more than 6 percent of the total faculty professional development funds for minority faculty development was coded "high minority faculty development funding." When this value is obtained, institutions in the sample realized higher ratios of minority hires to white hires.

IMPLICATIONS

The conclusions of our study lead us to argue that (1) improved minority hiring is critical to increased minority presence on faculties, and that (2) to correct the current underrepresentation, minorities must be hired in much greater proportions (relative to whites) than they are at present.

The most significant resistance to these arguments is likely to come from two directions. The first is from the public policy standpoint. What we recommend necessitates affirmative action to deliberately increase minority hiring, and to many this violates principles of merit and fairness to white faculty.

A second attack is likely to involve our underlying premise that it is within the power of academic institutions to simply hire more minority faculty. There are many who believe that a low rate of minority hiring simply reflects a low supply of qualified candidates and that, if this is the case, no amount of investment to increase minority recruitment will be effective.

These points of view—separately and in combination—actually underlie the problem of minority underrepresentation. Dealing first with the notion that there are not enough qualified candidates, that explanation for low minority presence was the one most frequently given by the institutions we surveyed, and the data show that it is negatively related to actual minority hiring. What is critical to the issue is that qualification in higher education—beyond mere credentialing—involves a high degree of subjectivity and ample room for the cultural biases of academic and tenure review committees. Because courts and other independent bodies largely defer to these subjective judgments, there can be no meaningful challenge to an assertion that applicants are unqualified.

If institutions cannot take affirmative measures to recruit and retain minority faculty, the barrier of nonrecognition will thwart minority faculty development for generations to come; the perception that minorities are simply not qualified will persist. In essence, the role of affirmative action is to buttress resources needed to overcome stereotypes and false perceptions. The elimination of affirmative action is likely to reinforce perceptions that there are not enough qualified minorities and to lure administrations into a complacency that virtually assures reduced minority recruitment and hiring.

Many may disagree with our conclusion that efforts to recruit are more important than efforts to retain minority faculty, citing conditions and circumstances that make academic institutions inhospitable to minorities. We certainly agree—and devote a substantial portion of this book to examining the issue—that institutional climates need a great deal of improvement in embracing diversity. Indeed, our data on individual minority faculty reveals a wide range of significant hardships either unique to or more acute for minorities in academia. However, our statistics show that, once hired, minorities do not depart at an excessive rate. We conclude, therefore, that hostile environment may not be the only cause of minority faculty leaving institutions, but it may well serve to discourage minorities from aspiring to these positions. We agree that the environment for minorities must be improved, but primarily because of its possible effect on recruitment, not retention.

Our statistical findings tell us that institutions can and should develop strategies to increase their minority hiring. In the previous chapter we saw evidence of the many hardships minorities face in pursuing academic careers, and in Chapter 6, we will see why they endure those hardships. The lessons here can be applied in the context of the old song: Institutions need to accentuate the positive and eliminate the negative.

6

WHY STAY? CURRENT REWARDS AND PROMISING EFFORTS

CURRENT REWARDS AND SATISFACTIONS

As we saw in Chapter 4, the faculty of color we interviewed offer convincing testimony of pervasive racial and ethnic bias in the academic workplace. Female faculty of color offer further testimony to the interlocking biases of gender and race/ethnicity. In our view, these data offer the reader a window into the professional lives of faculty of color and must not be dismissed as isolated anecdotes of malcontents unsuccessful in their careers. Two-thirds of the successful faculty of color participating in our study, as well as countless others noted in the literature who have fruitful academic careers, describe troubling instances of bias in their work lives.

Although minority scholars continue to report subtle discrimination as a source of stress, they also report many satisfactions that attract them to and keep them in academia. Foremost among the broad reasons for staying are intellectual challenge, freedom to pursue research interests, and the opportunity to promote racial/ethnic understanding. The findings show that despite the stress of subtle discrimination, faculty of color have many of the same reasons for staying in academe as their white counterparts, as well as reasons particular to minority and multicultural interests.

Despite concerns about a chilly climate, most of the faculty we interviewed indicate that they plan to stay in academia. The most commonly articulated personal rewards include:

- satisfaction with teaching
- supportive administrative leadership, mentor relationships, collegiality
- interaction with other faculty of color

The respondent comments presented in the following pages reflect the commitment of faculty of color to their academic careers, and describe the positive experiences that keep them in an academic environment. They also allude to ways in which colleges and universities can enrich the lives of faculty of color, and provide further impetus to stay. There are, of course, an infinite number of practical and personal reasons that drive individual career decisions, but in this chapter we focus primarily on the importance of positive workplace experiences commonly identified by our study respondents. As in Chapter 4, quotations—within the major themes—are presented by race and ethnic category. Here, however, the responses vary little across racial and ethnic groups, and it appears that what makes for success and retention is nearly universal. A healthy, supportive, rewarding environment is good for everyone.

Love of Teaching

Many faculty stress their love of teaching and their interactions with students as the most satisfying aspects of their work lives. For these faculty, recognition and reward for teaching may assist in their retention.

African American Faculty

I enjoy teaching—the contact with the students and especially when you make a difference in their lives...

Male African American tenured social sciences

I guess I love it!...I'm certainly not going to make any money being a teacher, but I enjoy it...being the kind of teacher to [my students] that I didn't have as a young student.

Female African American untenured humanities

It [college name] is an encouraging college for someone who wants to teach...This is a good place to be. You'll have support and time and an area in which you can make a contribution.

Female African American tenured social sciences

I believe in helping those who can't help themselves. I teach predominantly white students. I may be the only exposure they'll have to people of color. It's what I do—what I love to do...

Female African American tenured humanities

[The university] has been very positive. The enthusiasm from students is very positive. It is an opportunity for the institution to rectify minority education responsibilities. The response has been tremendous. Faculty are seeing that and students speak highly of all their experiences...They [the college] have addressed my concerns immediately. My department is quick to address my concerns, the administration not as quickly...

Female African American tenured humanities

Latino Faculty

I think most of my support comes from the students. I don't believe my colleagues have supported me very much. I've gotten some summer grants from the institution. I've gotten some support for my students three or four times, so I think research-wise I've been supported fairly well by the institution.

Male Latino untenured social sciences

I always saw myself as a professor, or as a teacher rather, of students of different backgrounds, but I wanted to work in a city that had a significant Latino experience...My job was to empower students rather than to radicalize them. If they knew how to think critically, they could decide to be as radical as they wanted to be.

Male Latino tenured social sciences

In my case, it is important to help the students. Because of that you put a lot of time into [teaching and advising].

Female Latina untenured humanities

Supportive Administrative Leadership

From our respondents' comments, it is evident that the university provost, the college dean, or the department chair plays an important role in encouraging and supporting faculty members to remain engaged. Study responses also compel us to broaden our understanding of academic departmental leadership. Although department chairs or deans may be nominal leaders, a great deal of power may also rest with influential senior-level faculty whether or not they occupy formal leadership positions.

The comments suggest that—whatever the source of power—a person of influence can do much to pave the way for faculty success. Positive leadership behaviors described by our participants can be characterized as reflecting an equitable approach to administration, that is, administrative decision making that at each decision point considers issues of equity along with other administrative concerns. Such an "equity mind-set" can and should be brought to bear, for example, when determining the composition of an influential committee, refining a job description, initiating a candidate search, making a hiring decision, promoting from within, or formally recognizing employee merit. Too often affirmative action principles come into play only at the point of approving or vetoing a hiring choice, but not at other more critical points such as deciding whether a department should be allowed to search, which departments should be encouraged to grow, how areas for a search should be determined, and how qualifications should be specified.

The importance of institutional leadership—including department chairs, college deans, and other high-level administrators—to retaining new faculty is borne out in the literature (Collins & Johnson, 1990; Creswell et al., 1990; Johnsrud & Heck, 1994; Wilson, 1992). Understanding the impact of leadership on the success of faculty of color is crucial to creating academic communities that truly welcome cultural diversity. Collins and Johnson note the critical role of university leadership in articulating and publicly supporting increased minority participation on college campuses. Johnsrud and Heck, in their faculty study identifying who will leave and who will stay, conclude the following about factors contributing to faculty retention:

> *Some are high cost items, such as quality of life and housing, but others are not. Chairs can be trained, tenure criteria can be clarified, and alienation and isolation can be lessened…leadership within the academic department can set a tone of collegiality, tolerance, and acceptance of differences. Deliberate efforts can be made to foster collaboration, intellectual cross-fertilization, and social interaction…Proactive responses may make a critical difference in retaining faculty, particularly women and ethnic minority faculty, who might otherwise leave. (p. 82)*

African American Faculty

[University name] has given me some modest support in developing proposals in the way of supporting the technology that I have; they've provided the equipment that I needed to get started, like computer equipment. The university has a nice infrastructure for helping faculty to develop proposals…The department chair has been very supportive and encouraging. He is a very seasoned person who has been in his role for sixteen years and knows the university inside out. He promotes us to get our work out.

Male African American tenured social sciences

That dean—I was hired under—he was a real good person. He was very supportive.

Female African American untenured social sciences

[about the minority faculty program] In one sense we are privileged because of the kind of financial support we get. The legislature has always supported the program. This is the 22nd year, so we're doing something right. It's a lot of work working with the scholarship recipients, but one thing that I find, though, is that the environment is just the right environment…When you have a dean like [name], the sky's the limit. So, mine [experience] has been positive.

Female African American tenured social sciences

The provost has been really supportive and helpful. Actually, he sought me out to sit on some committees. I think we have a healthy respect for one another, we don't always agree...There are about five teaching faculty who are African American. They've been very supportive. The other African American people on campus are terrific. They're wonderful to work with. They are very supportive of one another.

Female African American untenured social sciences

Asian American Faculty

The people here help me in every respect. Deans, chairpersons, they have matching money for me to do every possible thing they can, so I feel pretty happy here. I don't feel I'm in the minority. There's a lot of diversity in this college, but maybe not in some other colleges [in this university].

Male Asian American tenured sciences

...when a department has a position to hire from, the dean passes on lists and explicitly instructs the chair to write to departments trying to find candidates of color. Extra budgetary considerations are given to recruiting in, for example, there's an association of black psychologists, putting an ad in there—the fees are high—they want like a thousand dollars for one two-inch ad...but the administration is willing to come up with the money for that. Generally, we are allowed to bring in three candidates, but if we can identify a fourth candidate such that among our four is a person of color, we're allowed to bring in four candidates—so, I think they put their money where their mouth is...On the other hand, I don't think that there are very direct pressures to hire the candidate of color, pushing other considerations aside.

Male Asian American tenured social sciences

Latino Faculty

[My experience as a faculty member here] was very positive. Very, very positive because I had a lot of support from the dean and from [two nationally known and influential senior professors].

Male Latino tenured social sciences

This faculty member goes on to note that one of his mentors is a very influential scholar who carries a lot of "weight"—much more than the department chair. The mentor holds a position as an "Honored Scholar," which includes not only special status within the university but also carries a substantial amount of funding for research support. Supportive leadership can come from such faculty who have status within the university without holding formal administrative positions.

Sense of Accomplishment

A sense of personal accomplishment—as well as what we call a sense of accomplishment toward change—also fuels the desire to remain in academia.

African American Faculty

I set up a program within the college…I decided that we would use community people who had academic backgrounds [to teach, they] might be in business or what have you…I talked the college into setting up two fellowships for graduate students, to take them out of the TA role and give them primary experience in the classroom under the supervision of a seasoned master teacher, so that in their particular discipline they could teach as a faculty person and get paid for it part-time while they're working. Get that on their résumé, get the mentoring that goes along with that, so that at the time of graduating, not only did they have a degree, but they've had a significant teaching experience, not a graduate teaching assistantship sort of thing, but more like a faculty position.

Male African American tenured humanities college-level administrator

I have had a few things published…I've won a Fulbright Fellowship…A few years ago I got the award for the Outstanding Teacher at the college.

Male African American tenured humanities

American Indian Faculty

We initiated an endowment to establish an endowed chair for American Indian education and we managed after years of advocacy to get well over a million dollars for that chair. So the chair was finally established and [name] was recruited into that position. It will be forever more.

Female American Indian tenured social sciences

Asian American Faculty

I feel that I've been fortunate. I'm a [title] Professor, that's my title. It's a title that you are selected for by a special committee based on research and you hold it for six years...I received the Outstanding Teacher Award, which is a university-wide award. The special professorships, they include really big bonuses. It's like $5,000 a year...

Male Asian American tenured social sciences

They [the university] encourage you to work at conferences and to deliver papers at conferences, and to attend national professional groups and conventions as well. Having an academic job allows you some of that freedom to follow your own interests.

Female Asian American tenured humanities

Latino Faculty

It [postdoctoral experience] made me confident of my research skills and I had the freedom to establish a research agenda before embarking on an academic career. I had the opportunity to submit and receive grants so that I could "hit the ground running" during my academic career. As you move along, certain people start to look out for you in the process.

Female Latina untenured social sciences

Importance of Mentors

According to a publication of the National Education Association (1993), "mentoring may be defined as a process in which one person, usually of superior rank, achievement, and prestige, guides the development of or sponsors another person, who is seen as the protégé" (p. 17). Many of our respondents describe the impact of such mentor/protégé relationships on their professional lives.

American Indian Faculty

...he was a faculty member in ethnic studies and since then he's become the director of the program—he's wonderful—he's like my uncle. He encourages me. He really is a good mentor for me.

Female American Indian untenured social sciences

...if it wasn't for [name], he was president—he was a wonderful man who mentored [me] and was very, very interested in being helpful...

Male American Indian untenured social sciences

I have a number of professors out there that I consider mentors. I still can call up the associate dean and I'm on a first name basis with him. And there's other professors out there that I call and talk to—some on a regular basis.

Male American Indian untenured social sciences

Asian American Faculty

My mentor has been—there's a professor at [university name]. He was young and bright, he had just come from [elite private research university] and was just getting started into the new graduate school, and he was the most motivating force in my professional life. So it is very important to have a very good mentor...Whatever support I needed—the administration has helped, no question about it.

Male Asian American tenured sciences

I think that there certainly were several people in my career who counseled me at critical points. I did not go to them like a friend, constantly to seek advice, but they were pivotal junctures in my career where I needed council. These people did take me under their wings and gave me some good council and kept me in the academy and also got me into administration.

Male Asian American tenured sciences university-level administrator

Latino Faculty

"I had a professor at [elite private research university] who believed in me—a conservative guy who always had troubles with affirmative action and reverse discrimination and stuff, but he was nice to me. He took me under his wing and he said, "Look, I'm going to show you—if you are going to debate with me— I'm going to teach you a list of ground rules to follow in academia," and I've never, never forgotten that.

Male Latino tenured social sciences

Collegiality

Statements here focus on the importance of friendship and peer collaboration in setting a comfortable tone for these faculty of color.

American Indian Faculty

The university has always shown that they want me to be here. I never had a feeling that they were being adversarial to my being here...I felt very supported by my departments...I have good friends in the university and that's helpful.

Female American Indian tenured social sciences

It's been really pretty good. They've [department colleagues] been very supportive. Nearly all of them have an attitude that there's a need to look at diversity issues. The courses that I'm teaching, I'm team teaching, so that's good. There's been some collaboration. They seem to be open, it's been a very positive experience.

Male American Indian untenured social sciences

Latino Faculty

They were enthusiastic about my background. They were very friendly and called me several times for about 45 minutes to an hour. It was perfect. I was looking for and interested in research...I could teach and continue with my research. People were friendly.

Female Latina tenured social sciences

As far as being a minority, I have no problems at this university...I have been made to be very comfortable, in and out of my department. I was surprised at the downpour of memos and invitations to all kinds of activities and there always seems to be an open door.

Female Latina tenured humanities

[When I was hired here] God, I loved it! It was terrific. I felt so important and so smart. I really liked it. My colleagues were really good to me, especially those first couple of years...they took it easy on me. So, I was able to at least keep my head above water...From the very first day I loved it here.

Female Latina tenured humanities

[When I was hired] it was a good job, a good starting salary for the time, and there really wasn't any reason not to come. There were a couple people here whom I had worked with before in the same field in which I work, people whom I knew and felt comfortable working with. They gave me a call and said, "You know, we have this position. Would you like to apply?" So, I did, and that was the end of it.

Male Latino tenured sciences

An interesting issue is illustrated by this respondent. Although he attributes his comfort at his work site largely to his relationships with colleagues of long standing, he reports—in response to the direct question about mentoring—not having been mentored during his career. Although we did not probe for more insight about this response for our present inquiry, the distinctions between mentoring and supportive collegiality are worth further study in the future.

African American

I wanted to come here—You have a miracle when a faculty member can find, first of all, a place they want to live that matches up with where they want to teach and is a place where that institution wants to have them. Very difficult to get all three of those working together!

Female African American untenured sciences

Commitment to Community and Relating to Other Faculty of Color

Faculty had positive statements to make about the presence of other faculty of color in the workplace, about feeling less isolated and more a part of a community.

Asian American

> They were lucky to hire two minority faculty. There were two of us interviewed, and I believe we were both liked very much by the faculty at the time—and the dean offered both of us jobs…
>
> Female Asian American tenured social sciences

> I know a woman who's Chinese. She's in the [name of department] so we have no overlap in the field, but I and another woman in my college who's in computer science have sort of taken it upon ourselves to keep her from getting isolated. We're not even in her college, but we have lunch with her—I like her a lot, so she's become my friend, but we started this by just trying to keep her from being so isolated over there in the [name of department]. I feel so strongly about trying to combat isolation…It's sort of hard because we have families but…
>
> Female Asian American tenured sciences department-level administrator

> Well, my first department head when I came here was a person of color—and, I must admit, it was nice to see that. Although we disagreed on a number of things over the years, we're still very good friends…My second department head was an Hispanic woman—she's no longer here because she's the president at another college now. Her style was a very inclusive style. She tended to pull people into projects, planning, or whatever was going on.
>
> Female Asian American tenured social sciences

It is important to remember that these positive comments come from the same individuals whose negative experiences are presented in Chapter 4. To the degree that the positives they report here offset those negatives is very telling and important in identifying where efforts can be best targeted to create a welcoming climate. For these faculty, teaching provides intrinsic rewards. Supportive leadership from the university level to the departmental level is critical. A sense of scholarly accomplishment and creating space for future faculty of color is important, as is positive interaction with mentors, majority colleagues, and other faculty of color.

It is also important to note that their experiences document successes, not failures. All study participants have earned tenure-track and tenured positions in higher education. However, the narrative data overwhelmingly point to continued exclusion and isolation of these successful scholars, even for those who are tenured and hold high-level academic appointments. Our respondents are individuals who have succeeded in their academic careers, and who persevere despite the challenges of a racially biased environment—and we can, therefore, see that the picture is not entirely gloomy. We can move toward providing a supportive and rewarding work environment reflective of faculty responses when asked why they stay. In these remarks are the seeds of successful retention and development strategies.

RECOMMENDATIONS FROM THE FIELD: ACCENTUATING THE POSITIVE

As a somewhat overused African proverb goes, it takes a village to raise a child. It takes a department to nurture a junior faculty member. That's the strength as well as the weakness of a department. Some departments do that well and other ones don't...It's not really a programmatic thing, although I think one can move in that direction, because "nurturing" comes more from how individuals relate to one another than the output of a program. We need to begin to look beyond the mechanical [such as campus orientations] and to develop a culture within the department in which [all] look out for each other. You can't program that...the point is not just to make the person feel comfortable. The goal is to allow the person to become productive. Usually a comfortable person is productive.

Male Asian American tenured sciences university-level administrator

From the comments about the satisfactions of academic careers, as well as the recommendations to follow, it appears that the interpersonal environment and its contribution to "mattering" can really make a difference. Smith (1994) discusses the five qualities that contribute to mattering. These are:

1. Attention—the sense that we are noticed whether present or absent;
2. Importance—the belief that what we say or do has importance;
3. Ego extension—the feeling that other people will be proud or saddened by our successes or failures;
4. Dependence—the sense that a person or a group is counting on us;
5. Appreciation—the view that our efforts are appreciated.

> *...mattering can be described in terms of individual perceptions— the feeling that he or she matters—mattering can also be significant for groups...a group can matter and be made to feel that it matters in the institutional community. It can be noticed, depended on, and appreciated.*
>
> Smith (1994, p. 33)

Hill (1991) notes the importance of representation when building a community based on inclusion and—to use Smith's terminology— mattering:

> *Were a college or university truly committed to democratic pluralism, it would proceed to create conditions under which the representatives of different cultures need to have conversations of respect with each other in order to do their everyday teaching and research...Marginalization ends and conversations of respect begin when the curriculum is reconceived to be unimplementable without the central participation of the currently excluded and marginalized. (pp. 44–45)*

In this view of pluralism differences matter but are appreciated as parts of a whole rather than denigrated as deviations from a narrowly defined norm. This counters the notion that attention to differences leads to balkanization—that for a unified institutional or national culture we need to stress what we have in common (sameness) not difference (which is thought of as what divides us). The vision here is very different: What unifies us is a common attention to, respect for, dependence on, and appreciation of our differences. They matter! We share a culture that values our diversity, and we all have a stake in maintaining that culture. Conversely, an emphasis on sameness (e.g., conformity to dominant cultural norms) is divisive. It marginalizes and alienates those who feel or are perceived as different. Inclusiveness leads to unity. Conformity leads to division.

A number of faculty of color in our study recommend focusing on retention through the development of more positive and encouraging professional environments, and through targeted faculty development initiatives. The main recommendations advocate networks of scholars of color, senior faculty mentors, and support for research and publications.

SUGGESTED STRATEGIES

Asked to describe strategies that are—or would be—most helpful to faculty of color in having successful academic careers, respondents most frequently suggest:

1. networking, workshops, creating social ethnic groups
2. mentoring
3. better support for research and publication

Other strategies considered crucial to the success of faculty of color include providing special assistance for ABD (all-but-dissertation) students, providing postdoctoral fellowship experiences, improving spousal/partner support, and early incubation of potential future faculty. Some of these strategies will be further explored in the discussion of exemplary programs later in this chapter. Here we will present our respondents' suggestions, focusing on the three most common and emphatic recommendations.

Networking

Respondents recommend networking as a way to counterbalance the isolation that many minority faculty members experience in the academic workplace. It is viewed as a way to connect with minority colleagues from other institutions in the region. Several interviewees suggest that an organized sharing process might encompass both professional and personal aspects of academic life, and provide both personal connection and access to information.

African American Faculty

The first thing that pops into my mind is the whole notion of networking information, connecting with those faculty members of color who are out there—and maybe even some faculty members who are not of color could be part of the network, too, who have information, who are working on particular projects, who are at different stages of their academic careers. And the information, maybe it could be connected by Internet or E-mail…with this whole new boom in technology, I think that would be a real doable thing.

Male African American tenured social sciences

Minority faculty development persons would meet and share experiences on a monthly basis or every two weeks or every two months. But there would be a time when minority faculty development persons would be able to share and reflect. That gives support. You could problem-solve, you could brainstorm. Even though you are in different schools or departments, it would still serve to bond, rather than feeling like you're just out there…And then there needs to be time when minority faculty development persons can meet with the dean or the department chair—somebody who is talking to you and actually listening and not just for the facade…

Female African American untenured social sciences

Strategies—seminar or workshops in grant writing would be excellent…How to document things you do inside and out of the classroom…information about opportunities that are out there would be helpful.

Male African American tenured humanities

American Indian Faculty

There do need to be support mechanisms. You need much more in terms of support systems…because these environments are not of our culture, not of our world. Minority people, we are always fringe members of society, we're never fully accepted… This is America entering the twenty-first century. It's a racist society, period. That's an issue that many people don't want to address but that's the truth of it. So if there are going to be minority faculty, there needs to be support for them. Sometimes "traveling in packs" would help.

Male American Indian tenured social sciences

Asian American Faculty

I think it would be great to have a retreat where several of the faculty could get together and talk about their problems as well as the positive things. I think to share those ideas across the Midwest would be really great.

Female Asian American tenured humanities

Another respondent alludes to the friction that often exists between faculty members from different groups of color. He suggests that the various minority groups should stop being negative toward each other and form a network that could bring about improvements for everyone on academic and personal levels. The academic environment would do well to support this instead of fostering competition between groups. This response also provides a vision of unity in diversity as discussed earlier in this chapter.

They usually don't communicate too well...it's hard to put them all together as a force, as a group, a large group. Something needs to get them together, then they can contribute their different opinions, points of view, different strengths, different cultural backgrounds...So maybe a regional strategy, we should connect them together to become a positive force... Some organization needs to do this kind of thing. Hold mini-academic forums, discussions, put them together. Sometimes we can see the African, Asian, but they just don't come together.

Male Asian American tenured sciences

Connections are important to most minority faculty members because they don't come into the department with already built-in connections, especially if the person is the only minority faculty member in the department...

Male Asian American tenured sciences university-level administrator

Latino Faculty

What about going to workshops? It could be orientation and research, it could be adaptability to your field, if you feel that is necessary, it could be in many different areas. It could be in teaching.

Female Latina untenured social sciences

Another faculty member recommends that some networking be done on an intraracial/intraethnic basis in order to help combat the feelings of cultural isolation:

Formation of groups of Latino faculty, organizations of Latino employees. Meet with others, use our own language, share experiences in the classroom. Promoting individual organizations by racial or ethnic background.

Female Latina tenured social sciences

Mentoring

According to a number of the interview participants, designing and implementing mentoring programs would help new minority faculty become acclimatized to academia and the campus culture as a whole. Some suggest that mechanisms be created to enable department chairs and senior faculty to facilitate the success of minority faculty. Respondents from each referent group suggest establishing mentor relationships as a strategy.

African American Faculty

Well, get mentoring. That's definite...get as much mentoring—because if you are on a tenure-track position and supposedly they are hiring you with the idea of tenuring you, then they should also be willing to avail you of the things that would support your packet. It's not just enough to hire them and leave it at that.

Male African American untenured humanities

I would say, find a mentor. Another African American mentor, the person doesn't have to be in that school.

Female African American tenured humanities

American Indian Faculty

I particularly like the model which is...sponsored by the American Bar Association—Project CLEO, the Council for Legal Educational Opportunity in Washington, DC. They run a summer institute that blends into a continuing mentoring relationship. A real mentoring relationship. Not this: "Hi, let's get together, have lunch and tell me what you'd like." It's a real, structured mentoring relationship for law students. I think that's a wonderful model.

Male American Indian tenured social sciences
university-level administrator

Mentors. You know, people to tell them like [name] told me what to do. They need people like [name] who can tell new faculty or even old faculty, "Look, we do this—try this strategy. Try this, I know what you're talking about"...To have a mentoring program and to have friends that you can discuss these things with and meet, so you can feel part of, so that you have some kind of social network. You're not there all alone. I don't know what I would have done if I had to come here like I did—have no friends and no family. I would not have made it.

Female American Indian tenured social sciences

Asian American Faculty

He is my formal mentor, but I had to seek him out...when I came in about six years ago it was not such a formal process. Generally, the mentoring system, I believe, has been okay...I think what I would have liked was a more personal, socially supportive mentor, so a different type of mentoring...a more personal, social mentor in more of a classical, Greek sense, who is your adviser, and who helps you be safe—especially when there are those who experience both personal racism and institutional racism.

Female Asian American tenured social sciences

Latino Faculty

...if you could get something that would do what my mentor did for me, that would be the exact thing, but that's a difficult

thing. My mentor became very instrumental and very important in my life...[H]e took me on as a research assistant and so
I did some research for him...and then he offered me a postdoc
for two years. I coauthored with him. I had a really good mentor. He got me my first position...He's the one who was looking
out for me and he's the one who put me on the editorial board.
He's the one who gave my name to others and they put me on
editorial boards. I will always be grateful to him.

Male Latino tenured social sciences

My mentor knew that department and he knew how high they
could go on salary so I negotiated up in salary and got it. I
wasn't going to accept less because my mentor said not to. I was
also able to negotiate staying at [university a] and completing
my postdoc before accepting the position at [university b]. My
mentor had just left that department at [university b]. When
the position became available and I interviewed—part of the
motivation was to replace someone like my mentor and since I
had worked with him and had similar interests in research...
They liked him and wanted someone to take his place and
mentor students.

Female Latino untenured social sciences

Support for Research and Publication

African American Faculty

So, I find myself doing research at the same time I'm going to
school because I'm getting that message to..."publish or per-
ish," you know. You hear it at the faculty meetings, but they
say [to me] "You're a new faculty, don't worry about it." But at
the same time they say [to me] "You'd better start worrying
about it." I want to have a couple of things under my belt, so
when I finish the program, even though it's supposed to be tenure track, I've got a little insurance that they are going to say,
"Hey! We think we want to keep you!" So, there is that unspo-
ken pressure to be doing it all at the same time.

Male African American untenured social sciences

American Indian Faculty

We must have diversity in scholarship. Indians get censored even before we get in print. More outlets are needed to publish articles on minority concerns. An editor I know implied that research on Indians is second rate. Tribal sovereignty is not an interest of mainstream publications. But outlets to publish articles about minority concerns are growing, and growing with respect to respectability.

Male American Indian tenured social sciences college-level administrator

Asian American Faculty

Maybe there should be some sort of scholarly journals, publications, where minorities are expressed—and they can take these as their academic credential...I think there should be some sort of regional goals—not any one university. I mean, in the Midwest, that they publish new scientific ideas, or what needs to be done, things like that—anything. And people express it and they say, "Well, I published an article. I wrote." I think that— that gives you some confidence. That's the way I have built myself, that's the way many people have built themselves.

Male Asian American tenured sciences

Latino Faculty

I would like to see something like the Spencer Grants for the Midwest region targeted to assist faculty members of color. I am thinking, what would help me? I need time to work on something. Time that is your own during the six-year period. Buy out half-time or even a term. It is costly to implement but it would give us a leg up. This could be competitive and faculty could commit so they can't do other things. Try not to participate in other things on campus. Not increase [your] involvement in other things. Time to focus on your own work would be extremely helpful.

Female Latina untenured social sciences

The three principal strategies cited by our respondents— networking, mentors, and support for research and publications— are also widely acknowledged in the literature as effective strategies for improving faculty retention (Blackwell, 1989; Boice, 1993; Cross, 1991; Gainen & Boice, 1993; Harvey & Valadez, 1994; Padilla & Chavez, 1995; Stein, 1994; Tack & Patitu, 1992). These strategies are generally targeted to improving faculty retention but may well have positive effects on recruitment, too. Networking relates to the positive effects for collegiality and interaction with other faculty of color noted by study respondents when describing why they stay in academe. Mentoring is reiterated as an important factor in enticing faculty of color to remain in academe. Support for publication and research is a means to obtain the sense of scholarly accomplishment that causes our respondents to remain in academe. All of these factors contribute to the intellectual challenge, autonomy, and freedom to pursue their own interests—including the promotion of racial understanding, which our study and others have shown to be attractive to faculty of color. Clearly, improvements in these areas would contribute to a university climate healthier for everyone.

EXEMPLARY PROGRAMS

In addition to compiling the recommendations of our study respondents, we examined several programs designed to address the problem of the underrepresentation of faculty of color. Some of these programs are described and discussed in the remainder of this chapter, following a brief explanation of our approach.

Pavel, Swisher, and Ward (1994) define exemplary as meaning an "example for others. It may not be one of a kind or unique but [it is] a model which sets the standards for others" (p. 52). In their view, colleges and universities demonstrating commitment and achievement in addressing the needs of students, staff, and faculty of color can be labeled "exemplary."

Our research shows that there are a number of exemplary programs within institutions of higher education, some funded by philanthropic foundations, to address the underrepresentation of faculty of color. Exemplary programs range from graduate fellowships under the auspices of professional associations (e.g., graduate fellowships for African American, Latino, and American Indian students of political science) to consortia arrangements and specific institutional initiatives. As part of our study, we examined several such efforts, interviewing participants in one "grow your own" initiative. For other programs, we reviewed the program documents, brochures, evaluations, proposals, and reports. Although more evaluation and analysis are needed to determine which programs work and why, it is clear that most exemplary programs have two constraints in common. First, many of them are fully or partially funded on "soft monies;" second, due in part to inadequate funding for evaluation, little or no formative or summative evaluation is done to document cost and effectiveness.

Each of the following exemplary programs addresses at least one aspect of minority faculty development. They provide examples of support at the departmental, institutional, regional, multiregional, and national levels for the recruitment, retention, and promotion of faculty of color. The various emphases of the programs we reviewed can be divided into three categories: fellowships, special hiring programs/contracts, and mentoring and networking opportunities. We will briefly describe one program from each category, not judging the quality of the programs as better or worse than other such programs, but simply presenting them as examples, along with observations about the general strategy.

Fellowship Programs

Fellowship programs focus on the need to increase the pool of minority doctoral candidates and recipients as a means for increasing minority faculty representation in higher education.

One of the most ambitious and promising of such fellowship programs is the Compact for Faculty Diversity. Concerned about the underrepresentation of minority faculty across the nation, predicted shortages of faculty due to retirement, and the general problem of inadequate increase in minority Ph.D's, the New England Board of Higher Education (NEBHE), the Southern Regional Education Board (SREB), and the Western Interstate Commission for Higher Education (WICHE) joined together, with support from the Pew Charitable Trusts and the Ford Foundation, to develop a national strategy for increasing minority faculty representation.

In 1994, after an eighteen-month planning period, the regional compacts held discussions with many diverse stakeholders, including state and university officials. Published in *The Compact for Faculty Diversity* (p. 10), the following conclusions emerged: (1) The problem of minority faculty underrepresentation is a major issue at the state level; (2) states are not active participants in resolving the problem; (3) states and universities need to increase the base of financial support for minority doctoral study; (4) there needs to be greater utilization of multiyear support for minority graduate students; (5) academic units need incentives to create supportive environments for minority graduate students and to increase the mentoring of those students; (6) there need to be stronger networks among minority graduate students to promote teaching; and (7) recruitment should be better targeted to minority students.

The three regional organizations joined together to form the Compact for Faculty Diversity and developed a program with the following components:

- initial funding of minority doctoral scholarships that eventually would be funded by the states and universities through tuition waivers, student stipends, fellowships, and teaching or research assistantships;
- encouragement of multiyear funding, tuition waivers, and guarantees for support through the completion of the dissertation, with special targeting to ABD minorities as an untapped source of talent;
- provision of small awards to academic departments for mentoring and support to minority students;
- sponsorship of an annual institute to encourage networking and support for development of teaching excellence;
- development of improved recruitment procedures to better target talented minorities interested in pursuing graduate work.

This initiative casts its net broadly. As Pepion (1997) puts it, the compact differs from other programs because

> ...*more than a 'check and a handshake' approach taken by traditional fellowship programs, each scholar is guaranteed five years of financial support and a commitment by the host academic department to provide an orientation to the department's guidelines and expectations for students, along with quality mentoring, professional development opportunities, and activities designed to hone their classroom teaching skills. (p. 9)*

According to the compact, as of September 29, 1997, 29 states, 51 institutions of higher education, and 216 students have participated in the program. In its first three years of operation, 20 students completed the Ph.D. and at least three of those were placed in tenure-track faculty positions.

The compact intends to extend its support even further. There are plans to seek funding to follow the compact doctoral graduates and provide continued support through the tenure process. This is an excellent next step for such a program. A follow-up study of fellowship recipients who complete the doctorate will help identify postdoctoral hiring issues for compact graduates. Current compact activities confirm the importance of fellowship programs in increasing the number of potential faculty of color. The extended effort will address the issue that, even with degrees in hand, scholars of color face significant barriers in the academic search and hiring process, and that even with an academic position secured, they face many challenges in the workplace environment that must be overcome if tenure and promotion are to be attained.

The compact represents perhaps the best of what is known about recruitment and retention of minorities in graduate schools. It realistically deals with the host of problems confronted by minorities interested in pursuing doctorates, through financial support, mentoring, networks, and incentives to academic units. The compact promises—in the face of continuing national ambivalence about race-based scholarships—to provide exactly that: minority scholarships to produce more minority faculty.

The fundamental question inherent in the compact strategies remains whether these efforts necessarily increase the representation of minority faculty; and, similarly, whether these efforts are of intrinsic value, independent of their impact on minority faculty representation.

It is clear that there is a need to keep promising scholars moving through the pipeline to faculty positions. The real decline in African American Ph.D.'s during the 1980s is cause for alarm. Programs that fund long-term fellowships and provide incentives to departments have two obvious benefits: They will increase the retention of minority graduate students; they will increase the production of minority Ph.D.'s. But these benefits seem short term at best. There is no indication that states or even participating universities will pick up the financial burdens once foundation resources are depleted. The states may look to the several cases now before the U.S. Supreme Court and the courts of appeal for guidance on the constitutionality of race-based scholarships, and they may conclude that initiatives like those proposed by the compact will invite immediate challenge by white graduate students.

Even if minority scholarships can pass constitutional muster in the courts, there still remains the dilemma of institutional resistance, that is, that many white *faculty* may be opposed to them. Thus, the very persons being asked to mentor these new graduate students, the very individuals being asked to improve environments for completing of the Ph.D.'s—it is they who may be most philosophically opposed to the scholarships.

Moreover, increasing the number of minority Ph.D.'s does not guarantee that the new Ph.D.'s (1) will become faculty, (2) will get promoted once they become faculty, or (3) will stay in academia if and when they get promoted. Given the present political and social environment, the compact—although a vastly promising and efficient mechanism for producing minority Ph.D.'s—may not have a sustained, long-term effect on national minority faculty representation.

Quite distinct from the issue of whether the compact will increase minority faculty representation is the issue of whether it is desirable to improve the national coordination of minority fellowships and mentoring to improve the number of minority Ph.D.'s, regardless of their ultimate career goals. The answer is a resounding yes! There is every reason to believe that improved coordination among graduate institutions in the southern, western, and northeastern regions would help promote minority graduate student enrollments nationally. The market for doctorates is no longer a regional one. More and more institutions are seeking broader networks for the recruitment of new Ph.D.'s. The compact's program coordinates three regional initiatives. Each region provides scholarships and programs financed by states in its own region. A major disadvantage of this approach is the possibility that a region will produce doctorates without receiving ultimate benefits.

Take, for example, the problem of the Midwest, a net exporter of minority doctorates. If compact dollars were state dollars appropriated in a vacuum, the midwestern states would benefit through an increased production of Ph.D.'s even if the vast majority of those Ph.D.'s migrated to other parts of the nation. If, however, these state dollars were diverted from other initiatives, such as minority faculty development or research networks, there might be less net benefit to the midwestern states because they are net exporters of minority Ph.D.'s. Making the effort national, then, would avoid the calculus by which each state assesses its success based on how many dollars are returned.

Smith et al. (1996), in their study of labor market effects (discussed more fully in the next chapter), conclude generally that fellowship programs, such as the Compact for Faculty Diversity, are indeed valuable. Fellowship programs will provide more "qualified" potential faculty candidates, but efforts cannot end there. The road to successful recruitment, retention, and the development of faculty of color is fraught with many challenges barring the way to true representation of faculty of color.

Hiring Programs

What we characterize as hiring programs are efforts that focus on policies and resources to promote recruitment and retention of faculty of color. Various institutions have created funding pools or special contracts with faculty of color with support for development and research activities as special incentives in the recruiting process.

Of particular interest is the kind of hiring program commonly referred to as "grow your own." There is one such grow-your-own program for minority faculty development at a major research university, which promotes the identification and recruitment of potential faculty of color, sometimes from outside of academe. The university and prospective faculty members enter into a contract. The contract requires the individuals to complete their doctorates while teaching two sections of the same course, meaning only one course preparation. Each participant receives tuition for doctoral work, as well as an office, travel allowance, equipment resources, and fringe benefits on the basis of .75 FTE faculty member (minimum salary of approximately $21,000). Their positions are guaranteed for conversion to tenure track, with salary change from .75 to 1.00 FTE (and an option to negotiate salary level). There are no strings attached concerning the number of years the individual must agree to stay in the employ of the college. As of May 1994, the program exceeded its minimum goal of three minority faculty hires who have been converted to tenure track. The success of this program has resulted in its expansion to other colleges at the university.

Among the faculty we interviewed for our study were nine participants of that program. Their comments indicate that it is a praiseworthy effort, and they attribute much of the program's success to the commitment of the college dean. Their quotes give the flavor of the experience.

> I'm in a minority faculty development program where I'm hired at 75 percent of a full-time faculty person. And I'm in a doctoral program, which is part of the program at the [major research university]. I'm required to complete twelve to eighteen hours a year in this particular program toward my doctoral degree. And at the conclusion of four years, with the doctoral degree, I'm guaranteed a tenure-track program right within the university in the area that I'm in.
>
> Female African American untenured humanities

> I am an instructor with [department]. I was working as [position] and I was approached to participate in the [minority faculty development program]...I'm teaching and I'm in the Ph.D. program here at [the university]. I teach two classes and I'm expected to take a full load of graduate courses.
>
> Male American Indian untenured social sciences

> The [minority faculty development program] really is something I was looking for—I was teaching high school for the past ten years and I was looking for a program where I could teach and work toward a doctoral degree simultaneously.
>
> Female African American untenured humanities

> I was working at a community agency...and was asked if I would be interested in this program...It just kind of came to me...The school of [name] is very culturally diverse so I've never encountered any problems there but it was rather a cul-

ture shock for me in the classroom because we have 98 percent non-Latino students in the classroom.

Female Latina untenured social sciences

I was working as a counselor and just got ongoing encouragement...I liked the university system so I did not want to leave...one professor was very instrumental in getting people involved and I see him as probably one of the most important mentors for me on this campus.

Male Latino untenured social sciences

The [minority faculty development program] came about at a good time for me because I was working...and considering a career change...It's been five years since I've started here, teaching as well as working toward the doctorate and I am happy to say that I'm honing in now on the first phase of the dissertation.

Male African American untenured social sciences

Although appreciative of the opportunities provided by the minority faculty development program, participants encountered some struggles. These same respondents articulate these concerns:

I was a [school] teacher...and was asked if I would be interested in the minority faculty development program. It would mean that I would be hired ¾ time to teach methods and ¼ time to supervise student teachers...I took a tremendous cut in salary... In faculty meetings I still get a sense that it's still the back door. That it's not the real process...I wonder when I go to those meetings if my fellow colleagues look at me in terms of their equals or as just another project...At the same time the dean and the department chair say "you have full status" but it's not...

Female African American untenured social sciences

Be able to say no. I think that when you are new everyone's enthusiastic about your being here and so they want you to become involved in a lot of activities...Also, according to the rules of our contract, we were supposed to teach one preparation, two courses a semester. And from the beginning I've been teaching two different preparations. As a new person, I thought they were expressing confidence in me, which is fine. On the other hand, on the business side of it, perhaps there wasn't someone to teach that course and so they thought I was available...I would tell new faculty to be aware of what you are being asked to do and then be able to say no if it is not in your best interest...I think I've begun to understand that while people are very supportive of you, they are also deans, directors, and chairs and may need you to fill in slots. I feel that sometimes the newest faculty can be exploited...

Female Latina untenured social sciences

This is a great opportunity but they say we are ¾ time, but we work full-time. I'm teaching and am on a lot of committees.

Female African American untenured social sciences

Although deserving of praise and support, such grow-your-own institutional efforts need continuous feedback from participants to allow for program adjustments as unintended and unpredicted challenges surface. One study respondent in another institution's minority faculty development program notes, "There was not someone to show me the ropes and I'm still puzzled and that's the kind of situation I've been in all year."

Nonetheless, a number of tenured faculty of color in our study encourage grow-your-own efforts as an effective strategy for minority faculty development.

I think one issue that might be considered is paying more attention to home-growing your faculty...I think for people of color it might be more of an issue because if it's difficult to find a natural community in the area, the fact that you are away from your family and whatever community your family has built up over the generations becomes a hardship. So, I think paying more attention to making sure that those kids who grow up in the Midwest stick around in the Midwest as faculty would help a lot...

Male Asian American tenured social sciences

I think it's probably time to look internally for the solution…one of the ways you can develop faculty is to identify and nourish faculty from within. You have students in your master's and doctoral programs that have potential—capture and nourish them…

Female African American tenured social sciences

We have a minority predoctoral fellows program. A person teaches during the dissertation process, teaching a reduced load. [The] rest of [the] time they have time for research. That's one of the programs that [small private college] has to increase minority faculty.

Female African American tenured social sciences

Mentoring and Networking Programs

This program type has mentoring and networking opportunities as its primary focus. Other kinds of minority faculty development programs—including fellowship programs—may incorporate mentoring and networking components, but the programs described in this section have networking and mentoring as their primary program emphasis.

The Midwest Consortium for Latino Research (MCLR) is one such mentoring and network program. MCLR is a regional consortium housed at Michigan State University. It was originally conceived in 1986 as the result of discussions among scholars about the lack of research and training opportunities for Latino researchers, faculty, and students in midwestern colleges and universities. MCLR's mission is to provide leadership for the advancement of Latino scholars in midwestern institutions, and for research on Latinos in the Midwest. Nine midwestern colleges and universities are MCLR members: De Paul University, University of Illinois-Chicago, Indiana University-Bloomington, University of Iowa, University of Michigan-Ann Arbor, Michigan State University, University of Nebraska-Lincoln, University of Wisconsin-Madison, and Wayne State University. Membership dues and foundation grants finance the consortium's initiatives, which include:

MCLR Listserv—The first U.S. Latino electronic network provides a valuable source of information and scholarly exchange at the national level. Since 1995 the news network has reached international audiences.

MCLR WWW Home Page—MCLR is establishing a home page on the World Wide Web to supplement its current news network. The home page will highlight current and proposed MCLR work and, in addition, will devote a section to highlight member institutions and the work they are doing on behalf of Latinos in the Midwest.

MCLR Annual Roundtables focus on faculty development issues. The roundtables provide opportunities for establishing relationships, exchanging ideas, developing support networks, and building consensus. For example, the 1994 Scholars Roundtable held at Indiana University involved fifty-four Latino scholars from eight midwestern states. The theme for the meeting was "Partnerships for a Midwest Latino Academic Leadership Agenda." Out of the discussions came several general observations and recommendations:

1. Latino research in the arts and literature, social sciences, math and sciences, and education disciplines is in its infancy.
2. Challenges exist for Latino scholars to gain respect for their research.
3. Campus environments need to be improved to create greater respect for Latino research.
4. Prejudice toward Latino scholars makes them susceptible to the revolving door syndrome.
5. The tenure review process does not include scholars who can evaluate and assess quality in Latino research.
6. Isolation must be overcome through networking (e-mail, regional meetings, directory, etc.).
7. Institutional support in the form of resources should be given to departments to fund Latino research.
8. The tenure process should be reviewed to include a process in which Latino research is recognized.
9. Pipelines should be developed to increase future scholars in the profession.
10. The MCLR should continue. Other ongoing projects include the development of a Latino Faculty Survey to assess academic

environments, the development of a Latino resource directory and database, and the development of an MCLR reprint series highlighting scholarly articles reporting research on Latinos in the Midwest.

Although MCLR's strength is networking, other similar programs place more emphasis on mentoring. There are many institutional programs (such as the Center for Minority Faculty Development at Pennsylvania State University) that assign mentors to work with faculty of color in addition to providing faculty development through professional workshops and supplemental funding for research. The value of mentoring is clear, but it is a common and serious flaw of many mentoring efforts that they are often not implemented in every department of an institution and do not include every faculty member of color.

Tenure-Track Faculty Study (Bensimon, Ward, & Tierney, 1994), focusing on the experiences of women and people of color, emphasizes the importance of mentors and discusses the problem of unevenness in mentoring programs:

> *While some departments and colleges have mentoring programs, they are neither across-the-board nor institutionalized. Faculty who work with mentors find them useful and helpful for professional development...New faculty report needing advice about many aspects of their work—the tenure process, publishing, teaching, office politics, and the like—and one person cannot necessarily supply advice to meet all the needs of a junior faculty member...The Center for Minority Faculty Development, which provides information and collegial support for people of color, was highlighted as an important resource by those who used it. (p. 2)*

LEARNING FROM MISTAKES

As administrators and policy makers in higher education design programs to support faculty diversity, they must be aware of the myriad complexities that emerge around the implementation of such programs, which make the goal of inclusion so elusive. In their study of the Economic Development Administration's effort to create jobs in Oakland, Pressman and Wildavsky (1973) point to the many steps needed to move from a public policy initiative to implementation by bureaucratic agencies. The EDA effort was derailed due to miscues and missteps in translating policy to program, from idea to outcome. The title of Pressman and Wildavsky's book, *Implementation: How Great Expectations in Washington Are Dashed in Oakland,* tells the story. They grapple with the reality of trying to successfully implement a program that depends on the positive outcome of many interactions, a process that they dub "The Complexity of Joint Action." They conclude that "the probability of agreement by every participant on each decision point must be exceedingly high for there to be any chance at all that a program will be brought to completion" (p. 107).

A high level of commitment by people throughout the institution is essential. Proactive efforts can and must be increased. Institutions of higher education can boldly and critically examine themselves and make much needed changes. To achieve the goal of faculty diversity, everyone has a role to play in transforming the academic workplace environment into one that affirms and nurtures all of its members.

A dramatic and much publicized effort to diversify the faculty at Duke University provides one example of how good intentions can be derailed. The 1988 Black Faculty Initiative (BFI) called for an increase by at least one black faculty person in each of Duke University's academic hiring units by 1993. This goal was not accomplished. According to Applebome (1993), many blacks said that the main reason for the failed strategy was "that many departments never seriously tried to reach the goal and that high attrition revealed Duke as a place less than hospitable to Black faculty members...[Henry Louis Gates Jr., one of the nation's literary scholars, was quoted as saying] "It (Duke) was the most racist experience I ever had in my professional life," (p. 4A).

However, Franklin (1989), a distinguished historian and Duke emeritus professor, is quoted as saying, in Duke's defense:

> *Duke was much in the same (sic) position as other American universities: caught between a homogeneous past and a more heterogeneous future with no clear, cost-free path toward the latter...Everyone is stumbling and fumbling and groping for a way to make this work. Duke was frank enough and open*

enough to set a goal, which is more than most institutions have done. (p. 4A)

In January 1994, the Committee on Black Faculty of the Academic Council examined the effort to achieve the goals set forth in the 1988 BFI at Duke. Data collected over the five-year period from 1988 to 1993 were studied. Among the committee's conclusions were that the university had failed to increase the numbers of black faculty and that "serious deficiencies in nurturing young Black scholars accelerated the attrition of current Black faculty and made recruitment of potential Black faculty more difficult" (p. 2). Nonetheless, the committee also reaffirmed continued efforts by Duke, and other universities, to reach their faculty diversity goals:

It [is clear] that in order to achieve and maintain greatness as a University, an academic environment must be created in which Blacks and other minorities are fully represented, where the talents of all are maximally developed and valued and where the dignity and individual worth of every member of the University community is treasured and respected. (p. 1)

In general, major findings about the Duke experience were that:

• The monitoring of the BFI was ineffective.
• Retention was a problem because minority scholars were not supported.
• The only area of success was in the graduate school, which doubled enrollments of black Ph.D. candidates.
• Strategic planning beyond the BFI was needed if the institution's goal was achieving diversity.
• For some departments, the five-year plan was an unrealistic timetable because the pool of candidates was too small.
• Retention is important to help the recruiting efforts.
• Stronger monitoring was needed to increase black hiring at the departmental level.
• Committed leadership is essential at every level to eliminate barriers.
• Mentoring by senior faculty is critical to the retention and promotion of junior faculty.

Based on their findings, the Committee on Black Faculty of the Academic Council made specific recommendations, which include the following:

- If on-campus numbers need to be doubled, numbers of recruited candidates must be doubled.
- Incentive funds must be used to hire and provide opportunities for black faculty.
- The institution should consider hiring its own graduate students, especially if the pool of candidates is small.
- In order for retention to improve, mentoring and support programs must be developed.
- Mentoring must occur early on in graduate school.
- A vice provost or provost-level position should be created to monitor the implementation of these recommendations.
- Departments should submit yearly reports on efforts.
- An external review process should be developed to monitor departmental progress.

Conclusions from this report include the importance of monitoring the implementation of such strategic plans to diversify the professoriate. Incentives to accomplish goals and the serious involvement of top administration in the implementation process are also essential to the success of such initiatives. It is important to remember, too, that even when a university administration supports hiring faculty of color to achieve racial/ethnic balance, it is each department's faculty hiring committee that must implement such policies. If there is resistance at this level, the goal of faculty diversity will likely not be achieved. The hiring of faculty of color is clearly a prime example of "the complexity of joint action," and efforts to achieve faculty diversity must recognize that reality.

Despite Duke's failed attempt, however, an undiscouraged president, Nannerl O. Keohane, is quoted as saying that future plans "may succeed because of the failures of the past" (Magner, 1994, p. A23). Certainly, it seems, we can learn as much from our mistakes as our successes.

7

MARKET FORCES

Ph.D. Pipelines versus Competitive Wages

There are many possible causes for the underrepresentation of minority faculty in higher education. These range from a shortage of qualified applicants for faculty positions to the existence of institutional barriers that limit hiring and retention of people of color. To underscore the relative importance of the quantifiable causes of minority underrepresentation, this chapter explores a conventional labor market model of the supply of faculty and the relationship between the production of minority Ph.D.'s and the underrepresentation of minority faculty.

From the literature we know that many of the factors influencing the decisions of minority faculty extend back into their undergraduate years. However, several factors seem to have direct impact on faculty supply, for instance, the number of minority Ph.D.'s, and wages in academia versus wages in the private sector. The central analytical problem here is to isolate the relative contribution of premarket factors (development of a minority Ph.D. pool) from market factors (wage competition). We have found that an undersupply of minority Ph.D.'s has a statistically significant but tiny impact on minority faculty representation. Market wages exert a far greater influence on the underrepresentation of minority faculty in higher education.

These are strong and perhaps unconventional conclusions. Many administrators, when confronted with the evidence of the underrepresentation of minority faculty, almost reflexively say:

"The problem is not enough minority Ph.D.'s." Those analyzing the underrepresentation of minority faculty in higher education, however, have long recognized the dual influences on the supply of minority faculty. On the one hand, there is certainly a problem of insufficient numbers of qualified minority applicants for jobs. Policies that focus on this factor invariably seek ways to improve the movement of minorities along the Ph.D. pipeline. On the other hand, it is apparent that minority Ph.D.'s—particularly in sciences and engineering—are aggressively recruited by high-paying industries. The market competition for these talented minority scholars drives wages up and may undermine their recruitment to faculty positions. Strategies for addressing this aspect of the supply problem have been undermined by challenges to affirmative action, which now discourage "preferential treatment"—presumably including salary premiums for minorities.

In this chapter we evaluate econometric evidence supporting the wage competition arguments versus the pipeline, and analyze which market force has the greater effect on the presence of minority faculty in higher education: (1) the attractiveness of salaries in nonacademic jobs, or (2) a scarcity of minorities holding Ph.D.'s.

Our central conclusion is that the pipeline explanation does not hold up to careful scrutiny. This deeply rooted belief has energized substantial foundation and institutional support over the years but does not reflect current reality. Despite thirty years of public and private funding to train minority doctorates, many of these doctorates are still not in academic positions, and we find that market incentives play an enormous role in explaining the underrepresentation. This is particularly discouraging in light of the current hostility to any affirmative action measures that might use market incentives to attract and retain minority faculty. Pipeline initiatives are useful in supplying minority talent to government and private industry but do not cure the continuing underrepresentation of minority faculty on American campuses.

Although this chapter includes the sort of discussion usually found in technical journals, we have tried to first summarize our work in a way that will be palatable to the less technically inclined reader. The methods employed are the standard methods of empirical research in labor economics. We first provide a comprehensive summary of the results. For the more technically inclined, a detailed analysis follows the summary.

SUMMARY OF RESULTS

There is an undersupply of minorities in the Ph.D. pipeline.

At every point in the educational pipeline from the bachelor's to the doctoral degree, African Americans, Hispanics, and American Indians are substantially underrepresented. Asians are underrepresented but less severely so. Figure 7.1 illustrates the data.

The pool for the Ph.D. pipeline has increased over time.

Between 1977 and 1990, the number *and* share of bachelor's degree recipients increased nationally for Asians, Hispanics, and American Indians. For African Americans, though, the number increased slightly, whereas the share declined.

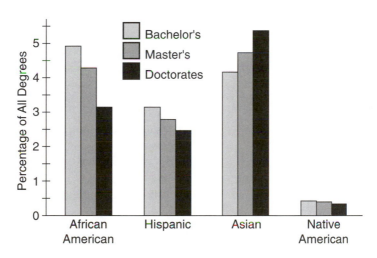

FIGURE 7.1   **Pipeline from Bachelor's to Doctorate All Fields, U.S. Citizens, 1990**

Source: U.S. Department of Education, National Center for Education Statistics, Digest of Education Statistics 1991, Tables 245, 247, and 249 (for 1977–1987 data) and "Race/Ethnicity Trends in Degrees Conferred by Institutions of Higher Education: 1980–81 through 1989–90, Tables 3–7 (for 1989 and 1990) data (based on IPEDS/HEGIS surveys of degrees conferred).

The gains in master's degrees and Ph.D.'s were generally weaker, and, for African Americans, the percentages declined. These results are elaborated here and are also illustrated in Figure 7.2.

- The share of all *bachelor's* degrees earned by Asians more than doubled; the share earned by Hispanics increased by 40 percent; the minuscule share earned by American Indians increased by 10 percent; and the share earned by African Americans declined by more than 11 percent.
- For Asians, Hispanics, and American Indians the increase in share of *master's* degrees awarded did not keep pace with the

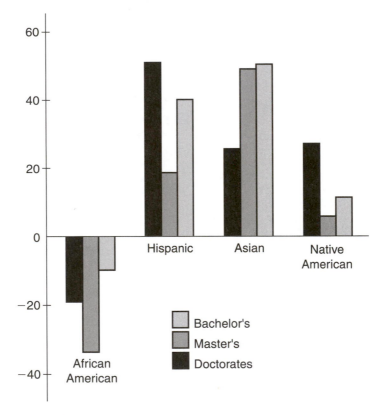

FIGURE 7.2   **Changes (Percentage Increase or Decrease) from 1977 to 1990 in Share of Degrees Received**

increase in share of bachelor's degrees awarded. The share of master's degrees earned by Asians less than doubled; the share earned by Hispanics rose by 18 percent, less than half the increase in the share of bachelor's degrees; and the share earned by American Indians barely increased by 6 percent—about half the increase in the share of bachelor's degrees earned. For African Americans the news was worse: The *number* of master's degrees earned by African Americans *declined* by 31 percent, whereas the share *declined* by one-third.

- For Hispanics the increase in the share of *Ph.D.* degrees—51 percent—outpaced the increase in the share of bachelor's and master's degrees. For Asians the increase in the share of Ph.D. degrees awarded—26 percent—did not keep pace with the increase in share of bachelor's or master's degrees. The tiny share earned by American Indians increased by 28 percent whereas the share earned by African Americans declined by 20 percent.

There is a considerable drop-off in the pipeline from Ph.D. to tenured faculty positions.

In the science and engineering fields, in which there has been a historic underrepresentation of African Americans, Hispanics, and American Indians, the pathways toward the Ph.D. differ for each minority group nationally. But at the critical juncture at which doctorates move to faculty tenure at four-year colleges and universities, there is a drop-off among *all* minority groups, including Asians, who are adequately represented at earlier points along the pipeline (see Figure 7.3).

- African American, American Indian, and Hispanic shares of tenured science and engineering faculty at four-year colleges and universities around the country are considerably below their shares of bachelor's degree recipients in science and engineering. This is not true of Asians, for whom the share of tenured faculty is greater than the share of bachelor's degree recipients.
- All minority groups are represented at lower percentages among tenured science and engineering faculty at four-year colleges and universities than among employed science and engineering Ph.D.'s.

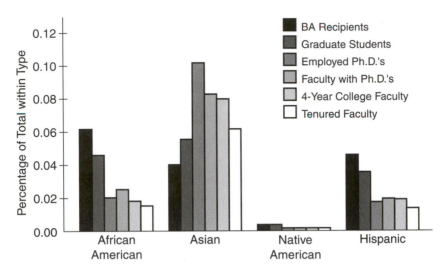

FIGURE 7.3   **Pipeline from BA Recipiency to Tenure by Race and Ethnicity, U.S. Citizens, 1991**

The undersupply of minority Ph.D.'s is not the cause of the underrepresentation of minority faculty.

Low faculty salaries have a greater effect on the representation of minority faculty members than does availability of minority Ph.D.'s.[1]

- Increasing the supply of minority Ph.D.'s would have only small effects on their representation rates among faculty members. In some cases, it would have negative effects.
- The supply of faculty is very responsive to earnings potential in academia. This responsiveness is much more pronounced among nonwhites as a group than among whites, especially in MHEC states.
- The reduction of minority faculty supply resulting from increased private sector wages is of a smaller magnitude than the increase in supply resulting from increased faculty salaries.

---

[1]Figures 7.5 and 7.6, and Tables A.7.4 and A.7.5, in the chapter appendix, show the elasticities of representation with respect to Ph.D. production and with respect to faculty and private sector wages.

Quite simply, the results, although revealing a pipeline problem, are not consistent with the view that the pipeline problem is the cause of minority faculty underrepresentation. Instead, market forces seem to dominate, particularly in the form of the relative attractiveness of faculty salaries. Although fixing the pipeline problem may be useful in its own right, the fix will have little impact on the persistent underrepresentation of minority faculty.

DETAILS OF THE ANALYSIS

Pipeline Effects

There is ample evidence of substantial underrepresentation of blacks, Hispanics, and American Indians along virtually every part of the pipeline toward faculty positions: underrepresentation among college graduates in science and engineering fields and in nonprofessional fields; underrepresentation in graduate school enrollment; and underrepresentation in Ph.D.'s received. There is no doubt that increasing the supply of minority faculty will require increasing the stocks and flows along the pipeline.

Bachelor's Degrees

In 1977 of the 928,228 persons earning bachelors' degrees in science and engineering, health fields, and nonscience and engineering fields, 13,907 were Asian, 58,700 were blacks, 27,043 were Hispanic, and 3,328 were American Indian or Alaskan Native. By 1990, 1.06 million persons earned bachelor's degrees; 38,027 were Asian, 59,301 were black, 43,864 were Hispanic, and 4,212 were American Indian.[2] The share of all bachelor's degrees earned by Asians more than doubled; the share of all degrees earned by Hispanics increased by 40 percent; the minuscule share earned by American Indians increased by 10 percent, and the share earned by African Americans declined by more than 11 percent.

---

[2]Table 1, *Science and Engineering Degrees, by Race/Ethnicity of Recipients: 1977–1991*, National Science Foundation NSF 94-306.

Master's Degrees

By way of contrast, in 1977 there were 318,241 master's degrees earned, with 5,145 awarded to Asians, 21,041 awarded to blacks, 7,071 awarded to Hispanics, and 968 awarded to American Indians. In 1990, of the 324,947 master's degrees earned, 9,994 were awarded to Asians, 14,473 were awarded to blacks, 8,495 were awarded to Hispanics, and 1,050 were awarded to American Indians.

The share of master's degrees earned by Asians nearly (but less than) doubled, the share earned by blacks declined by a third, the share earned by Hispanics rose by half the percent that bachelor's degrees increased, and the share earned by American Indians barely increased by 6 percent—just about half of the increase in the share of bachelor's degrees earned. All four racial/ethnic groups earned a declining share of master's degrees awarded relative to their shares of bachelor's degrees awarded. In the case of Asians, Hispanics, and American Indians, the growth of master's degree recipients did not match the growth of bachelor's degree recipients. This slowing of the pipeline could be due to many market-related phenomena, but it has dire consequences for the production of Ph.D.'s and ultimately the supply of faculty. In the case of African Americans, the reversals mean not a slowing of the pipeline but a dramatic and alarming reversal of the flow.[3]

Of course, these trends could be reversed if there are major year-to-year changes in the shares of bachelor's and master's degrees awarded to minorities. For example, the absolute decline in master's degrees awarded to African Americans—on a long-term decline since the late 1970s—was curbed in 1991, but just barely. In addition, much of the decline in shares in master's degrees can be attributed to increases in the share of all degrees awarded to noncitizens and persons of unknown race/ethnicity, and not to increas-

---

[3]See Table 24, *Science and Engineering Degrees by Race/Ethnicity of Recipients: 1971–1991*, National Science Foundation, NSF 94-306.

ing shares awarded to white non-Hispanic U.S. citizens and permanent residents.

There is an obvious lag between the receipt of a bachelor's degree and emergence in the faculty market with a Ph.D. However, the small growth of minority Ph.D.'s awarded even between 1977 and 1990 reveals a substantial problem long in the making. In 1977 the share of all doctorates[4] awarded by U.S. universities was only 2.87 percent among Asian Americans, 3.76 percent among blacks, 1.49 percent among Hispanics, and 0.21 percent among American Indians. The remaining 91.67 percent went to whites and foreign nationals. By 1990, there was some improvement. Asians' share increased to 3.61 percent; American Indians' share increased to 0.21 percent; and Hispanics' share increased to 2.25 percent representing relative increases of 25.85, 27.94, and 50.61 percent. Blacks' share dropped to 3 percent, representing a decline of 20 percent. The effect, then, is that minorities' share of all Ph.D.'s increased by less than 10 percent from 8.33 percent to 9.13 percent. There was little change in the entire thirteen-year period in the share of all U.S. Ph.D.'s awarded to American minorities. Thus, even without taking into account the time gap between receipt of the bachelor's degree and receipt of the Ph.D., we see relatively small increases in the shares of minority Ph.D.'s who are prepared to enter the academic job market.[5]

Figure 7.2 graphically shows that the pipeline problem is not identical for all racial groups. Although there has been a drop-off all along the pipeline among African Americans, there is steady movement up the pipeline among other groups, as Bowen and Rudenstine (1992) have shown in Figure 7.3.

The recent downsizing of the defense industry, changes in the manufacturing sectors of the economy, and important increases in joblessness among scientists and engineers serve to substantially slow efforts to increase minority enrollment in Ph.D. programs or to provide what may appear to be advantages to minority group

---

[4]Including science and engineering and nonscience and engineering doctorates, but excluding professional degrees such as M.D.'s, J.D.'s, and Ed.D.'s.

[5]Science Resource Studies Division, National Science Foundation. *Science and Engineering Doctorates 1960–91, Detailed Statistical Tables* NSF 93-301 (Washington, DC: NSF, 1993).

members when many majority group members are facing employment difficulties.[6]

Market Forces

There is extensive literature documenting the impacts of economic and market forces on the decisions to pursue the Ph.D. and to enter academia.[7] These forces include attraction to other professions such as law and medicine, preference and perception about life in academia and the demands of entering the profession,[8] the high cost of graduate education,[9] and a variety of other deterrents to the pursuit of the Ph.D.[10] Because most faculty positions—particularly at major research universities—require the doctoral degree, barriers to pursuing a Ph.D. also serve to limit entry to faculty positions. Ehrenberg, one of the nation's leading analysts of academic labor markets, concludes that the earnings in academia are among the strongest determinants of the production of Ph.D.'s and, indirectly, of the supply of faculty. He surveys the wide range of econometric

[6]The case for increased production of Ph.D.'s, especially minority Ph.D.'s, rests not just on the need to improve representation of minorities on college campus, but also to stem a forecast of faculty shortage predicted by such prominent educational leaders as William Bowen, former president of Princeton University and head of the Mellon Foundation, and Neil L. Rudenstine, president of Harvard University. *In Pursuit of the Ph.D.,* Princeton, NJ: Princeton University Press, 1992.

[7]Excellent reviews of this literature include Breneman and Youn (1988) and Ehrenberg (1991).

[8]For example, the view of preparation as an "extended pledgeship at subsistence levels of income...and problematic prospects of attaining tenure." Bowen and Schuster, (1986), p. 154.

[9]See "Road Blocks to Graduate School: Black Americans Are Not Achieving Parity," William F. Brazziel, *Educational Record,* Fall 1987–Winter 1988, citing high costs of graduate study and low faculty pay as causes for low black faculty production.

[10]One important deterrent is the length of time that it takes to obtain the degree. See "A Stock Flow Model of Academic Supply," Ronald G. Ehrenberg, *Modern Labor Economics Theory and Public Policy* (1991) p. 159. Among African Americans, moreover, who often take longer than average to complete the Ph.D., there is evidence of considerable dissatisfaction with the graduate school experience. See "The McKnight Black Doctoral Fellowship Program: An Evaluative Study," S. David Stamps and Israel Tribble, 1993, finding overall levels of dissatisfaction comparable between students with financial aid and those without.

evidence on the determinants of Ph.D. production and concludes that Ph.D. supply is extremely responsive to earnings in the field and to alternative earnings opportunities.[11]

Even if production of Ph.D.'s can be improved, there still exists the problem of large numbers of Ph.D.'s choosing to enter other professions. Bowen and Schuster (1988) note that there has been a sharp drop in the share of Ph.D.'s who enter academic work. The following table shows this to be the case in science and engineering Ph.D.'s employed in higher education from the 1960s to 1980.

Percentage of Ph.D. Recipients Employed in Academic Positions

	1960-1964	*1977-1980*
Sciences	54%	34%
Social Sciences	71%	54%

Bowen and Schuster (1986, p. 180).

Any model designed to capture the factors contributing to the underrepresentation of minority faculty in higher education must account for two factors: (1) the production of Ph.D.'s; and (2) the attractiveness of other nonacademic employment prospects. Figure 7.4 sketches one such model. Preferences and opportunities—which may involve such factors as financial aid for graduate study, family obligations, alternative earning opportunities, and a host of other demographic factors—affect the pursuit of a doctorate. Inducements as well as constraints combine to determine whether new doctorates decide to seek academic, public service, or private sector jobs.

The relative attractiveness of the alternatives is at least partially a function of expected earnings. Along with the demographic factors

---

[11]He finds elasticities in the range of 0.82 to 3.00 for earnings in the same field; and –1.04 to –2.8 for earnings in other fields, Ehrenberg (1991). Studies cited by Ehrenberg supporting these findings can be found in Clotfelter, Ehrenberg, Getz, and Siegfried (1991) and include Freeman (1971), Freeman (1975), Scott (1979), Kuh and Radner (1980), Hoffman and Low (1983), Alexander and Frey (1984), Hoffman and Orazan, (1985), Baker (1989), and Stapleton (1989).

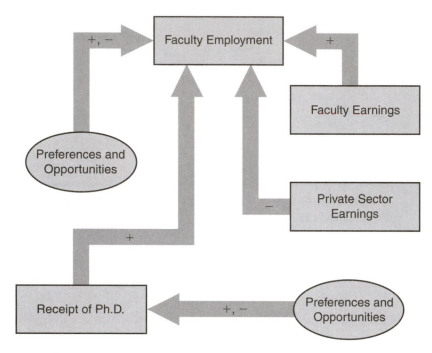

FIGURE 7.4   Model of Faculty Supply

affecting preferences and opportunities, the three factors that most directly affect the choice of an academic career in this simple model are (1) the receipt of the Ph.D., (2) faculty wages, and (3) wages in the private sector.

We have simplified matters considerably in order to estimate a straightforward relationship between the Ph.D. pool, other factors, and faculty employment. For example, we have ignored demand-side factors, which affect decisions by academic departments to hire faculty, such as student enrollment and fiscal resources. We have also ignored the wide range of alternative routes to faculty positions, although we will return to this issue again in our discussion of recommendations.[12]

---

[12]We have also not included public sector earnings in the model. This is due to empirical convenience. We found that public sector wages were highly correlated with private sector wages. Inclusion of both in our regression model—along with faculty wages—introduced substantial multicollinearity.

Despite these simplifications, the model can be useful in assessing the effectiveness of programs designed to increase minority Ph.D.'s. By separately estimating the impact of Ph.D. production on faculty employment for various groups, we can estimate the effects of pipeline efforts on minority representation.

To understand this reasoning, suppose that a policy—such as an increase in financial assistance for graduate study—increases both minority and nonminority attainment of the Ph.D. And suppose that there is a uniform increase in the percentages of minority and non-minority Ph.D.'s. The financial assistance program might provide extra aid to, let's say, African American graduate students in order to make the *number* of African American Ph.D.'s equal to the number of white Ph.D.'s. This sort of intervention—extra financial aid—is advocated by economists such as Ehrenberg who contend that the borrowing patterns of African American graduate students seriously impede both their pursuit and completion of the Ph.D.[13]

What we need to examine is: "Suppose there is a uniform percentage increase in the receipt of Ph.D.'s by minority and non-minority persons in the same qualifications group. What would happen to the minority faculty representation ratios?" The answer depends on whether existing hiring patterns in academia versus other sectors result in larger, smaller, or equal increases in minority faculty employment than nonminority faculty employment. Generally speaking, for uniform increases in Ph.D.'s to result in greater minority faculty representation, increases in minority faculty hiring would have to be greater than the nonminority increase in hiring.

In order to answer the question, we considered two different comparisons. The first is a comparison of faculty share to population share. The second is a comparison of faculty share to share of the subpopulation of employed persons with master's or doctorate degrees. In the first comparison, we included as independent variables age, marital status, gender, presence of children or elderly adults, immigration status, and receipt of the Ph.D. We estimated a model of the probability of faculty employment and then computed the

[13]Ehrenberg (1991), p. 228. "Black dependent students from each family income class are much *less* likely to have taken out college loans than students from other race/ethnic groups...Black independent students in each income class are also less likely to have loans...However, the loan burdens that these black students acquire are a much larger share of their income (.637) than are the loan burdens of any other group."

How We Computed Representation Ratios

Let R^k denote the representation ratio for the kth group, where:

$$R^k = \frac{P^k(\text{Fac})}{P(\text{Fac})} \text{ , where } P(\text{Fac}) = \frac{1}{1 + \exp - (\sum \beta_i x_i)}$$

The slope of the faculty probability, $P(\text{Fac})$, with respect to a factor x_i (such as the receipt of the Ph.D.), is given by $\beta_i P(1 - P)$. The elasticity of $P(\text{Fac})$ with respect to x_i is given by $\beta_i(1 - P)x_i$.

How We Computed the Effects of Factors on the Representation Ratios

To compute the effect of x_i on R^k, we derive:

$$\partial R^k / \partial x_i \quad \text{and} \quad \partial R^k / \partial x_i \cdot x_i / R^k.$$

But note that

$$\partial R^k / \partial x_i = [\partial P^k / \partial x_i \, P - \partial P / \partial x_i \, P^k] / P^2,$$

which may be negative even when $\partial P / \partial x_i < \partial P^k / \partial x_i$ when $P^k > P$, as is the case with Asian Americans.

Computation of Faculty Shares

The comparison of the share of faculty to the share of the population is the same as the comparison of the probability that a minority is a faculty member to the probability that a person is a faculty member.

Let $P^k(\text{Fac})$ = probability that a minority is a faculty member and $P(\text{Fac})$ is the probability that any person is a faculty member.

$$P^k(\text{Fac}) \approx \#\text{Fac}^K / \#\text{Pop}^k$$

and $P(\text{Fac}) \approx \#\text{Fac} / \#\text{Pop}$,

or the ratios of faculty to populations.

But note that:

$$P^k(\text{Fac}) / P(\text{Fac}) = (\#\text{Fac}^K / \#\text{Pop}^k) / \#\text{Fac} / \#\text{Pop})$$
$$= (\#\text{Fac}^K / \#\text{Fac}) / (\#\text{Pop}^k / \#\text{Pop})$$

impact of an increase in the production of Ph.D.'s on the faculty representation ratios for whites, blacks, American Indians, Asians, and Hispanics. We partitioned the data set to examine just the subset of cases from the MHEC member states and reestimated the equations and similarly derived the impact of Ph.D. production on faculty representation ratios.

Figure 7.5 shows the responsiveness of faculty representation to changes in the Ph.D. production. It shows what would happen to the national and the MHEC representation ratio for blacks, Asians, and Hispanics if there were a 1 percent increase in Ph.D. attainment

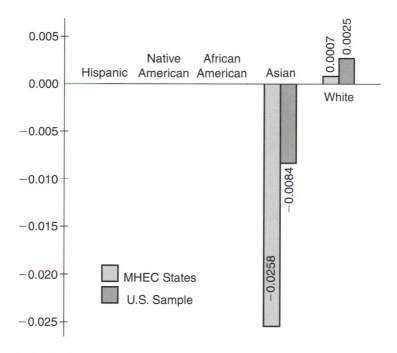

FIGURE 7.5   Elasticities of Representation Ratios with Respect to Ph.D. Production

Source: Appendix D, Table D.24 (3% of 5% PUMS U.S.) Sample. Population ages 24–70).

The elasticities of representation ratios with respect to Ph.D. is the percentage change in the representation ratio as a result of a 1 percent change in Ph.D.

for each group.[14] The responsiveness of faculty supply both at the national level and among MHEC member states is negligible. A 1 percent increase in the production of Ph.D.'s would only marginally increase the representation of African Americans, American Indians, and Latinos in higher education employment. Although there would be a slight reduction in the representation ratios of Asian Americans, even that change would be quite small.

As noted, this analysis compares faculty and the general population, and it may be more legitimate to compare faculty numbers with the pool of potentially qualified individuals, such as those with master's and doctoral degrees. About 5 percent of all persons with MA's or Ph.D.'s are employed as faculty members in colleges or universities. What would happen to the faculty employment if there were an increase of 1 percent in the numbers of persons in that pool who had Ph.D.'s? And how would the impact of increasing the Ph.D. pool compare with the impact of potential earnings in private and academic sectors?

Figure 7.6 reveals that, even using the second comparison population, faculty representation ratios are not particularly responsive to increased Ph.D. attainment. The figure shows that a 1 percent increase in minority Ph.D.'s would have only small effects on their representation ratios, and in some cases negative effects.[15]

But what about the impacts of market incentives, such as faculty wages and earnings in private sector jobs? To assess these impacts, we first estimated log-wage equations for wage and salary incomes reported by employed professionals in 1989. We excluded medical professionals and lawyers, whose salaries are considerably higher than those of typical master's and Ph.D. recipients. The sample was partitioned into four industry-occupation classifications: faculty employed in higher education, professionals employed in

---

[14]American Indian calculations, based on a limited number of observations, are not displayed here. The full results are found in Table A.7.4. of the appendix.

[15]The reason for the negative effects on African Americans is that the slopes of faculty employment with respect to increased Ph.D. recipiency are smaller than average. This means that just simply increasing the numbers of blacks who have Ph.D.'s will not assure that they will become employed or will want to become employed as faculty members at the same rate as whites or Asians who have considerably higher rates of employment as faculty. Full details are given in Table A.7.8 of the appendix.

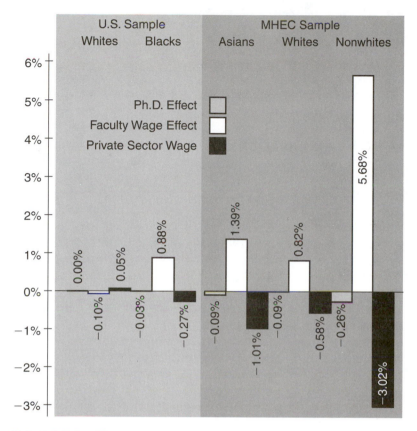

FIGURE 7.6 **Elasticities of Representation Ratios with Respect to Ph.D.'s, Faculty Wage, and Private Sector Wage**

Source: Tables D.20 and D.21.

Elasticity of representation ratio (*r*) with respect to variable *x* is defined as the percentage change in *r* as a result of a 1 percent change in *x*.

nonpublic sector jobs, professionals employed in public sector jobs, and all others. We estimated wage equations within each sector, controlling for hours worked, age, gender, and a host of other factors. The coefficients from these equations were used to predict expected earnings for persons in the entire sample of professional employees. In short, we computed what a person could expect to earn in each of the sectors. Not surprisingly, we found higher wages in private sector employment and lower wages in higher education employment. We also found that the earnings of racial minorities tended to be lower than those of whites.

Again, Figure 7.6 reveals the results of our computations. Generally speaking we find minority faculty representation increases as faculty salaries increase, and that faculty representation falls as private sector salaries increase. We find, also, that the increase in minority faculty representation due to increased faculty wages is greater than the decrease in faculty representation due to high private sector wages. The effect, then, is more a push from academia due to low salaries than a pull from the private sector due to high salaries, and we cannot conclude that the blame for low minority faculty representation lies with high salaries in industry; part of the blame rests on the unattractive salaries in academia. If faculty salaries were to rise, the corresponding increase in minority faculty employment would be greater than if private sector salaries were to fall.

The full details of these computations are presented in a technical appendix. Suffice it to say that effects of Ph.D. production on minority faculty supply are swamped by the effect of market incentives. There is every reason to believe that some persons would decide to pursue an academic career at any level of earnings. Conversely, there is every reason to believe that some would refuse to work in a college or university regardless of the salary or wage. But our findings suggest that overall, there is a significant responsiveness of faculty supply to earnings potential in academia and that this responsiveness is much more pronounced among many nonwhites than among whites. Higher salaries in academia would improve the representation of minorities in higher education.

APPENDIX: THE DATA

The Public Use Microdata Samples (PUMS) were prepared by the Bureau of the Census using the 1990 Census of Population and Housing. PUMS contain records representing 5 percent or 1 percent samples of the housing units in the United States without regard to legal status or citizenship. Citizens who maintained usual residence outside the United States were not included. The Bureau of the Census either acquired a commercial mailing list, which is updated by the United Postal Service and the census staff, or surveyed and listed each address in the area before census day. All were sent the short census form containing basic demographic questions, referred to as the 100-percent questions. A sample of the population was sent the 100-percent questions with additional detailed questions such as income and occupation. Three sampling rates procedures were used to determine housing units that were to receive the long questionnaires. The enumerations were obtained from the returned self-reports.

The sampling size was based on the sampling rate of the population area. The purpose of the sampling rate was to produce more reliable estimates for smaller areas and to reduce the work of those in more densely populated areas. When sampling rates were taken into account, approximately one in six housing units was surveyed. The 5 percent PUMS sample includes every state and each subdivision/county with at least 100,000 persons. The 1 percent sample contains the full census sample for each state for metropolitan areas. The 1 percent sample was selected at random from the sample size of each state.

In the MHEC project, 3 percent of full U.S. PUMS sample was used (0.15 percent, which is 413,119 observations). The 1 percent U.S. sample used to calculate predicted wages was restricted to persons who had a master's or a Ph.D. degree (20,195 observations), between and including ages twenty-four to seventy, and who earned income in 1989. From this sample, multiple regressions were employed to predict wages that faculty might receive if they worked in different sectors of the economy. Faculty was defined as persons not enrolled in school, who reported their occupation as a postsecondary teacher, and whose industry is in a college or university. The remaining persons were grouped into the private sector or the public/nonprofit sector. The data are presented in Tables A.7.1 through A.7.8.

TABLE A.7.1   Definitions of Regression Variables

Source of data	3% of the 5% U.S. PUMS file; full 5% for individual states
Population	Limited to persons between and including ages 24–70 in 1989 with master's or Ph.D. degree, and earned income in 1989
Faculty	Persons not enrolled in school, who reported their occupation as a postsecondary teacher, and whose industry is in a college or university
Predicted wage	Multiple regressions used to predict wages that faculty might have received if they worked in different sectors of the economy. All workers with MA/Ph.D. degrees divided into three groups: 1. Worked in private sector 2. Worked in public/nonpublic sector 3. Faculty members White and non-Hispanic predicted wages were based solely on actual coefficients. The U.S. total, white, and non-Hispanic variables were calculated for all workers in the sample. Black and Asian variables were calculated only for workers in those racial groups.
Age	Person's age
Combination of sex and marital status	1. Bachelor: single men 2. Single F: single women 3. Wife: married women (4. Married men—not coded)
Region of country	Based on four regions in Census Bureau 1. West 2. MWest: Midcentral states 3. East: Northeast 4. South (not coded)
Week '89	Number of weeks person worked in 1989
Language	Language spoken at home—English/Not English
Over 60	Any person(s) 60 years old or over who lived in household
R–18 Under	Any person(s) under 18 years old who lived in household
PHD	Had Ph.D.
Immigration	1. Pre-1986: immigrated before 1987 2. Post-1986: immigrated after 1987

TABLE A.7.2 Maximum Likelihood Estimates in Logistic Model of Faculty Probability (Master's/Ph.D. 1% PUMS U.S. Sample) (t-statistic in parentheses)

	Total	White	Blacks	Indian**	Asian	Hispanic**
Constant	-2.2255 (6.0303)	-1.5591 (-5.3707)	-11.1996 (-8.5867)	61.6844 (4.7156)	-5.5822 (-4.5446)	8.8296 (3.9503)
Age	0.0398 (6.0303)	0.0375 (5.2817)	0.1280 (3.4225)	-2.4341 (-5.8724)	0.0221 (0.7727)	-0.0365 (-6.2424)
Age squared	-0.0002 (-2.8571)	-0.0001 (-1.3184)	-0.0010 (-2.5000)	0.0259 (5.7556)	0.0000 (0.1183)	0.0037 (6.1667)
Sex	0.1219 (6.5187)	0.1930 (9.6020)	-0.4608 (-5.6401)	-7.2633 (-5.6572)	-0.3126 (-3.3868)	-0.8611 (-5.8380)
Persons under 18 in household	0.0511 (3.1350)	0.0357 (2.0284)	0.5836 (7.5694)	6.9909 (5.1268)	-0.0722 (-0.9863)	0.2031 (1.7524)
Persons over 60 in household	0.0273 (0.9750)	0.0071 (0.2305)	0.0101 (0.0758)	2.8644 (4.9065)	0.6323 (6.7698)	-3.0812 (-10.3327)
Other language spoken in home	-0.2717 (-10.3702)	-0.2955 (-9.2344)	0.1726 (1.4714)	-4.5167 (4.7917)	0.4158 (4.3768)	-0.5499 (-4.4240)
Unmarried female with children under 18	-0.4324 (-7.6396)	-0.2474 (-3.9458)	-0.1942 (-1.3211)	-12.4598 (-0.4588)	-5.1347 (-1.8802)	-6.8344 (-1.6023)
Immigrated before 1987	-0.1166 (-4.2711)	0.0044 (0.1354)	-0.3109 (-2.7248)	n/a	-0.8584 (-7.1474)	0.0915 (0.6224)
Immigrated after 1987	0.3309 (0.5170)	0.3576 (4.8194)	2.8491 (8.1055)	1.2793 (0.0216)	-0.1494 (-0.6349)	0.8902 (2.3809)

(continued)

TABLE A.7.2 *Continued*

	Total	White	Blacks	Indian**	Asian	Hispanic**
Ph.D.	2.5151	2.5557	2.1090	2.8629	1.9581	3.2721
	(66.7135)	(62.1825)	(12.2119)	(1.0381)	(11.3711)	(11.0919)
Predicted faculty wage	0.2401	0.1310	1.1496	15.0827	1.6939	0.8504
	(2.4575)	(1.2300)	(2.6910)	(3.3432)	(3.7212)	(1.0411)
Predicted private wage	−0.5128	−0.4651	−0.7822	−16.1581	−1.5685	−1.5533
	(−7.3153)	(−6.0797)	(−2.5529)	(−4.7304)	(−4.7201)	(−2.6001)
N. Central/Midwest				−16.2842		2.1324
				(−1.0884)		(10.8519)
East region						0.4965
						(2.5646)
West region						0.5682
						(3.2487)
Probability (*p*)	0.0588	0.0615	0.0423	0.0510	0.0487	0.0408
Representation ratio		1.0471	0.7199	0.8685	0.8294	0.6944
Chi-square	34,914.106	29,982.329	1,979.501	393.675	2,459.688	1,392.406
% correctly classified	94.06	93.75	95.89	97.26	95.18	95.9
No. observ. (weighted)	421,542	352,581	27,709	1,607	26,737	12,717
No. observ. (unweighted)	20,195	17,209	1,143	80	1,195	562

Source: 1% PUMS sample restricted to persons with a master's or Ph.D., age 24–70, and who earned income in 1989.

Probability (*p*) is the conditional probability that a person with a master's/Ph.D.is a faculty member.

**For Indians and Hispanics, regional dummy variables were used in regression.

TABLE A.7.3 Maximum Likelihood Coefficients in Logistic Model of Faculty Probabilities (Master's/Ph.D. 1% MHEC subsample) (t-statistic in parentheses)

	Total	White	Nonwhite
Age	0.0403 (6.1061)	–0.0682 (–3.9195)	–0.2899 (–115.9600)
Age squared	–0.0002 (–2.8571)	0.0009 (4.5000)	0.0025 (3.5714)
Sex	0.1278 (6.8342)	0.1398 (1.4794)	–0.6392 (–2.7062)
Persons under 18 in household	0.0457 (2.8037)	0.1701 (3.5145)	0.2834 (1.6297)
Persons over 60 in household	0.0153 (0.5464)	–0.0220 (–0.2937)	1.6647 (6.5669)
Other language spoken in home	–0.2671 (–10.1559)	0.0900 (1.0514)	–1.4643 (–8.3057)
Unmarried female with children under 18	–0.4235 (–7.4823)	0.6701 (4.5308)	–5.6720 (–0.8589)
Immigrated to U.S. before 1987	–0.1178 (–4.2993)	–0.4647 (–6.2544)	2.0714 (9.2185)
Immigrated to U.S. after 1987	0.3029 (0.4733)	0.7673 (4.3721)	5.5777 (10.7305)
Ph.D.	2.4779 (63.8634)	2.4272 (12.0576)	0.7483 (1.8071)
Predicted faculty wage	0.2426 (2.4406)	1.1236 (2.0366)	6.1847 (6.0533)
Predicted private wage	–0.5219 (–7.3198)	–1.1403 (–2.7234)	–3.6631 (–5.0976)
Probability (p)	0.0653	0.0679	0.0448
Representation ratio (r)		1.1551	0.7630
Chi-square	35,001.8790	6,302.3510	1,084.7730
% Correctly classified	94.05	92.89	96.81
No. observ. (weighted)	421,542	57,700	7,183
No. observ. (unweighted)	20,195	2,651	287

Source: 1% PUMS sample restricted to MHEC states (8) persons with a master's or Ph.D., ages 24–70, and who earned income in 1989.

Probability (p) is the conditional probability that a person with a master's/Ph.D. is a faculty member.

TABLE A.7.4   Elasticities of Faculty Probability and Representation Ratio with Respect to Ph.D. and Wages

	Total	White	Black	Indian*	Asian	Hispanic**
Ph.D.						
slope (*p*)	0.1391	0.1476	0.0854	0.1386	0.0908	0.1281
elastic (*p*)	0.3314	0.3358	0.2020	0.2988	0.3353	0.1569
slope (*r*)		0.0326	–0.2502	0.3035	–0.4186	0.5356
elastic (*r*)		0.0044	–0.0348	0.0384	–0.0908	0.0386
Predicted Faculty Wage						
slope (*p*)	0.0013	0.0008	0.0047	0.0727	0.0078	0.0033
elastic (*p*)	0.2260	0.1229	1.1010	14.3131	1.6113	0.8157
slope (*r*)		–0.0107	0.0632	1.2173	0.1142	0.0407
elastic (*r*)		–0.1031	0.8750	14.0871	1.3854	0.5897
Predicted Private Wage						
slope (*p*)	–0.0028	–0.0026	–0.0031	–0.0761	–0.0071	–0.0059
elastic (*p*)	–0.4827	–0.4365	–0.7491	–15.3336	–1.4921	–1.4899
slope (*r*)		0.0047	–0.0190	–1.2546	–0.0816	–0.0684
elastic (*r*)		0.0462	–0.2664	–14.8509	–1.0094	–1.0073

Source: 1% U.S. PUMS sample (20,195 cases) and restricted to persons with a master's or Ph.D., between and including the ages 24–70, and who earned income in 1989.

Elasticities (*p*) of faculty probabilities with respect to Ph.D.'s is the percentage change in the faculty probabilities as a result of a 1 percent change in Ph.D.'s.

Elasticities (*r*) of representation ratios with respect to Ph.D.'s is the percentage change in the representation ratios as a result of a 1 percent change in Ph.D.'s.

Elasticities (*p*) of faculty probabilities with respect to predicted wages is the percentage change in faculty probabilities as a result of a 1 percent change in predicted wages.

Elasticities (*r*) of representation ratios with respect to predicted wages is the percentage change in representation ratios as a result of a 1 percent change in predicted wages.

* For Indians, the North Central/Midwest regional variable was used in regression.

** For Hispanics, all regional variables were used in regression.

TABLE A.7.5   Elasticities of Faculty Probability and Representation Ratio with Respect to Ph.D. and Wages

	Total	White	Nonwhite
Ph.D.			
slope (p)	0.0186	0.1535	0.0320
elastic (p)	0.0399	0.3167	0.1141
slope (r)		–0.1211	–1.2608
elastic (r)		–0.0147	–0.2644
Predicted Faculty Wage			
slope (p)	–0.0014	0.0071	0.0265
elastic (p)	–0.2111	1.1473	5.9075
slope (r)		0.0945	0.4339
elastic (r)		0.8214	5.6815
Predicted Private Wage			
slope (p)	0.0013	–0.0070	–0.0155
elastic (p)	0.2087	–1.0629	–3.4989
slope (r)		–0.0655	–0.2276
elastic (r)		–0.5802	–3.0162

Source: 1% U.S. PUMS sample (20,195 cases) and restricted to persons with a master's or Ph.D., between and including the ages 24–70, and who earned income in 1989.

Elasticities (p) of faculty probabilities with respect to Ph.D. is the percentage change in the faculty probabilities as a result of a 1 percent change in Ph.D.

Elasticities (r) of representation ratios with respect to Ph.D. is the percentage change in the representation ratios as a result of a 1 percent change in Ph.D.

Elasticities (p) of faculty probabilities with respect to predicted wages is the percentage change in faculty probabilities as a result of a 1 percent change in predicted wages.

Elasticities (r) of representation ratios with respect to predicted wages is the percentage change in representation ratios as a result of a 1 percent change in predicted wages.

TABLE A.7.6 Maximum Likelihood Coefficients in Logistic Model of Faculty Probabilities (3% PUMS Sample U.S. Population 24–70 Years old) (t-statistics in parentheses)

	Total	White	Black	Indian	Asian	Hispanic
Age	0.2313 (15.6284)	0.0603 (3.9671)	0.3530 (15.4148)	-0.1518 (-2.5091)	0.0159 (0.8154)	-0.0136 (-0.5354)
Age squared	-0.0023 (-11.5000)	-0.0005 (-2.5000)	-0.0035 (-17.5000)	0.0010 (1.4286)	0.0001 (0.2600)	0.0003 (1.0000)
Sex	0.1203 (3.1658)	0.2078 (4.8438)	-0.1388 (-2.3133)	1.6415 (6.9467)	0.1302 (2.1956)	0.6308 (8.2135)
Persons under 18 in household	-0.0140 (-0.3373)	-0.1661 (-3.4822)	0.5486 (9.2047)	-1.8705 (-7.7775)	-0.1761 (-3.0520)	-0.0742 (-0.9298)
Persons over 60 in household	0.1445 (2.3458)	-0.0004 (-0.0057)	0.2394 (3.0000)	-0.0122 (-0.0389)	0.1443 (1.9553)	-0.9402 (-6.2141)
Other language spoken in home	-0.2287 (-3.1588)	0.1523 (1.8109)	0.4023 (3.7989)	2.7104 (12.0946)	0.3000 (3.6855)	-0.2158 (-2.2716)
Unmarried female with children under 18	-1.9356 (-9.0831)	-1.1620 (-5.2770)	-0.3019 (-2.9921)	-7.4535 (-1.0296)	-5.5666 (-2.6022)	-1.9462 (-8.1911)
Immigrated to U.S. before 1987	0.0070 (0.0933)	-0.5144 (-5.7156)	-0.4027 (-3.7919)	-7.3055 (-0.4278)	-0.2372 (-2.6041)	0.1262 (1.4674)

Immigrated to U.S. after 1987	−0.7541 (−3.4418)	0.2903 (1.8339)	0.8370 (3.9762)	−8.3908 (−0.1380)	−0.0620 (−0.5223)	0.8465 (6.2890)
Ph.D.	4.8098 (122.3868)	5.0681 (114.4041)	5.3130 (90.2037)	7.4322 (20.9535)	4.3957 (75.5275)	6.1685 (78.0823)
Probability (p)	0.0041	0.0047	0.0018	0.0024	0.0059	0.0011
Representation ratio (r)		1.1453	0.4306	0.5930	1.4353	0.2796
Chi-square	11,226.783	11,112.581	6,092.790	671.352	5,622.340	4,206.69
% corr. classified	99.5900	99.5300	99.8200	99.7100	99.4100	99.8900
No. observ. (weighted)	833,758	633,535	877,407	57,403	283,254	753,171
No. observ. (unweighted)	41,515	32,216	37,244	3,219	13,582	35,700

Source: 3% PUMS sample.

Probability (p) is probability that a person in the 24–70-year-old sample is a faculty member.

TABLE A.7.7 Maximum Likelihood Coefficients in Logistic Model of Faculty Probabilities* (3% MHEC States PUMS Subsample, 24–70 Years Old) (t-statistics in parentheses)

	Total	White	Black	Asian	Hispanic
Age	0.8430 (71.4407)	0.0830 (6.5873)	2.5152 (7.6683)	-0.3057 (-5.0529)	-0.3991 (-5.1036)
Age squared	-0.0006 (-8.5714)	-0.0006 (-7.9010)	-0.0299 (-7.4750)	0.0038 (6.3333)	0.0049 (5.4444)
Sex	0.3308 (10.0547)	0.3409 (9.7960)	1.2471 (5.4530)	-0.3187 (-1.6979)	-1.7565 (-5.7085)
Persons under 18 in household	0.1027 (2.9093)	-0.0173 (-0.4589)	2.3288 (8.8514)	1.4211 (7.5071)	-0.1389 (-0.5363)
Persons over 60 in household	0.2291 (4.1429)	-0.2612 (-4.3752)	-5.5770 (-1.2374)	0.3096 (1.3345)	-0.7257 (-1.8859)
Other language spoken in home	0.1467 (2.4991)	-0.1075 (-1.5468)	-3.1728 (-8.8725)	0.3447 (1.1825)	-0.3386 (-1.1572)
Unmarried female with children under 18	0.2676 (2.8468)	-0.0981 (-0.8508)	0.5818 (2.7456)	-6.7090 (-0.7205)	-5.1732 (-0.4750)
Immigrated to U.S. before 1987	0.1785 (3.1371)	-0.1845 (-2.6395)	4.3431 (17.0988)	5.0777 (0.5987)	1.8598 (6.0977)
Immigrated to U.S. after 1987	0.9978 (9.6220)	0.9644 (8.1178)	-5.1303 (-0.0734)	5.6619 (0.6675)	-5.2094 (-0.3372)

Ph.D.				
5.3355	5.4062	4.3974	4.5023	7.2991
(158.7946)	(151.4342)	(16.9915)	(24.8746)	(16.7104)
Probability (*p*)				
0.0038	0.0040	0.0015	0.0102	0.0031
Representation ratio (*r*)				
	1.0479	0.3954	2.6872	0.8066
Chi-square				
21,384.4480	19,417.3010	1,153.5760	832.6870	679.7200
% corr classified				
99.61	99.59	99.89	98.98	99.79
No. observ. (weighted)				
1,366,323	1,169,882	130,058	20,014	40,330
No. observ. (unweighted)				
68,212	60,525	4,877	866	1,598

Source: 3% of 5% PUMS (0.15%) sample restricted to eight MHEC states.

Probability (*p*) is probability that a person with a master's/Ph.D. is a faculty member.

*Regression for American Indians did not converge due to the small number of observations (unweighted observations = 332).

**TABLE A.7.8   Elasticities of Faculty Probability and
Representation Ratio with Respect to Ph.D.**

	Total	White	Black	Indian	Asian	Hispanic
*U.S.						
slope (*p*)	0.0196	0.0237	0.0094	0.0181	0.0258	0.0071
elastic (*p*)	0.0335	0.0504	0.0000	0.0000	0.0874	0.0000
slope (*r*)		0.2914	0.2218	1.5609	–0.6052	0.3846
elastic (*r*)		0.0025	0.0000	0.0000	–0.0084	0.0000
**MHEC Subsample						
slope (*p*)	0.0203	0.0215	0.0066	**	0.0456	0.0224
elastic (*p*)	0.0532	0.0538	0.0000		0.1337	0.0000
slope (*r*)		0.0728	–0.3655		–2.3083	1.5822
elastic (*r*)		0.0007	0.0000		–0.0258	0.0000

Source: 3% of 5% (0.15%) PUMS U.S. and MHEC subsample.

Elasticities (*r*) of representation ratios with respect to Ph.D.'s is the percentage change in the representation ratios as a result of a 1 percent change in Ph.D.

Elasticities (*p*) of faculty probabilities with respect to Ph.D.'s. is the percentage change in faculty probabilities as a result of a 1 percent change in predicted wages.

Elasticities (*p*) of faculty probabilities with respect to predicted wages is the percentage change in faculty probabilities as a result of a 1 percent change in predicted wages.

Elasticities (*r*) of representation ratios with respect to predicted wages is the percentage change in the representation ratios as a result of a 1 percent change in predicted wages.

*Elasticities for blacks, American Indians, and Hispanics are zero because mean Ph.D. values for these groups are approximately zero.

**Regression for American Indians did not converge due to the small number of observations. The elasticities for black, Indian, and Hispanic groups are zero because mean Ph.D. values for these groups are approximately zero.

8

MOVING BEYOND MYTHS AND TOWARD COMMUNITY DIVERSITY

Conclusions and Reflections

The statistical and narrative data show the continued underrepresentation and exclusion of faculty of color in the nation's colleges and universities. Our study and many others show the presence of subtle discrimination and bias based on racial and ethnic difference. This book underscores the importance of addressing two areas of concern:

1. the relative scarcity of faculty of color
2. issues of the academic workplace environment for faculty of color.

We focus particularly on the workplace environment problems identified by study respondents, statistical analyses, and a comprehensive examination of the literature.

The dominant view has been that underrepresentation is primarily a problem of too few qualified minority Ph.D.'s. Our findings challenge the premise that this contributes substantially to the continued scarcity of minority faculty.

Still, the pipeline strategy continues to prevail as the major focus in increasing minority faculty. Why this is so—as we learned from examining the roles of the Midwestern Higher Education

Commission and reviewing other regional organizations' plans—is deeply rooted in a narrow perception that the problem *necessarily* rests with the deficiencies of minorities. To transcend such biases, we will examine some of the alternatives that have been offered.

FRESH APPROACHES

Our evidence suggests that there is a greater need for mentoring, networking, and research support. There exist several alternatives to pipeline projects that achieve some of the intended goals of those projects without relying so heavily on the notion of under-supply. For example, one study of the productivity of minority and nonminority scientists found a substantial correlation between the number of predoctoral publications, the number of postdoctoral as-sistantships, the time available for research, and the production of scholarly articles and books.

Although there seems to be an inverse relationship between race and productivity, some—if not most—of the race effect might be attributable to the scarcity of postdoctoral assistantships at the disposal of minority faculty, or the lack of time for research because of teaching, mentoring or "diversity" responsibilities. Others have noted that minority faculty have greater demands placed on their time, and that this affects their productivity, but there seems to be no general consensus on how to improve minority faculty produc-tivity and at the same time maintain a level playing field with non-minority faculty. A number of advocates suggest that institutions restructure tenure requirements so that faculty are rewarded for time spent mentoring minority students and providing community services (Carter & O'Brien 1993, p. 2). Others propose that the "ser-vice" component of the "teaching, research, and service" require-ments for tenure be taken more seriously. If faculty recruitment, promotion, and reward structures were to recognize the value of ac-tivities related to promoting racial understanding, not only would many faculty of color directly benefit from receiving credit for work they are already doing, others—minority and nonminority alike—might be encouraged to undertake such activities as well. Such a reward structure would also be visible evidence that an institution values and is committed to creating an environment that is nurtur-ing and welcoming to all.

Would restructuring tenure requirements in this way mean that minorities would be judged against a lower standard than nonminorities for research and productivity? It seems appropriate to look directly at what promotes productivity among scholars—both minority and nonminority. Productivity studies clearly show that research assistance and time devoted to research are key. Two means to increase minority faculty productivity, then, are to provide increased research assistance and to reduce teaching and service loads. These are precisely the major recommendations of minority faculty themselves, and such efforts hold great promise for increasing faculty productivity.

The relationship between increased minority faculty productivity and minority faculty retention has not been tested in our research or definitively demonstrated elsewhere. In theory, at least—especially in the presence of high market demands for exceptionally qualified minority scholars—increased productivity might *reduce* retention rates if it resulted in the more productive minority faculty being lured away by higher salaries or more prestigious positions elsewhere.

One obvious strategy for improving minority faculty productivity while avoiding academic brain-drain is to provide increased research assistance and reduced teaching and service loads in exchange for commitments to stay. This sort of quid pro quo has obvious ethical and moral dimensions, but it has great potential as a regional strategy. Funds for increased research assistance and release time might come from a regionwide minority research network in the same way external grants are awarded to colleges and universities now. The faculty obligation might be to remain within the cooperating-institution network for a period equal to the award period, perhaps with a payback provision. A faculty member might, for example, receive an award from the Regional Minority Research Network for one quarter-time leave each year for four years plus research assistance. This faculty member could take another position within the region and avoid any payback obligation. A faculty member wishing to move to a nonmember institution would have to put in one full year's service before leaving to compensate for the four quarters' leave. The payback is service to the employing institution for the amount of leave awarded through the network. Of course, if the person did not obtain tenure, there would be no payback required.

In many respects this alternative permits valuation of the research and service time of minority faculty without appearing to create promotion and tenure rules that differ for minority and non-minority faculty. There are also financial incentives to the participating institutions because the costs of replacing the released faculty members may often be lower than payments from the network, which are based on the faculty salaries.

Although we present this as a possible strategy, we realize that it does not challenge the traditional academic reward process but merely reflects that process and the values underlying it. Present faculty recruitment and retainment processes and practices in higher education have produced an unrepresentative professorate. It appears that new ways of doing business must be pursued in order to produce different outcomes. Change in the professorate, for instance, might be attained if an equal weight was placed on the research, teaching, and service contributions of all faculty, including faculty of color. Valuing faculty contributions toward building a racially and ethnically diverse academic environment would be a step toward addressing issues of discrimination in the workplace. The literature on minority faculty retention and the results of our studies suggest that teaching and service to the community as well as research are very important to faculty of color. However, the overwhelming emphasis on research for promotion and tenure forces all faculty into a homogenous way of achieving academic "success" or tenure while placing little or no value in attempts to create and nurture a racially diverse academic community. Some proponents for tenure reform might call for the elimination of tenure altogether. However, we contend that any change or even the elimination of the tenure and promotion process will not solve the issues confronted by faculty of color as reflected in this book. Criteria for faculty rewards and mobility along a career ladder will continue to be needed. The workplace environment must be free from racial/ethnic discrimination to effectively address issues described here.

MINORITY FACULTY IN HIGHER EDUCATION: ACADEMIC ANGST COMPOUNDED

Pursuing a career in academia is not easy. There are rigorous requirements, both explicit and implicit. In addition, persons of color face many obstacles not experienced by their white colleagues.

That such additional obstacles do indeed exist is supported by the fact that nearly all of the participants in our interviews and focus groups expressed this view. Whether tenured or tenure track, in the fields of science, social science, or humanities, at two-year or four-year institutions, similar experiences were reported. These informants cannot be simply dismissed as disgruntled individuals. Many seasoned veterans who have been successful in their academic careers commented on the additional difficulties encountered by persons of color. It is also clear that women of color suffer the double burden of race and gender bias.

For faculty of color, the general academic angst is aggravated by the dynamics of race and gender. The sense of being expected to work harder and achieve more weighs heavily, often leading to despair and diminished self-confidence; having colleagues and students pay more attention to color than to credentials is wearing; being held forth as an example of institutional benevolence engenders feelings of anger and resentment; rarely—if ever—receiving support or full recognition for research on minority issues not only devalues that research but undermines the will to achieve excellence in that research or in other academic pursuits. Feelings of isolation are reinforced by a scarcity of other minorities at an institution. And, finally, the issue of tenure—problematic for all faculty in higher education—is exacerbated for faculty of color by the suspicion that race or ethnicity may figure prominently (if subtly) in this very subjective decision.

Despite the reports—by our respondents and throughout the literature—that chilly institutional climates limit satisfaction, productivity, and advancement, a not entirely gloomy picture emerges when these same faculty of color describe why they remain in academia. Positive workplace experiences strengthen the commitment of faculty to stay. They report that they receive great satisfaction from teaching, appreciate supportive administrative leadership, and often revel in a sense of accomplishment. They emphasize the importance of mentors and colleagues, and of being part of academic communities of color. In the literature, faculty of color report that they remain in academe for reasons of intellectual challenge and the freedom to pursue their own interests. Promotion of racial understanding is also widely mentioned as an important personal goal.

What makes for success and retention appears to vary little by racial and ethnic group. Healthy, supportive, rewarding environments allow everyone to flourish even in a challenging and stressful environment. Unfortunately, for many faculty of color, the positives are greatly overshadowed by the negatives.

Nearly all our survey participants agree that there must be a focused strategy if their circumstances are to improve. None of the informants express the desire for special treatment or for reducing any of the existing academic standards; rather, they believe that strategies are needed to help level the playing field and neutralize some of the additional demands placed on faculty of color.

STRATEGIES FOR IMPROVING THE REPRESENTATION AND CIRCUMSTANCES OF FACULTY OF COLOR

Networking, mentoring, and research support stand out as major strategies for addressing the problems faced by faculty of color.

Networking is a particularly effective way to deal with problems of isolation, and there are a number of approaches to making this strategy successful. It must be recognized, too, that each minority group has its own specific needs. Networking along ethnic lines allows members to relate in the areas of shared culture and language and as academicians as well. For women of color, networking is necessary to address the complex issues surrounding race combined with gender.

Ideally, networks should develop to the point that they are organized not only around racial/ethnic commonalities but also link those who are in similar institutional settings, recognizing that circumstances vary greatly by institutional type. For example, two-year institutions have a heavy emphasis on teaching, and student evaluations are of particular importance to faculty success. This means that a network of two-year faculty would tend to focus on faculty concerns in that area. Four-year faculty also need to be concerned with teaching and student evaluations, but often there is more emphasis on research and publication.

Mentoring has been a powerful force in the lives of some informants. They attribute much of their success to past and present mentor relationships. Mentoring that is so positive and helpful for some would likely be positive and helpful for many others, but many informants reported having had very little or no mentoring in their academic lives. Given the documented positive effect of mentoring and other faculty development activities on the job satisfaction and retention of faculty of color, it bears restating that only 5.9 percent of the institutions in our sample had minority faculty development programs.

Initiating an effective and meaningful mentoring program would help reduce some of the extra burdens by faculty of color. Effectiveness would depend on making good matches between mentee and mentor because each must be able to deal with the other on many levels.

For those whose academic success depends on research and publication, there needs to be increased support for research. The most promising strategies for increasing minority recruitment and retention are ones that create greater access to publication opportunities, increase faculty time and resources for undertaking research projects, provide for careful peer review, and support travel for professional development and research networking activities.

The grow-your-own approach is a strategy that shows promise. Committed institutions have achieved moderate success through identifying need by disciplinary area, aggressively recruiting graduate students of color in those disciplines, and then hiring them as junior faculty upon the completion of their studies: the "grow-your-own" philosophy. As we have shown, however, such programs can also have drawbacks if they are not supported university-wide. Faculty in grow-your-own programs can be marginalized when they are perceived to have traveled a different road to obtain their positions. However, if the career paths of ordinary (not "grow-your-own") faculty were examined, we might find that many of them were nurtured in and began their careers in their own doctorate-granting departments. This is not of primary importance here, although such a finding might counter the notion that a "grow-your-own" approach for minority faculty is either unprecedented or unfair to nonminorities.

What is of major importance here is the extent to which higher education is willing to aggressively address the problem of underrepresentation of faculty of color. If there is a strong willingness to move on, then a grow-your-own approach is one way for academic departments to be a part of the solution.

The departmental role is critical in promoting diversity among its faculty. Departmental performance in hiring, retaining, and providing a supportive workplace environment for faculty of color needs to be examined. Mickelson and Oliver (1991) challenge hiring departments to broaden their faculty hiring criteria. If this were accomplished, there could well be many more qualified applicants making the short list and being hired for faculty positions.

A department's success rate in granting doctorates to minority scholars should also be carefully scrutinized, and departmental rewards and sanctions brought to bear in order to achieve an institutional mission for promoting diversity. As Olivas (1988) noted, in academia "consumers are also the producers" (p. 7). When a department says that the problem is that there are no qualified minority candidates for faculty positions, the institution should determine if the department is preparing and credentialing minority scholars in appropriate numbers. If not, the department can and should become part of the solution.

The grow-your-own approach gives all departments the means to solve any supply problem it has with respect to minority faculty. Even without a grow-your-own policy, initiatives at the departmental level to increase minority doctoral recipients are important to increase the overall availability of faculty of color.

Finally, in considering fresh approaches, we are encouraged by the commendable efforts of the Compact for Faculty Diversity in its regional effort to support minority graduate scholarship (see Chapter 6, "Exemplary Programs"). The compact developed—and includes in its brochure—a set of strategy recommendations based on its own experience. We feel they have broad utility, and these recommendations follow: "The Compact for Faculty Diversity must depend on cooperative action of interested parties. It cannot address the problem alone. The following suggestions describe how key players can help insure diversity."

For States:

- Regional programs should be funded on a long-term basis.
- States should encourage universities that grant doctoral degrees to participate in the program.
- Strategies should be developed to help place program graduates.
- The participation in the compact should be linked to other significant higher education policy issues.

For Universities:

- Universities should participate in the regional programs.
- Institutions should support minority graduate students financially in the fourth and fifth years of study. (The compact provides financial support, in most cases, for three years of the student's doctoral program.)
- Institutions must increase the pool of candidates to improve recruitment.
- Universities should encourage faculty members to serve as mentors.

For Departments:

- The department should provide the graduate students with assistantships.
- A supportive environment should be created within the department.
- Departments should guarantee faculty mentors.
- Department heads should diversify teaching staff.

For Compact:

- Seek funding from states, foundations, and corporations.
- Continue to administer regional doctoral scholar programs and coordinate national programs and activities.
- Continue to see that minority graduate students receive financial support.
- Continue to hold annual Institute on Teaching and Mentoring for scholars and their faculty mentors from all three regions.
- Develop program evaluation and monitoring processes for the assessment of the program and student progress.

THE ROLE OF AFFIRMATIVE ACTION

It is apparent that we cannot continue along those paths that have resulted in so little systemic change. Despite civil rights legislation and institutional efforts to improve faculty diversity, faculty of color remain severely underrepresented among the ranks of the

The data contradict J. E. Blackwell's conclusion that:

> ...*many who oppose affirmative action are not racially biased but firmly believe that the opportunity structure, which served them well in the past, will also serve racial and ethnic minorities if they meet the traditional criteria for getting jobs and moving upward.*
>
> Blackwell (1988, p. 424)

general professorate. The well-articulated experiences of study respondents as well as extensive testimony emerging from literature point to the continued exclusion and isolation of minority scholars. It is important to note that regardless of tenure status or professional standing, the stories are all too similar.

The small success that has been achieved is attributable to the many commendable efforts to address the underrepresentation of faculty of color in academe. That these efforts have made a difference is attested to, in part, by faculty respondents describing why they stay. We argue against discontinuing these efforts, including affirmative action, out of hand.

This is not to say that affirmative action policies and practices are not to be questioned. We do need to examine the viability of affirmative action for addressing the underrepresentation of people of color in educational institutions. Even with affirmative action policies in place, the small degree of change in the presence of faculty of color suggests that such policies are not sufficient to effect diversity. Affirmative action has definite limitations, particularly in addressing the underrepresentation of faculty of color. Mickelson and Oliver (1991) note that:

> *Affirmative action policies have limitations because greater numbers of minority faculty per se are not their direct goal. Rather their primary objective is to open up the recruitment process by advertising widely and stating explicitly the employers' nondiscriminatory intentions. Affirmative action programs have been relatively unsuccessful in increasing the proportion of minority faculty in this country precisely because of the way in which qualified candidates are identified, screened, and selected for the short list, the points at which affirmative action policies are relevant and operate most directly. (p. 161)*

Certainly, such criticisms need to be taken seriously, and affirmative action should be examined with a view toward improving policies and practices to produce a more diverse professorate. Nevertheless, to dismantle affirmative action without confronting the issues it was meant to address would be to abandon the progress—however small—we have made. The focus should be improvement, not retreat.[1]

There is no question that sustained action is necessary to advance the diversity agenda, an agenda that requires broad changes in the structure and culture of institutions. A truly inclusive climate can be created only when the culture in which the faculty core resides has undergone a transformation. In a truly inclusive university, faculty could not do their everyday teaching and research (let alone do them in ways that exemplify excellence) without being in conversation with individuals from a variety of cultures. In the words of Hill (1991), curricula must be "…reconceived to be unimplementable without the central participation of the currently excluded and marginalized" (pp. 44–45).

ORGANIZATIONAL CHANGE PROCESS

Data on the perceptions and experiences of faculty of color point to the need for institutional change if the recruitment, retention, and development of faculty of color is to improve. Academic administrators and policy makers need to understand the bidirectional nature of faculty socialization, how faculty learn to be faculty. Not only do people adapt to organizations, organizations continually adapt to their members. Thus far, the accent has been on adapting faculty of color into present organizational structures, processes, and values. Organizational solutions, such as mentoring programs, to the recruitment and retention of faculty of color have focused on changing them while maintaining the status quo. Token numbers of faculty of color can offer little force to promote institutional change. This view underscores the potential benefit of developing faculties of diverse backgrounds, namely, that these individuals serve to shape as well as be shaped by the university. As this process takes place, a new university structure and culture will arise.

---

[1]For a comprehensive and optimistic discussion of affirmative action, see *Affirmative Action's Testament of Hope: Strategies for a New Era in Higher Education*. M. Garcia (Ed.) (1997).

Many in the academic community will welcome the opportunity for self-examination and the energetic dialogue that must accompany institutional change. For some, efforts to transform the culture of higher education will be embraced as a long overdue renaissance. Others who have invested much of their lives to building the institution as it now exists will experience change as a kind of death or great loss. These strong reactions—as well as more moderate versions—are both predictable and understandable.

Organizational theorists say that change is simply painful, and that it is natural for change to bring discomfort on many levels. Change alters role stability, creates confusion, and causes people to feel incompetent and powerless. It generates conflict and creates winners and losers. Finally, it creates loss of meaning and purpose as attachments to symbols are severed (Bolman & Deal, 1991).

> *Analysts of academic systems have noted that academic sites often reek with lofty doctrines that elicit emotion, in a secular version of religion.*
>
> Clark (1983, p. 74)

Change will not be an easy process, in part because it will raise questions about closely held values and assumptions relating to the academic enterprise. We know that academic culture, particularly the culture of major research universities, is very strong. Peterson and Spencer (1990) note that culture is changed "primarily by cataclysmic events or through slow, intensive, and long-term efforts" (p. 6). The history of higher education reveals both types of organizational change events, and the issue of diversity provides another opportunity for institutions to reexamine their missions and values. Strong statements in support of diversity from faculty and administrative leaders are helpful. However, strong actions that change the "way things are usually done around here" will do far more to nurture open and inclusive climates. Inclusiveness must mean more than "come on in, but don't change anything" (Martha Minnow in *Carnegie Foundation,* 1991, p. 35).

Marginalization is perpetuated if new voices are added while the priorities and core of the organization remain unchanged. Newcomers who question institutional assumptions and conventions threaten established authority and "must be taught to see the organizational world as do their more experienced colleagues if the traditions of the organization are to survive" (Van Maanen & Schein, 1979, p. 211). In order for education to meet the fast-changing needs of contemporary society, it appears the "newcomers" must link with "old-timers." If all faculty work together as equal partners in restructuring the nature of interactions that occur in the daily life of the academy, there is a better chance that the next generation will enjoy a very positive academic climate that captures the best of what higher education is all about. The beneficiaries will be not only faculty of color, but students, staff, administrators, and faculty of all colors and ethnic backgrounds.

Disinterest in working collaboratively is a major stumbling block to creating the "inclusive university" described by the Committee on Policy for Racial Justice (1993): "[The inclusive university would provide an environment which nurtures]…appreciation of diversity and respect for differences while at the same time encouraging efforts to search for and understand shared values among different cultures" (p. 1). In order to realize this vision every facet of the university must undergo change.

To achieve campus cultures that are truly inclusive, then, institutions must emphasize cooperation, collaboration, and community. This is important because, as Duster (1991) notes, "Seeing others from a distance and being seen from a distance" allow individuals to maintain their stereotypes of each other (p. 15). University, college, and departmental administrators can provide opportunities and incentives for diverse groups of students, faculty, and staff to collaborate on various campus endeavors (teaching, research, curriculum design, etc.). It is also important to establish institutional rewards for contributing to collaborative and community-building activities. Although this approach may challenge the traditions of higher education, in which competition and individualism are entrenched values, such challenges are nevertheless necessary. We agree with Smith's observation that we may have "gone too far in encouraging competitive and highly individualistic practices at the expense of concern for the community and at the expense of good learning" (1989, p. 58).

Although the efforts to effect change must involve all members of an institutional community, special collaboration among faculty of color remains important. Faculty of color in higher education must form coalitions with one another in order to promote diversity, raise their own common issues, and ensure that they are represented throughout the entire higher education system, not just

> *Together we must work at dispelling the myth…we must lobby and press for a reexamination of the criteria for review, promotion, and tenure, for a redefinition of scholarship, and for inclusion of so-called "minority journals" among those classified as premier journals.*
>
> Reyes and Halcon (1988, p. 311)

in marginalized areas. In the end, as Reyes and Halcon (1988) express it: "We must be each other's biggest fans" (p. 312).

We must note here a list of elements that can cause even the best-intended programs to fail. Pressman and Wildavsky (1973) observe that "in order to make concrete an otherwise abstract notion we provide a list of reasons why participants may agree with the substantive ends of a proposal and still oppose (or merely fail to facilitate) the means for effectuating it" (p. 99). Their list includes (1) direct incompatibility with other commitments, (2) no direct incompatibility but a preference for other programs, (3) simultaneous commitments to other projects, (4) dependence on others who lack a sense of urgency in the project, (5) differences of opinion on leadership and proper organizational roles, (6) legal or procedural differences, and (7) agreement coupled with lack of power. We believe that these elements must be addressed in each institution attempting to achieve faculty diversity. Institutions can note if their goals are directly incompatible with faculty diversity, if stated or unstated preferences present barriers to faculty diversity, and so on. Overcoming these barriers to change is crucial in order to assure that all institutional participants are working together toward the same goal.

The effect of racial and ethnic bias is not explicitly addressed in Pressman and Wildavsky's list of barriers to change, but in our view, such bias may either generate or reinforce the barriers. Blackwell (1988) addresses this issue with the following observation on the role of racism in preventing organizational change in higher education:

> *If one accepts the symbolic racism thesis that minorities are attempting to violate "cherished values" of meritocracy and white privilege in a racially stratified society, and if minorities pose a threat to the economic rewards generally received by whites, then it is understandable how these attitudes influence affirmative action policies in higher education at levels controlled by whites. (p. 424)*

DIVERSIFYING ACADEMIA: THE NEED FOR "EXTRAMURAL" SUPPORT

The inclusive university is described as hospitable, engaging, and supportive, providing increased opportunities for all historically disadvantaged groups. The Committee on Policy for Racial Justice (1993) concludes an essay with this encouraging statement: "To the extent that these purposes are realized, the education levels and productivity of the next generation of adults will be enhanced and the entire society will gain, at home and in its dealings with other nations" (p. 2). However, the committee asserts that academe cannot accomplish this alone. Several elements necessary to support such a change include institutional commitment, public and private sector support, and the continued engagement of communities of color.

To achieve faculty diversity we must recognize that institutional efforts cannot be viewed in isolation. Scholars must broaden their scope to examine the practices of professional organizations as well as the editorial processes of scholarly journals.

> *It's more than just the departmental climate at [university]. Climate also involves the reception among students, professional organizations, and editors of journals. One must be accepted in these arenas and at these levels, too. If one does not get accepted at these levels, one does not get accepted for tenure.*
>
> Male American Indian tenured social
> sciences college-level administrator

Russell (1994) addresses the role of one professional organization—the American Educational Research Association (AERA)—in achieving diversity in academe and describes some of AERA's efforts to promote diversity among its ranks, which include the following:

- Since 1972, the AERA council has adopted resolutions to attain diversity among its leadership and programs.
- In 1978, the association created the Committee on the Role and Status of Minorities in Educational Research.
- Since 1991, AERA has provided funds to support four minority doctoral fellows each year.
- In 1993 AERA received a three-year grant to conduct a national fellowship competition to financially support doctoral students as well as provide a set of educational experiences for selected students.

According to Russell, sustained and systematic attention to achieving diversity in academe at every level, including among professional organizations, is imperative. He concludes, as does the Committee on Policy for Racial Justice, that "Every segment of society has a vital role in addressing the problem. But the sum will be significantly greater than its parts if the efforts are coordinated, systemic, and guided by an overall national initiative" (p. 28).

As many others have expressed,[2] we hope that the ideal of community with diversity can be achieved even in the midst of great resistance and conflict. In order for such visions to become reality, academe will need the sustained efforts of society as a whole. Internal institutional efforts toward change must be encouraged and supported by forces external to these institutions.

MYTHS AS BARRIERS TO PROBLEM SOLVING

Our studies lead us to conclude that we must move forward from where we are today to address underlying assumptions—within ourselves as individuals and within our institutions—that compel us to maintain the status quo. Many of these assumptions are reflected in societal myths that present invisible but significant barriers toward achieving the goal of faculty diversity.

We need not examine here all of the racial/ethnic stereotypes, misconceptions, and animosities inherent in our national culture. Although as an ethnically diverse society we are slowly moving toward some greater understanding of one another, these barriers are still very real in academia as they are in all parts of our society.

In academia, general misconceptions about various minority groups are compounded by myths that they are unqualified and unavailable for faculty positions. Our study and others have shown that although the pool of qualified minorities is small, it is also underutilized. As we have shown in our statistical analyses, minorities are underrepresented on faculties, not just in terms of their pres-

---

[2]Hill (1991), who writes about conversations of respect; Smith (1994) who writes about "mattering"; Tierney and Rhoads (1993) who write about building communities of difference; Rosaldo (1994) who writes about cultural citizenship as a right to be different and to belong; Light (1994) who writes about the importance of valuing difference in academe.

ence in the general population, but—much more to the point—with respect to the number of minorities holding doctorates.

Others scholars have attacked the availability/qualifications myth. In 1988 Olivas documented its effects on the hiring of law professors. As a result of his analysis of new hires in law he found:

> *A powerful myth permeates law hiring, as it does hiring in nearly all academic fields—that there are too few minority candidates for too few positions, and they possess unexceptional credentials... [the data demonstrates that] for most schools, white candidates with good (but not sterling) credentials are routinely considered and hired, while the high demand/low supply mythology about minorities persists. (p. 7)*

Evidence supporting this contention is also provided by Smith et al. (1996) who examine the academic labor market experiences of over 200 recent doctoral graduates. The authors sought to explore the current labor market theories, which argue that the lack of success in diversifying faculty is due to a scarcity of minorities available for hire and, as a result, bidding wars exist in which only a few wealthy and prestigious institutions can attract the available faculty of color. In their book entitled *The Pipeline for Achieving Faculty Diversity: Debunking the Myths,* the researchers conclude that although the 200 graduates were generally doing well and most were in faculty positions, their experiences contradicted six prevalent myths about the academic labor market. First, the authors found the supply and bidding arguments to be grossly overstated. In fact, only 11 percent of the scholars of color in Smith's study were sought after. Difficulties of the job market and limited options affect most candidates. The authors also found that many of the hard science graduates were in postdoctoral positions rather than faculty positions in higher education. Postdoctoral work is required in order to attain faculty positions in many of the hard sciences. Additionally, Smith et al. state that their study respondents expressed a wide range of preferences for desired position, region of the country, and institutional type. When people move, reasons often focus on unresolved issues with the institution, dual-career choices, and questions of appropriate fit more so than on financial packages and institutional prestige. They conclude that choices to leave academe were as often a function of the problems of academe as they were the result of lucrative offers elsewhere. Furthermore, they found that in most cases in which white men had difficulty finding a regular faculty appointment it was because the fields in which they specialized had virtually no openings. Another interesting point is that white men who had expertise related to diversity had a significant advantage in the job market.

THE IMPORTANCE OF ACKNOWLEDGMENT: THE PRIVILEGE OF IGNORANCE, THE IGNORANCE OF PRIVILEGE

The sheer invisibility of racism to white people makes it difficult to perceive (and correctly interpret) the reality of organizational life as it exists for people of color. Since this invisibility is historic as well as contemporary, white people also often are blind to their enmeshment in well established patterns of racial advantage and disadvantage, and to the privileges they and their ancestors have gained thereby... Thus, patterns of institutional racism often operate without white people being aware of them and without their conscious intent. Nevertheless, these patterns of racism reproduce themselves: they are aided by the ways in which people with power and advantage in the society, white people and people with wealth, cannot see racism clearly, deny responsibility for action to remove it, and thus passively if not actively contribute to the maintenance of the status quo.

Chesler and Crowfoot (1989, p. 2)

Based on our study results, we conclude that it is essential to acknowledge the importance of race and ethnicity within organizations as we attempt to implement equitable practices in college and university contexts. Higher education cannot remain ignorant of the ways in which its organizations perpetuate exclusionary practices. The acceptance of race and ethnicity as salient issues is critical to promoting the inclusion of diverse voices in higher education.

Many scholars agree that the issues identified here—by our study participants and throughout the literature—must be acknowledged by the white academic community. They also point out that what is hard to understand at a personal level becomes even harder to fathom at the institutional level: how organizational rules and norms perpetuate the status quo. Racism, as defined by Weinberg (1977), is

Minorities are more aware of racial tension...because they...must depend on constant interracial contact in social, learning, and work spheres on predominantly white campuses.

Hurtado (1992, p. 562)

...the doctrine of racial or ethnic superiority, including the justification of differential rewards based on the presumed differences. Racism without privilege would be mere individual prejudice. The social impact of racism derives from its role as a policy, not as an individual attitude. Racism is thus always collective and thereby institutional. (p. 352)

Chesler and Crowfoot (1989) do not casually dismiss lack of knowledge as a reason for the "invisibility of racism." They assert that

...lack of information is neither accidental nor individual. It is socially constructed ignorance, and is created by the separate cultures, life experiences and responsibilities of whites and people of color—in the society, in the neighborhood and in the university. Moreover, it was ignorance that was permitted to exist because most individuals did not inquire proactively into the conditions of life of students [or faculty] of color: there was no payoff for such concern and no sanctions for such ignorance. (p. 9)

Anyone who says "race doesn't matter to me," is probably (1) white and (2) unaware of the luxury of being able to make that statement. The option to focus on or ignore race as one chooses is the most fundamental privilege of dominance in a racist society. Members of the dominant group—even those who feel bound by conscience or morality to concern themselves with issues of racism—can ultimately walk away from it.

In 1988 McIntosh wrote a working paper, since published, in which she discusses the concept of "white privilege." Her work helps explain the "invisibility" of racism cited by Chesler and Crowfoot. McIntosh (1988) says:

> *I realized that I had been taught about racism as something which puts others at a disadvantage, but had been taught not to see one of its corollary aspects, white privilege which puts me at an advantage...I have come to see white privilege as an invisible package of unearned assets which I can count on cashing in each day...white privilege is like an invisible weightless knapsack of special provisions, assurances. (p. 1)*

Olson (1992) gives us another way to understand the importance of acknowledging the problem of racism and working for change when she says:

> *The first step toward change, always, is to understand the problem. Ours has two faces: prejudice is the active side of discrimination; privilege is the passive side. We can address prejudice only when we make ourselves open to the truth of other people's experience and when we join hands to eliminate it. (p. 30)*

Terry (quoted in Olson) states it most succinctly: "The fundamental privilege of being white is that we can ignore the fact that we are white" (p. 30).

Privilege exists for those who need not concern themselves with the painful sense of "otherness" on a daily basis, and can remain blissfully ignorant of what that experience is. Likewise, members of a dominant group can be oblivious to their own comfort in "belonging" and be unaware that others are deprived of it.

The faculty of color we interviewed cited examples of daily slights, large

---

While delivering a keynote address for a conference recently, I began to feel unaccountably so comfortable and so "like myself" in the process that I pushed my notes aside and engaged the audience as though I were conversing with them. Then I realized that this was the first time in a decade of being a faculty member that I—a woman of color—had had the privilege of addressing a large group audience of my peers—primarily faculty and graduate students of color. This is a privilege that, I would guess, goes largely unnoticed for majority faculty for whom such an experience is the norm.

Caroline Turner, coauthor

and small, that demand their attention and emotional energy beyond the inevitable friction of professional and personal interaction. They recount stories about having to prove to support staff outside their departments that they are faculty members, having students openly surprised at receiving a professor of color, not being invited to participate in collaborative research relevant to their fields, or having their work go unacknowledged in departmental reports. Such incidents force faculty of color to decide day by day—and probably hour by hour—"Is this [indignity, person, demand, slight, racist remark, incident of exclusion, lack of professional opportunity, etc.] important enough to give it my energy?" Majority faculty are free of these exhausting stressors of subtle racism, leaving psychic and emotional energy available for other activities.

Moreover, faculty of well-represented groups—even if sympathetic to issues of diversity and equity—may lack empathy for the experiences of faculty of color and be bewildered by their responses to what seems "trivial" or "innocent." For example, if a minority faculty member is disturbed by some occurrence, a majority faculty member may wonder, "How would I react in this case?" and quite honestly conclude that her minority colleague reacted unreasonably, that the minority faculty member "overreacted" or was "too sensitive." Her conclusion may well ignore, however, that her colleague operates from a totally different cultural context, and that it takes significant effort, as well as intellectual and emotional openness, to transcend her own reality and world view. Because of a disinclination to make the investment, such occurrences are all too likely to be exercises in resentment and frustration rather than opportunities for mutual respect and enlightenment.

That is not to say that faculty of color cannot be oversensitive or overreact—or simply be unreasonable human beings in any context. It is also not to suggest that everyone should—or can—be tuned into every other culture's history and nuances. But at least it must be understood that the experience of minorities in this country is vastly different from that of the dominant group, and that, for people of color, any situation is likely to involve complex symbolic (and often painful) content that is at first glance lost on anyone who has not shared the experience.

A supportive climate in which faculty of color can flourish will require efforts to bridge those gaps between what faculty of color may perceive as hostile and threatening, and white faculty may not. For members of a dominant group, being on the receiving end of racial or ethnic bias may occur so rarely that it is an anomaly, not taken personally or internalized and certainly not having the cumulative effect of lifelong repetition. In short, majority faculty members have the privilege of ignoring incidents that faculty of color must process and react to. All of us make mistakes and misjudgments when we enter the reality of others. We must expect to do that and then also expect to learn from our errors and misassumptions.

Knowledge is constructed from different experiences and contexts. For example, a podium looks, from the audience's perspective, to be a solid wood object. However, if you have seen the other side of the podium you know that it is hollow, and that there are shelves on which to place things. Your reality of a podium is different from people who have experienced it differently.

Both minority and majority members in academe can better understand each others' perspectives if institutions of higher education commit to—as one of their guiding missions—inclusion and empowerment of all groups in the academic community.

Many colleges and universities have made some progress in their goals to attract and retain faculty of color. But there is no room for complacency. We listen to the assurances. We look at the statistics. We hear some departments complain that they have no faculty of color because there are no qualified candidates, but their failure to attract and mentor graduate students of color assures that the problem will continue.

We believe it is true that the ugly bias of racism disappears by changing one mind at a time, but we are also convinced that institutional intervention and expectations are absolutely crucial in creating the environment in which the existence of racism can first be acknowledged and then can become intolerable. Institutional policies and practices, both formal and informal, shape, in many ways, individual reactions and responses to one another.

INSTITUTIONAL EFFORTS

Despite the significant steps that individuals, both of minority and majority representation, must and should make in creating a more respectful environment for diversity, individual efforts will go farther and have more effect in creating shared understandings if institutions of higher education seriously commit to the inclusion and empowerment of all groups in the academic community as one of their guiding missions.

If the subtle processes that work against the success and retention of graduate students and faculty of color are going to change, institutional rewards systems must change to explicitly acknowledge and reward the contributions of faculty of color in mentoring students of color, in representing ethnic diversity for the university, and so on. Colleges and universities must also reward the successes of individuals who recruit and support faculty of color.

As long as faculty of color occupy a token status, they will continue to represent their entire racial or ethnic group and to act as a mentor for all in that group. They will continue to work under a microscope and be treated as anomalies on campus. Their every success or mistake becomes an opening or a closing door for their racial/ethnic group's success or failure. With these added expectations, striving toward tenure can be even more stressful and lonely than it is for junior faculty in general. The institution will expect them to serve its ethnic representation needs but will usually not reward such service in the tenure and promotion process (Padilla, 1994). In order to alleviate this situation, colleges and universities need not only to increase the representation of faculty of color but also must reevaluate hiring, promotion, and tenure policies with the goal of rewarding a wider variety of accomplishments and types of research, teaching, and service than are traditionally recognized.

Colleges and universities should be at the forefront of preserving such legislative imperatives as affirmative action. Currently, external pressures have caused the institution to begin moving away from the goals of diversity for fear of lawsuits, and many academicians see little continued purpose to be served by affirmative action. While it is true that affirmative action policies have done little to change the overall pattern of hiring and retaining university faculty, they have still facilitated the entrance of a few faculty of color whose voices and contributions to the academic dialogue would not otherwise be there. If the programs that support the initiatives to recruit faculty of color are abandoned, many scholars, including ourselves, see a trend back toward the time before the civil rights era. Creating a critical mass of scholars of color is vitally important in continuing to correct the underrepresentation of faculty of color, in retaining present faculty, and in enhancing their contributions to their respective disciplines. For example, Harvard University's Afro-American Studies Department, though not representative of Harvard's other disciplines, shows the impact such an approach can make.

Colleges and universities need to address directly the disconnect between the problems confronted by faculty of color and the proposed solutions. As one colleague observed, "A lot of time is spent on racial and ethnic bias. That's an institutional problem. The solutions...answer pipeline and access issues. We've got to figure out a way that the solutions answer what's found in the data." Higher education must design remedies to address issues of workplace environment and deficient promotion and tenure practices, at the same time finding ways to encourage more students of color to engage in the process that will result in becoming faculty of color.

Designing and implementing mentor programs would help new faculty of color become acclimatized to academia and to the campus culture as a whole. Mechanisms must be created to enable department chairs and senior faculty to facilitate the success of new faculty of color. Where academic success depends on research and publication, increased support for research is necessary along with careful peer review, greater access to publication opportunities, and support for travel.

College and university departments should deliberately sponsor conscious-raising sessions. As noted in Brewer (1990), such sessions would meet Style's criterion that colleges and universities should provide everyone, students and faculty alike,

> ...with both mirrors and windows. Windows provide new perspectives; they encourage [participants] to look beyond their existing views. But mirrors are also essential. They allow us to see ourselves and our own culture through role models and culturally connected materials and experiences. The problem with our current educational system is that too many [participants] of color have many windows but not enough mirrors, while white [participants] have too many mirrors on the dominant culture but not enough windows into different perspectives. (p. 4)

Colleges and universities are now in the process of designing faculty development leaves for tenured faculty. Such leaves might also include incentives for majority senior faculty to place themselves for a period of time in situations in which they are really a minority. One white senior faculty member notes that whites "do not see color until they are in a position where they are in the minority and then you do see color." This faculty member goes on to state that she was placed in such a situation and learned "that I did not exactly know how to behave here—the rules might be different—I did not want to behave in ways in which I would be overly noticed." In her view, learning to live in a multicultural community "takes time and experience just like any other skill you might have. White faculty, who may be unaware of their own unconscious biases, must live through their own experience and acknowledge ignorance in this regard." To achieve a healthy, safe climate for growth, majority members must be willing to suspend their own quick judgments about what something means to them or how something looks from their perception, sincerely asking for more information and making the imaginative effort to exercise empathy.

Part of such sessions and other activities should be training so that all faculty and administrators can recognize and acknowledge the ways in which we are privileged and not privileged within our higher education institutions. Recognizing and naming examples of privilege and lack of privilege can help us all to begin to work on leveling the higher education playing field and resisting the forces that leave us immobilized by these situations.

Higher education institutions can explicitly encourage and support faculty collaboration across colleges and disciplines, thus making research activities that are less mainstream more visible. In this environment, should faculty of color find that their research interests are not supported by their department, they can develop partnerships in other areas of the university without being penalized for doing so. Typically at a large research university there are many pockets of research activities, and almost certainly some of them will provide overlapping research interests. Furthermore, from data presented here, it appears that faculty of color must be prepared to take the first step—over and over again—toward collaboration, toward collegiality, toward a mentoring relationship, toward friendship. It is not fair, but the alternative—waiting to be noticed—is not effective nor psychologically healthy. First steps need to be taken and rewarded at the institutional as well as the individual level.

The faculty—all of the faculty—must support all individuals who may need some up-front nurturing before they can go on to develop into productive and contributing scholars.

Although it seems unconventional, universities need to begin addressing the subtle and subjective processes of creating belonging simultaneously with the process of dismantling the subtle and subjective processes of exclusion. An Asian American tenured science professor observed, "As a somewhat overused African proverb goes, it takes a village to raise a child. It takes a department to nurture a junior faculty member.... Some departments do that well and other ones don't.... It's not really a programmatic thing, although I think one can move in that direction, because 'nurturing' comes more from how individuals relate to one another than the output of a program.... The point is not just to make the person feel comfortable. The goal is to allow the person to become productive. Usually a comfortable person is productive."

Colleges and universities need to clearly articulate and find ways to move toward environments that honor diversity, not by creating homogeneous politically correct groupings, but by creating a community in which all groups can maintain integrity of identity while participating with equal power in the larger community. As Duster (1991) states, "It will mean knowing how to be 'different' and feeling comfortable about it; being able to be the 'insider' in one situation and the 'outsider' in another.... Everyone [must do] some changing" (p. 54). Such changes would contribute to the creation of a university climate healthier for everyone.

Colleges and universities must simultaneously guard against balkanization by building an inclusive environment and dominant culture in which differences matter. Rather than stressing what we have in common (sameness), the emphasis is on a common attention to, respect for, dependence on, and appreciation of differences as life enhancing and inherently valuable. When we share a culture that values our diversity, then we all have a stake in maintaining that culture. Conversely, an emphasis on sameness (e.g., conformity to dominant cultural norms) is divisive. It marginalizes and alienates those who feel or are perceived as different. Inclusiveness leads to unity. Conformity leads to division.

BUSINESS AS UNUSUAL, NOT BUSINESS AS USUAL

Higher education remains resistant to change, even though there is insurmountable evidence that something is wrong and continues to be wrong despite continuing efforts to make things right.

Study after study, statistic after statistic document the continuing and undeniable underrepresentation of faculty of color in higher education. Year after year little, if any, progress is made. Must we conclude that in spite of the great expectations arising in Washington in the 1960s there is no commitment—no will at all—to create a professorate that fairly represents all racial and ethnic groups that now make up this country? This hope has been all but dashed because, despite many earnest efforts, the progress has been so minimal. Data emerging from our research underscore the need to begin doing business as unusual rather than continue doing business as usual. We need to take a hard look, not only at the organizational dynamics that continue to produce the same outcome in higher education, but at the spirit behind those dynamics. To change the dynamics we will have to take an open-minded and open-hearted look at our institutions, and commit to embarking on a course to implement business as unusual, not business as usual.

> *We need to begin to look beyond the mechanical to develop a culture within the department in which [all] look out for each other. You can't program that.*
>
> Male Asian American tenured
> sciences university-level
> administrator

Glimmers of hope appear, but thus far academia has failed to reach to the heart of the problem. In the struggle to establish communities of difference in the academy, we need to design ways in which diversity and pluralism can become realities. What are some steps that can lead us in that direction? We have attempted to address this question in this book.

It is clear that increased diversity in academia requires significant organizational and cultural change, and that only serious institutional commitment can achieve it. Many of the recommendations offered in this book are familiar ones; however, it is helpful when examining them to keep in mind several complex but interrelated processes.

First, organizational culture, behavior, and change theory says changes are very disruptive and often personally painful. Second, the vision of a truly inclusive academic climate must include space for all individuals to maintain their cultural identities while participating fully in the institution. The task of the university is to "provide all...with a range of safe environments and options where they can explore and develop terms which they find comfortable for inter-ethnic/cultural contacts" (Duster, 1991, p. 15). Third, strategies can be developed but will not be effectively or efficiently implemented until higher education is able to see well beyond prevailing myths that hinder or block cultural diversity in the academic workplace. Fourth, subtle discrimination, encountered and described by faculty of color, must be acknowledged by the rest of the higher education community. Concomitantly, the rest of the higher education community must be made aware that their exemption from such discrimination constitutes the privilege of not having to react to strong and extraneous stressors. Finally, if the preceding issues are not addressed, the elements contributing to failure may sabotage whatever well-intended programs, policies, and practices are attempted.

> *Clearly [changes in the structure and culture of institutions] will not be easy: as the multicultural agenda has made headway strong forces have surfaced to challenge it...Whether or not institutions of higher education will generate the political will, technical skill and person power to persevere in this effort remains to be seen.*
>
> Chesler and Crowfoot (1997, p. 34)

Many strategies have been suggested and some may be implemented. In many instances they go a long way in assisting an individual struggling for success in academia. Even so, one important underlying problem remains to be addressed. What can be done about an unwelcoming and inhospitable college climate? In our analysis, racial and ethnic bias stood out as the greatest challenge to the success and well-being of minority faculty. Institutions must go a long way in order to transform the overall climate into one that encourages and nurtures all of its members. Faculty members of color have strongly reported that they are ready and willing to do what is necessary to be the best they can be. They in turn need to see a bona fide institutional commitment to change.

Although mentoring, networking, and research support efforts will not eliminate racism or bias on college campuses, these efforts do hold promise for strengthening minority faculty's capacity to help build better campus climates. With minority faculty as co-equal partners in restructuring the nature of the daily interactions of academic life, there is a better chance that the next generation will face a less chilly climate than the current generation of faculty experience.

For racial and ethnic groups to maintain their integrity of identity while participating as equals in the large community requires change. No matter how difficult such change may be, it is important that institutions of higher education find ways to successfully meet the needs of their diverse communities. If newcomers are able to join forces with influential senior faculty, institutional change can occur in a collaborative environment. However, most members of the higher education community, ourselves included, have been educated and socialized in institutional cultures resistant to change. Creating a campus environment that increases the participation and success of faculty of color will challenge all, and we must be creative and introspective as we determine our roles in the organizational change process. Creating diverse and pluralistic campus environments will require both learning and unlearning. But faculty working together to restructure the daily interactions of academic life can improve the chances that the next generation will enjoy a richer, more positive, and more stimulating academic climate. The beneficiaries will be not only minority faculty, but all students, staff, administrators, and faculty, regardless of color and ethnic background. This is the future we can build.

BIBLIOGRAPHY

Adams, H. G. (1988, January). *Tomorrow's professoriate: Insuring minority participation through talent development today.* Paper presented at the Engineering Dean's Council Student Pipeline Workshop, American Society for Engineering Education, Washington, DC.

Affirmative action on the line: A special report. (1995, April 28). *The Chronicle of Higher Education,* A11–A33.

Aguirre, Jr., A., (1987). An interpretive analysis of Chicano faculty in academe. *The Social Science Journal, 24(1),* 71–81.

Aguirre, Jr., A., & Martinez, R. O. (1993). *Chicanos in higher education: Issues and dilemmas for the 21st century* (ASHE-ERIC Higher Education reports, No. 3). Washington, DC: The George Washington University.

Allen, W. (1988). Improving black student access and achievement in higher education. *The Review of Higher Education, 11,* 403–416.

Alpert, D. (1985, May/June). Performance and paralysis: The organizational context of the American research university. *Journal of Higher Education, 56(3),* 241–281.

Altbach, P. G., & Lomotey, K. (Eds.). (1991). *The racial crisis in American higher education.* Albany: State University of New York Press.

American Association of University Professors. (1982, January/February). Affirmative action plans. *Academe,* 15A–20A.

Applebome, P. (1993, September 19). Goal unmet, Duke reveals perils in effort to increase Black faculty. *The New York Times,* 1.

Applebome, P. (1993, September 25). Duke in spotlight as minority plan fails: Move to add black faculty members falls far short of goal. *The Star Tribune,* 4A.

Arenson, K. W. (1997, April 24). 62 top colleges endorse bias in admissions. *The New York Times,* A17.

Astin, A. W. (1982). *Minorities in American higher education, recent trends, current prospects, and recommendations.* San Francisco: Jossey-Bass.

Astin, H. S., Antonio, A. L., Cress, C. M., & Astin, A. W. (1997, April). *Race and ethnicity in the American professoriate, 1995–96.* Los Angeles: Higher Education Research Institute, Graduate School of Education & Information Studies.

Baker, B. (1997, September). Forcing Americans to keep faith: Historian accepts President's charge to lead national discussion of race. *AARP Bulletin, 38,* 20, 8.

Banks, J. A., & Banks, C. A. (Eds.). (1995). *Handbook of Research on Multicultural Education.* New York: Macmillan.

Begala, P. (1997, September). I'm white and they're wrong. *George, 88.*

Bensimon, E. M., Ward, K. A., & Tierney, W. G. (1994, May). *Tenure-track faculty study.* Prepared for the Penn State Commission for Women. University Park, PA: Penn State University.

Berry, G. L., & Asamen, J. K. (1989). *Black students: Psychosocial issues and academic achievement.* Newbury Park, CA: Sage Publications.

Bjork, L. G., & Thompson, T. E. (1989). The next generation of faculty minority issues. *Education and Urban Society, 21(3),* 341–351.

Blackwell, J. E. (1988). Faculty issues: The impact on minorities. *The Review of Higher Education, 11(4),* 417–434.

Blackwell, J. E. (1989). Mentoring: An action strategy for increasing minority faculty. *Academe, 75(5),* 8–14.

Blauner, R. (1972). *Racial oppression in America.* New York: Harper & Row Publishers.

Boice, R. (1992). *The new faculty member: Supporting and fostering professional development.* San Francisco: Jossey-Bass.

Boice, R. (1993). New faculty involvement for women and minorities. *Research in Higher Education, 34,* 291–340.

Bolman, L. G., & Deal, T. E. (1991). *Reframing organizations: Artistry, choice and leadership.* San Francisco: Jossey-Bass.

Bond, H. M. (1972). *Black American scholars: A study of their beginnings.* Detroit: Belamp Publishers.

Bowen, H. R., & Schuster, J. H. (1986). *American professors: A national resource imperiled.* New York: Oxford University Press.

Bowen, W., & Rudenstine, N. L. (1992). *In pursuit of the Ph.D.* Princeton, NJ: Princeton University Press.

Brazziel, W. F. (1987–1988, Fall–Winter). *Educational Record.*

Breneman, D. W., & Youn, T. I. K. (1988). *Academic labor markets and careers.* New York: Falmer Press.

Brewer, C. (1990, Spring). *Minority student success in college: What works?* Olympia, WA: Evergreen State College, Washington Center for Improving the Quality of Undergraduate Education.

Bronstein, P. (1993). Challenges, rewards, and costs for feminist and ethnic minority scholars. *New Directions for Teaching, 53,* 61–70.

Brown, S. V. (1988). *Increasing minority faculty: An elusive goal.* Princeton, NJ: Educational Testing Service.

Brown, S. V. (1994). The impasse on faculty diversity in higher education: A national agenda. In M. J. Justiz, R. Wilson, & L. G. Bjork (Eds.), *Minorities in higher education* (pp. 314–333). Phoenix, AZ: Oryx Press.

Carnegie Foundation for the Advancement of Teaching. (1991). *Campus life: In search of community.* Lawrenceville, NJ: Princeton University Press.

Carter, D. J., & O'Brien, E. M. (1993). *Employment and hiring patterns for faculty of color.* (American Council on Education Research Briefs v4, n6). Washington DC: American Council on Education Research, Division of Policy Analysis and Research.

Carter, D. J., & Wilson, R. (1996). *Minorities in higher education: Fourteenth annual status report.* Washington, DC: American Council on Education, Office of Minorities in Higher Education.

Chase, S. E. (1995). *Ambiguous empowerment: The work narratives of women school superintendents.* Amherst: University of Massachusetts Press.

Chesler, M. A., & Crowfoot, J. (1989, November). Racism in higher education I: An organizational analysis. (*CRSO Working Paper Series #412*). Ann Arbor: University of Michigan, Center for Research on Social Organizations.

Chesler, M. A., & Crowfoot, J. (1997, June). Racism in higher education II: Challenging racism and promoting multiculturalism in higher education organizations. (*CRSO Working Paper Series #538*). Ann Arbor: University of Michigan, Center for Research on Social Organizations.

Cho, S. (1996, March). Confronting the myths: Asian Pacific American faculty in higher education. *Ninth Annual APAHE Conference Proceedings,* 31–56. San Francisco, California.

Clague, M. W. (1992, October/November). Hiring, promoting and retaining African American faculty: A case study of an aspiring multi-cultural research university. Paper presented at the annual meeting of the Association for the Study of Higher Education, Minneapolis, Minnesota.

Clark, B. R. (1983). *The higher education system: Academic organization in cross-national perspective.* Berkeley, CA: University Press.

Clotfelter, C. T., Ehrenberg, R. G., Getz, M., & Siegfried, J. J. (Eds.). (1991). *Economic challenges in higher education.* Chicago: University of Chicago Press.

Collins, M. (1990, Fall). Enrollment, recruitment, and retention of minority faculty and staff in institutions of higher education. *Action in Teacher Education,* 57–62.

Collins, R. W., & Johnson, J. A. (1990). One institution's success in increasing the number of minority faculty: A provost's perspective. *Peabody Journal of Education, 66,* 71–76.

The Committee on Black Faculty of the Academic Council. (1994, January). *A strategic plan for black faculty development.* Durham, NC: Duke University.

Committee on Policy for Racial Justice. (1993). *The inclusive university: A new environment for higher education.* Lanham, MD: University Press of America.

The compact for faculty diversity. (1994). New England Board of Higher Education, Boston, MA; Southern Regional Education Board, Atlanta, GA; Western Interstate Commission for Higher Education, Boulder, CO.

The compact for faculty diversity: Institute 1995. (1995, October). Second Meeting, Tucson, Arizona.

Cooper, R., & Smith, B. L. (1990, October). Lessons form the experience of the Evergreen State College: Achieving a diverse faculty. *AAHE Bulletin,* 10–12.

Creswell, J. W., et al. (1990). *The academic chairperson's handbook.* Lincoln: University of Nebraska Press.

Crosby, F., & Clayton, S. (1990). Affirmative action and the issue of expectancies. *Journal of Social Issues, 46,* 61–79.

Cross, K. P., & Shortman, P. V. (1995, Summer). Tribal college faculty: The demographics. *Tribal College,* 34–37.

Cross, T. (1994). Black faculty at Harvard: Does the pipeline defense hold water? *The Journal of Blacks in Higher Education, 4,* 42–46.

Cross, W. T. (1991, January). Pathways to the professoriate: The American Indian faculty pipeline. *Journal of American Indian Education, 30(2),* 13–24.

Daniels, L. A. (1991). Only the appearance of diversity: Higher education and the pluralist ideal in the 1980's and the 1990's. *Policy Perspectives,* Pew Higher Education Research Program, Philadelphia, PA.

Delgado, R. (1989). Minority law professors' lives: The Bell-Delgado survey. *Harvard Civil Liberties Law Review, 24,* 349–392.

Dill, D. D. (1982). The management of academic culture: Notes on the management of meaning and social integration. *Higher Education, 11*, 303–320.

The Diversity Project. (1991, November). *Final report: Institute for the study of social change*, University of California, Berkeley.

Duster, T. (1976, May). The structure of privilege and its universe of discourse. *The American Sociologist, 11*, 73–78.

Duster, T. (1991, November). *The diversity project: Final report.* Institute for Social Change: University of California, Berkeley.

EEOC: 1991 EEO-6 Higher education staff information, Table III.

Ehrenberg, R., & Smith, R. (1991). *Modern Labor Economics: Theory and Public Policy.* New York: HarperCollins.

Elmore, C. J., & Blackburn, R. T. (1983). Black and white faculty in white research universities. *Journal of Higher Education, 54(1)*, 1–15.

Escueta, E., & O'Brien, E. (1991). *Asian Americans in higher education: Trends and issues.* (American Council on Education Research Briefs v2, n4). Washington DC: American Council on Education Research, Division of Policy Analysis and Research.

Ethridge, R. W. (1997). There is much more to do. In M. Garcia (Ed.), *Affirmative action's testament of hope: Strategies for a new era in higher education* (pp. 47–74). Albany: State University of New York Press.

The federal civil rights enforcement effort. (1974). In *To preserve, protect, and defend the Constitution, VII*, 64–65. Washington, DC.

Finnegan, D. E., Webster, D., & Gamson, Z. F. (Eds.). (1996). *Faculty and faculty issues in colleges and universities.* Needham Heights, MA: Simon and Schuster Custom Publishing.

Fleming, J. (1988). *Blacks in college.* San Francisco: Jossey-Bass.

Fleming, J., Gill, G. R., & Swinton, D. H. (1978). *The case for affirmative action for blacks in higher education.* Washington: Howard University Press.

Franklin, J. H. (1989). *Race and history: Selected essays (1938–1988).* Baton Rouge: Louisiana State University Press.

Freeman, R. (1976). *The overeducated American.* New York: Academic Press.

Freeman, R., & Breneman, D. (1974). *Forecasting the Ph.D. labor market.* Washington, DC: National Board on Graduate Education.

Frierson, H. T. (1990). The situation of black education researchers: Continuation of a crisis. *Educational Researcher, 19(2)*, 12–17.

Gainen, J., & Boice, R. (Eds.). (1993). *Building a diverse faculty.* San Francisco: Jossey-Bass.

Garcia, M. (Ed.). (1997). *Affirmative action's testament of hope: Strategies for a new era in higher education.* Albany: State University of New York Press.

Garza, H. (1993). Second class academics: Chicano/Latino faculty in U.S. universities. *New Directions for Teaching and Learning, 53*, 33–41.

Granger, M. W. (1993). A review of the literature on the status of women and minorities in higher education. *Journal of School Leadership, 3*, 121–135.

Graves, S. B. (1990). A case of double jeopardy? Black women in higher education. *Initiatives, 53*, 3–8.

Green, M. F. (Ed.). (1989). *Minorities on campus: A handbook for enhancing diversity.* Washington, DC: American Council on Education.

Gregory, S. (1995). *Black women in the academy: The secrets to success and achievement.* New York: University Press of America.

Griffiths, S. (1995, October 13). A class sister act. *The Times Higher Education Supplement, 1197*, 20.

Guralnik, D. B. (1970). *Webster's new world dictionary of the American language.* New York: The World Publishing Company, 1495.

Hankin, J. N. (1984). Where the (affirmative) action is (or is not): The status of minorities and women among the faculty and administrators of public two-year colleges, 1983–1984. *Journal of College and University Personnel Association, 35(4)*, 36–39.

Harvey, W. B. (1991, Fall). Faculty responsibility and tolerance. *Thought & Action, 7*, 115–136.

Harvey, W. B., & Valadez, J. (Eds.). (1994). *Creating and maintaining a diverse faculty: New directions for community colleges.* San Francisco: Jossey-Bass.

Hill, P. J. (1991, July/August). Multiculturalism: The crucial philosophical and organizational issues. *Change, 23*, 38–47.

Hispanic Association of Colleges and Universities. (1996, October). *The voice of Hispanic higher education, 5.*

Hu-DeHart, E. (1983). Women, minorities, and academic freedom. In C. Kaplan & E. Schrecker (Eds.), *Regulating the intellectuals: Perspectives on academic freedom in the 1980's* (pp. 141–159). New York: Praeger.

Hune, S., & Chan, K. S. (1997, April). Special focus: Asian Pacific American demographic and educational trends. In D. J. Carter & R. Wilson (Eds.), *Minorities in higher education: Fifteenth annual status report*, 39–67. Washington DC: American Council on Education.

Hurtado, S. (1992, September/October). The campus racial climate: Contexts of conflict. *Journal of Higher Education, 63*, 539–569.

Ideta, L. M. (1996). *Asian women leaders in higher education: Tales of self-discovery from the ivory tower.* UMI Dissertation Services. (University Microfilms No. 9713953).

Jackson, K. W. (1991). Black faculty in academia. In P. G. Altbach & K. Lomotey (Eds.), *The racial crisis in American higher education.* Albany, NY: State University of New York Press.

Johnsrud, L. K. (1993). Women and minority faculty experiences: Defining and responding to diverse realities. *New Directions for Teaching and Learning, 53*, 3–16.

Johnsrud, L. K., & Des Jarlais, C. D. (1994). Barriers to tenure for women and minorities. *The Review of Higher Education, 17(4)*, 335–353.

Johnsrud, L. K., & Heck, R. H. (1994). A university's faculty: Identifying who will leave and who will stay. *Journal for Higher Education Management, 10(1)*, 71–84.

Justiz, M. J., Wilson, R., & Bjork, L. G. (Eds.). (1994). *Minorities in Higher Education.* Phoenix, AZ: Oryx Press.

Karabel, J. (1997, September/October). Can affirmative action survive? *Tikkun, 12*, 29–30.

Kerlin, S. P., & Dunlap, D. M. (1993, May/June). For richer, for poorer: Faculty morale in periods of austerity and retrenchment. *Journal of Higher Education, 64*, 348–377.

Kulis, S., & Miller, K. A. (1988). Are minority women sociologists in double jeopardy? *The American Sociologist, 19(4)*, 323–339.

LaNoue, G. R., & Lee, B. A. (1987). *Academics in court: The consequences of faculty discrimination litigation.* Ann Arbor: University of Michigan Press.

Leap, T. L. (1995). *Tenure, discrimination, and the courts.* Ithaca, NY: Cornell University Press.

Lennon, T. (Producer). (1988). *Racism 101: Racial prejudice on America's best college campuses.* Frontline with Judy Woodruff. Network Public Television Station, WGBH.

Leon, D. J. (1993). *Mentoring minorities in higher education: Passing the torch.* Washington, DC: National Education Association.

Light, P. (1994). Diversity in the faculty "not like us": Moving barriers to minority recruitment. *Journal of Policy Analysis and Management, 13(1),* 163–186.

Louis, K. S., & Turner, C. S. (1991,Winter). A program on institutional research on graduate education. *New Directions for Institutional Research, 72,* 49–64.

Magner, D. K. (1994, February 16). Duke tries again. *The Chronicle of Higher Education, 40,* A23.

Magner, D. K. (1996, September 13). Fewer professors believe western culture should be the cornerstone of the college curriculum. *The Chronicle of Higher Education, 43,* A12–A13.

Martinez Aleman, A. M. (1995). Actuando. In R. V. Padilla & R. C. Chavez (Eds.), *The leaning ivory tower: Latino professors in American universities* (pp. 67–76). Albany, NY: State University of New York Press.

Matier, M. W. (1990). Retaining faculty: A tale of two campuses. *Research in Higher Education, 31,* 39–60.

Matier, M. W. (1991). Recruiting faculty: Complementary tales from two campuses. *Research in Higher Education, 32,* 31–44.

Mazon, M. R., & Ross, H. (1990). Equality of educational opportunity: Myths and realities. Minorities in the higher education pipeline: A critical view. *The Western Journal of Black Studies, 14(3),* 159–165.

McClelland, K. E., & Auster, C. J. (1990, November/December). Public platitudes and hidden tensions: Racial climates at predominantly white liberal arts colleges. *Journal of Higher Education, 61,* 607–642.

McIntosh, P. (1988). *White privilege and male privilege: A personal account of coming to see correspondences through work in women's studies* (Working paper no. 189). Wellesley, MA: Wellesley College, Center for Research on Women.

Menges, R. J., & Exum, W. H. (1983). Barriers to the progress of women and minority faculty. *Journal of Higher Education, 54(2),* 123–144.

Mezey, S. G. (1992). *In pursuit of equality: Women, public policy, and the courts.* New York: St. Martin's Press.

Mickelson, R. A., & Oliver, M. L. (1991). Making the short list: Black candidates and the faculty recruitment process. In P. G. Altbach & K. Lomotey (Eds.), *The racial crisis in American higher education* (pp. 149–166). Albany, NY: SUNY Press.

Midwestern Higher Education Commission (MHEC). (1995, May). *Minority Faculty Development Project: Final Report.*

Milem, J. F., & Astin, H. S. (1993, March/April). The changing composition of the faculty: What does it really mean for diversity? *Change,* 21–27.

Mitchell, J. (1982). Reflections of a black social scientist: Some struggles, some doubts, some hopes. *Harvard Educational Review, 52(1),* 27–44.

Moore, K. M., & Johnson, M. P. (1989). The status of women and minorities in the professoriate: The role of affirmative action and equity. *New Directions for Institutional Research, 63,* 45–63.

Myers, Jr., S. L. (1997, July/August). Why diversity is a smoke screen for affirmative action. *Change,* 24–32.

Myers, Jr., S. L., & Turner, C. S. (1995, May). *Midwestern Higher Education Commission minority faculty development project.* Prepublication Report. Minneapolis, MN: Midwestern Higher Education Commission.

Nakanishi, D. T. (1989, November/December). A quota on excellence? The Asian American admission debate. *Change,* 38–47.

Nakanishi, D. T. (1993). Asian Pacific Americans in higher education: Faculty and administrative representation and tenure. *New Directions for Teaching and Learning, 53,* 51–59.

Nakanishi, D. T. (1995). Asian Pacific Americans and Colleges and Universities. In J. A. Banks & C. A. Banks, *Handbook of research on multicultural education* (pp. 683–695). New York: Macmillan.

Nakanishi, D. T., & Nishida, T. Y. (Eds.). (1995). *The Asian American Educational Experience.* London: Routledge.

National Education Association. (1993). *Mentoring minorities in higher education.* Washinton, DC: National Education Association Office of Higher Education.

National Research Council. 1991 Survey of Doctorate Recipients. (Table 1, Appendix F).

Nelson, S., & Pillett, G. (Producers). (1997). *Shattering the silence: Minority professors break into the ivory tower.* Public Broadcasting Service.

Nettles, M. T. (1990, August). Success in doctoral programs: Experiences of minority and white students. *American Journal of Education, 494–522.*

Neufeldt, V., & Guralnik, D. B. (1994). *Webster's New World Dictionary of American English.* New York: Prentice Hall.

Njeri, I. (1989, September 20). Academic acrimony: Minority professors claim racism plays role in obtaining tenure. *Los Angeles Times, 1,* 4.

Nkomo, S. M. (1992). The emperor has no clothes: Rewriting race in organization. *Academy of Management Review, 17,* 487–513.

Noel, L. (1990). Leadership and values: Retention secrets? *Recruitment and Retention in Higher Education, 4,* 6–7.

Office of Information and Regulatory Affairs, 1997. Revisions to the Standards for the Classification of Federal Data on Race and Ethnicity. Washington DC: Office of Management and Budget.

Olivas, M. A. (1988, May/June). Latino faculty at the border: Increasing numbers key to more Hispanic access. *Change,* 6–9.

Olson, R. A. (1992, November). *Eliminating white privilege in schools: An awesome challenge for white parents and educators.* (Paper prepared by SDS participants, no. 2). St. Paul, MN: Supporting Diversity in Schools.

Olson, R. A. (1996, March). Ants can build mountains. In M. D. Cohen (Ed.), *Valuing each other: Perspective on culturally responsive teaching* (pp. 28–39). Grand Forks, ND: Center for Teaching and Learning, University of North Dakota.

Opp, R. D., & Smith, A. B. (1992, April 11). *Minority faculty recruitment programs at two-year colleges.* Paper presented at the Annual Meeting of the Council of Universities and Colleges, Phoenix, AZ.

Oppelt, N. T. (1990). *The tribally controlled Indian college: The beginnings of self-determination in American Indian education.* Tsaile, AZ: Navajo Community College Press.

Padilla, A. M. (1994). Ethnic minority scholars, research, and mentoring: Current and future issues. *Educational Researcher, 23(4),* 24–27.

Padilla, R. V., & Chavez, R. C. (1995). *The leaning ivory tower: Latino professors in American universities.* Albany: State University of New York Press.

Paisano, E. L. (1993, September). *We the American...Asians.* Washington, DC: U.S. Department of Commerce, Economics and Statistics Administration, Bureau of the Census.

Paisano, E. L. (1993, September). *We the American...Blacks.* Washington, DC: U.S. Department of Commerce, Economics and Statistics Administration, Bureau of the Census.

Paisano, E. L. (1993, September). *We the American...Hispanics.* Washington, DC: U.S. Department of Commerce, Economics and Statistics Administration, Bureau of the Census.

Paisano, E. L. (1993, September). *We the American....Pacific Islanders.* Washington, DC: U.S. Department of Commerce, Economics and Statistics Administration, Bureau of the Census.

Paisano, E. L. (1993, September). *We the...First Americans.* Washington, DC: U.S. Department of Commerce, Economics and Statistics Administration, Bureau of the Census.

Pascerella, E. T., & Terenzini, P. T. (1991). *How college affects students.* San Francisco: Jossey-Bass.

Pavel, M., Swisher, K., & Ward, M. (1994). Special focus: American Indian and Alaska native demographic and educational trends. *Minorities in Higher Education, 13,* 33–56.

Pepion, K. (1993). *Ideologies of excellence: Issues in the evaluation, promotion, and tenure of minority faculty.* Doctoral dissertation, University of Arizona.

Pepion, K. (1997). Building a stairway to parity: The west and south prepare diverse faculty. *Hispanic Outlook in Higher Education, 7 (21),* 9–11.

Peterson, M. W., & Spencer, M. G. (1990). Understanding academic culture and climate. In W. G. Tierney (Ed.), *New Directions for Institutional Research: Assessing Academic Climates and Cultures* (pp. 3–18). San Francisco: Jossey-Bass.

Peterson, S. (1990). Challenges for black women faculty. *Initiatives, 33–36.*

Pierce, C. M. (1989). Unity in diversity: Thirty-three years of stress. In G. L. Berry & J. K. Asamen (Eds.), *Black students: Psychosocial issues and academic achievement* (pp. 247–311). Newbury Park, CA: Sage.

Ponterotto, J. G. (1990). Racial/ethnic minority and women administrators and faculty in higher education: A status report. *New Directions for Student Services, 52,* 61–72.

Pressman, J. L., & Wildavsky, A. (1973). *Implementation.* Los Angeles: University of California Press-Berkeley.

Pruitt, A. S., & Isaac, P. D. (1995). Discrimination in recruitment, admission, and retention of minority graduate students. *Journal of Negro Education, 54(4),* 526–536.

Reyes, M., & Halcon, J. J. (1988). Racism in America: The old wolf revisited. *Harvard Educational Review, 58(3),* 299–314.

Reyes, M., & Halcon, J. J. (1991). Practices of the academy: Barriers to access for Chicano academics. In P. G. Altbach & K. Lomotey (Eds.), *The racial crisis in American higher education* (pp. 167–186). Albany: State University of New York Press.

Rockwell, R. C. (1975). Applications of the 1970 census public use samples in affirmative action programs. *The American Sociologist, 10,* 41–46.

Rosaldo, R. (1994). Cultural citizenship and educational democracy. *Cultural Anthropology, 9,* 402–411.

Ross, K. (1990). Eight myths about minorities in higher education. *The College Board Review, 155,* 12–47.

Russell, W. J. (1994, December). Achieving diversity in academe: AERA's role. *Educational Researcher, 23,* 26–28.

Sands, R. G., Parson, A. L., & Duane, J. (1992). Faculty-faculty mentoring and discrimination: Perceptions among Asian, Asian American, and Pacific Island faculty. *Equity & Excellence, 25(2–4),* 124–129.

Scheurich, J. J., & Young, M. D. (1997). Coloring epistemologies: Are our research epistemologies racially biased? *Educational Researcher, 26(4),* 4–16.

Schneider, A. (1997, June 20). Proportion of minority professors inches up to about 10%. *The Chronicle of Higher Education,* A12–A13.

Schuster, J. H. (1990). Faculty issues in the 1990's: New realities, new opportunities. *New Directions for Higher Education, 70,* 33–41.

Sherry, S. (1996). The sleep of reason. *The Georgetown Law Journal, 84,* 453–484.

Smith, D. G. (1989). *The challenge of diversity: Involvement or alienation in the academy?* ASHE-ERIC Higher Education Report, No. 4. Washington, DC: School of Education and Human Development, George Washington University.

Smith, D. G. (1994). Community and group identity: Fostering mattering. *Higher Education Exchange,* The Kettering Foundation, 29–35.

Smith, D. G., et al. (1996). *Achieving faculty diversity: Debunking the myths.* Washington, DC: Association of American Colleges and Universities.

Smith, E., & Witt, S. L. (1993). A comparative study of occupational stress among African American and white university faculty: A research note. *Research in Higher Education, 34(2),* 229–241.

Spann, J. (1990). *Retaining and promoting minority faculty members: Problems and possibilities.* Madison: University of Wisconsin System.

Stamps, S. D., & Tribble, I. (1993, October). If you can walk, you can dance; If you can talk, you can sing: A successful African American doctoral fellowship program. *Black Issues in Higher Education, 13(16),* 30–33.

Stein, W. (1994, Spring). The survival of American Indian faculty: Thought and action. *The National Education Association Higher Educational Journal, 10(1),* 101–114.

Tack, M. W., & Patitu, C. L. (1992). *Faculty job satisfaction: Women and minorities in peril* (ASHE-ERIC Higher Education Reports, No. 4). Washington, DC: George Washington University.

Takaki, R. (1993). *A different mirror: A history of multicultural America.* Toronto: Little, Brown and Company.

Thomas, G. E. (1992, March). Participation and degree attainment of African-American and Latino students in graduate education relative to other racial and ethnic groups: An update from OCR data. *Harvard Educational Review, 62,* 45–65.

Tierney, W. G. (1993). *Building communities of difference: Higher education in the twenty-first century.* Westport, CT: Bergin & Garvey.

Tierney, W. G. (1996). Affirmative action in California: Looking back, looking forward in public academe. *Journal of Negro Education, 65,* 122–132.

Tierney, W. G. (1997). The parameters of affirmative action: Equity and excellence in the academy. *Review of Educational Research, 67,* 165–196.

Tierney, W. G., & Bensimon, E. M. (1996). *Promotion and tenure: Community and socialization in academe.* Albany: State University of New York Press.

Tierney, W. G., & Rhoads, R. A. (1993). *The socialization of women faculty and faculty of color: Enhancing promotion, tenure and beyond* (ASHE-ERIC Higher Education Reports, No. 6). Washington, DC: George Washington University.

Turner, C. S. (in press). Promotion and tenure for faculty of color: Promoting business as unusual. Paper presented at Keeping Our Faculties: Addressing the Recruitment and Retention of Faculty of Color in Higher Education, a national symposium held in Minneapolis, MN, October 18–20, 1998.

Turner, C. S., Garcia, M., Nora, A., & Rendon, L. I. (Eds.). (1996). *Racial and ethnic diversity in higher education.* Needham Heights, MA: Simon and Schuster Custom Publishing.

Turner, C. S., & Myers, Jr., S. L. (1997). Faculty diversity and affirmative action. In M. Garcia (Ed.), *Affirmative action's testament of hope: Strategies for a new era in higher education* (pp. 131–148). Albany: State University of New York Press.

Turner, C. S., Myers, Jr., S. L., & Creswell, J. W. (1999, January/February). Exploring underrepresentation: The case of faculty of color in the Midwest. *Journal of Higher Education, 70(1),* 27–59.

Turner, C. S., & Seashore, L. K. (1996, May). Society's response to differences: A sociological perspective. *Remedial and Special Education, 17,* 134–141.

U.S. Department of Commerce, Bureau of the Census. (1990). *General Population Characteristics: Sex, Race, and Hispanic Origin.*

U.S. Department of Education. (1991, April). *National Survey of Postsecondary Faculty (NSOPF)*, 1987–88, Table 22.

Valdes, M. I., & Seoane, M. H. (1995). *Hispanic market handbook: The definitive source for reaching this lucrative segment of American consumers.* New York: Gale Research.

Van Maanen, J., & Schein, E. H. (1979). In B. M. Staw (Ed.), *Toward a theory of organizational socialization research in organizational behavior.* Greenwich, CT: JAI Press.

Verdugo, R. R. (1995). The segregated citadel: Some personal observations on the academic career not offered. In R. V. Padilla & R. C. Chavez (Eds.), *The leaning ivory tower: Latino professors in American universities* (pp. 101–109). Albany, NY: State University of New York Press.

Villalpando, O. (in press). Scholars of color: Are they really a part of the emerging composition of the professoriate? *UCLA Journal of Education and Information Studies, 6(1).* UCLA: Regents of the University of California.

Wagner, U. (1991). How to increase the number of minority Ph.D.s. *Planning for Higher Education, 19,* 1–7.

Washington, V., & Harvey, W. (1989). *Affirmative rhetoric, negative action.* Washington, DC: School of Education and Human Development, George Washington University.

Weekly compilation of presidential documents (no. 986). (1975, September 15). Washington, DC.

Weinberg, M. (1977). *A chance to learn: The history of race and education in the United States.* New York: Cambridge University Press.

Wey, N. (1980). Asian-Americans in academia. In Y. H. Jo (Ed.), *Political participation of Asian Americans* (pp. 38–49). Mental Health Research Center.

Williams, P. J. (1991). *The alchemy of race and rights: Diary of a law professor.* Cambridge: Harvard University Press.

Wilson, R. (1987, February). Recruitment and retention of minority faculty and staff. *AAHE Bulletin,* 11–14.

Wilson, R. (1992, Spring). [Review of the book *Fostering minority access and achievement in higher education*]. *Harvard Educational Review, 62,* 79–87.

Wilson, R. (1994). The participation of African Americans in American higher education. In M. J. Justiz, R. Wilson, & L. G. Bjork (Eds.), *Minorities in higher education.* Phoenix, AZ: Oryx Press.

Wilson, R. (1995, May). *Affirmative action: Yesterday, today, and beyond.* American Council on Education.

INDEX

A